More Praise for
How to Land a Top-Paying Federal Job

"This book pulls together needed and hard-to-find information on ways to get a job in federal government. It is a very helpful resource."

—Sandy Hessler, Director of Career Advancement, Harvard Kennedy School

"This book is a must-read. Anyone who aspires to a federal position or promotion within the federal service will find Whiteman's advice invaluable as they prevail over obstacles of entry and advancement throughout their federal careers. Whiteman gives her readers access to a wide range of information on the federal service application process, interview techniques, and how to successfully sell your 'résumé' to hiring managers. Her 'hot tips' are excellent resources that are appropriately positioned throughout the book to help the reader gain additional insights. This is a superb reference book and action plan for all prospective and current federal employees."

—Farrell J. Chiles, former Chairman of the Board,
National Organization of Blacks in Government

"This book will become an instant classic. It is chock full of make-or-break advice—available nowhere else—about every phase of the job-search process and about getting ahead in government."

—Kelly Paisley, former Deputy Director of Vice-President Al Gore's
National Partnership for Reinventing Government

"An excellent resource for undergraduate and graduate students who are interested in securing an internship in the public sector . . . A great resource for new-career professionals and mid-career professionals who seek a federal career and are interested in 'insider' tips to navigate the federal hiring process . . . describes the myriad of diversity programs for women, minorities, and disabled job seekers . . . provides for easy reading and a straightforward approach . . . will almost certainly ensure that job-seekers submit an A+ application . . . . Anyone looking for a federal job, or any job for that matter, would definitely benefit by reading this book."

—*Journal of Public Management & Social Policy*

"This book is essential reading for anyone who wants to decipher the federal government's hiring system. Don't apply for a federal job without it."

—Paul C. Light, Paulette Goddard Professor of Public Service,
Robert Wagner School of Public Service, New York University

"Most books on how to find a federal job are about as interesting as the tax code. But [this book] offers a mountain of helpful advice in a visually appealing, easy-to-read format."

—*Government Leader*

"Whiteman's enlightening, entertaining book will teach you everything you need to know about how to put the right spin on your credentials on paper and in person."

—Ray Kurzweil, recipient of the National Medal of Technology; best-selling author of *The Singularity Is Near: When Humans Transcend Biology*

"This book will change how you conduct a job hunt not just for a federal job, but how you can improve the odds of landing a job almost anywhere. Perhaps the most valuable aspect of the book is that many of the strategies and techniques recommended are often highly pragmatic and easily implemented. Absorb this information and watch your confidence grow as your success ratio of calls to interviews rises dramatically."

—George Selby, President of the National Association of Government Communicators

"In summary, this book rocks. This is not a book you read at the bookstore over 10 minutes. This is a book you buy. Read. Read again. And reference. If anyone asks you how to get a federal job, just tell them to buy this book. And if you are already in the federal system, this is an essential career guide as it tells you how to navigate the waters, find your next job, get promoted, and negotiate your salary (yes you can do this as a fed)."

—Steve Ressler, cofounder of Young Government Leaders and manager of GovLoop.Com, a popular networking site for government professionals

"Peppered with cartoons and a touch of wit, Whiteman's book is the layman's field guide to a federal job search. . . . The book is based on hundreds of interviews with federal hiring managers and job hunters. Unlike other similar guides, it focuses on process rather than just aggregating information about agencies. This book provides step-by-step instructions on crafting successful résumés, cover letters, and essays that get applicants out of the pile and into the interview. As readers gear up for the hot seat, Whiteman lets them in on the do's and the don'ts of interviewing for a federal job. And when an offer does roll around, readers can find tips on negotiating salary and climbing the ranks."

—*Roll Call*, the newspaper of Capitol Hill since 1955

HOW TO LAND A
TOP-PAYING FEDERAL JOB

Your Complete Guide to Opportunities, Internships,
Résumés and Cover Letters, Application Essays (KSAs),
Interviews, Salaries, Promotions, and More!

LILY WHITEMAN

AMACOM

American Management Association
New York • Atlanta • Brussels • Chicago • Mexico City • San Francisco
Shanghai • Tokyo • Toronto • Washington, D.C.

Special discounts on bulk quantities of AMACOM books are available to corporations, professional associations, and other organizations. For details, contact Special Sales Department, AMACOM, a division of American Management Association, 1601 Broadway, New York, NY, 10019.

Tel.: 212-903-8316.   Fax: 212-903-8083

Web site: www.amacombooks.org

This publication is designed to provide accurate and authoritative information in regard to the subject mater covered. It is sold with the understanding that the publisher is not engaged in rendering legal, accounting, or other professional service. If legal advice or other expert assistance is required, the services of a competent professional person should be sought.

This book represents the views of Lily Whiteman and not the views of the U.S. National Science Foundation.

Library of Congress Cataloging-in-Publication Data

Whiteman, Lily.

How to land a top-paying federal job : your complete guide to opportunities, internships, résumés and cover letters, application essays (KSAs), interviews, salaries, promotions, and more! / Lily Whiteman.—1st ed
p. cm.
Includes bibliographical references and index.
ISBN-13: 978-0-8144-0172-9
ISBN-10: 0-8144-0172-4
1. Civil service positions—United States—Handbooks, manuals, etc.
2. Career changes—United States—Handbooks, manuals, etc.
3. Internship programs—United States—Handbooks, manuals, etc.
4. Job hunting—United States—Handbooks, manuals, etc. 5. Vocational guidance—United States—Handbooks, manuals, etc. I. Title.

JK692.W45 2008
351.73023—dc22

2008003809

Printing Number

10   9   8   7   6   5   4   3

CONTENTS

PART III
THE TALKING STAGE

PART IV
ACCELERATING YOUR ASCENT

DOCUMENTS ON THE CD

Directory of Internships and Special Recruitment Programs for Young Professionals

Directory of Internships That Are Specially Recruiting Women, Minorities, and People with Disabilities

Directory of Fellowships for Experienced Professionals (Nonfeds and Current Feds)

Cheat Sheets for Application and Interview Prep

KSA & Interview Prep Cheat Sheets

Résumé Prep Cheat Sheets

Going Global in Government

Get Ahead Cheat Sheets

Lily Whiteman's *Washington Post* articles on Federal Internships, Interview Skills, International Opportunities, and Networking in Professional Organizations

FOREWORD

Lily Whiteman's neat, well-organized book demonstrated that my 18 years on the subcommittee with direct oversight over federal employees haven't taught me all I want to know. This nugget of a book will tell you what you don't know, what you need to know, and what you may not have thought to ask about federal employment and promotion. Whiteman, herself a federal writer who has served as a federal hiring manager, is skillful in culling the essentials and meticulous in providing accurate information. She draws on other federal experts on the inside as well to provide information not easily available elsewhere. At the same time, this readable paperback has much to offer a wider audience seeking up-to-date approaches to employers in today's competitive job and promotion market.

The book's breadth (interns to manager as well as Congress and agencies) is matched by attention to detail. Yet, Whiteman does not take you in the weeds. Discussion that could get complicated, such as job qualifications and the ranking of applicants, is uncannily concise. In plain-speaking language, she concentrates on the basics for a fruitful federal job and promotion search while also offering helpful tips and insights.

Whiteman's book is being issued as federal employment is becoming more attractive and more available. The historic election of Barack Obama is likely to draw a new crop of talent to every level of federal employment as public service becomes more appealing. The collapse of prestigious companies has made the private sector less glamorous. Federal jobs seem a lot more inviting today as the country experiences the most serious economic crisis since the 1930s.

However, this good news about federal employment also assures a large pool of applicants. More Americans seeking jobs and promotions are likely to be attracted by government stability and benefits. Baby boomers, who have been quick to retire, may respond to the poor economy and its impact on retirement savings by stating in place longer. As federal job and promotion opportunities become more competitive, the information in these ages will grow even more valuable.

The varied and increasingly important missions of the federal sector virtually assure that the federal sector will grow. Federal employment offers a version of virtually all the major job categories in the private sector. No single employer has this range of opportunities for jobs and promotions and locations in the U.S. and overseas. *How to Land a Top-Paying Federal Job* is an invaluable tool for the federal job and promotion search, but the guidance in these pages will serve the reader wherever good jobs are available.

—**Congresswoman Eleanor Holmes Norton**
(D–Washington, DC)

This book is dedicated to the **Whiteman** and **Gregg** wings of my family,
a band of survivors who have again and again intrepidly soldiered
on through adversities—and in memory of my young nephew,
Lucian Gregg, an adventurous climber who literally and
figuratively reached great heights in his short life.

PREFACE:
Common Myths About Federal Jobs

1. **Government salaries are low. No!** Studies and anecdotal reports show that federal salaries compare very favorably to private sector salaries. And federal "benies" and job security are unparalleled. Plus, some feds receive up to $60,000 in student loan repayments. This book provides the most complete, accurate guidance available anywhere on federal salaries.

2. **Federal salaries are nonnegotiable. No!** Federal salaries are usually negotiable. This is the *only* book that explains how to negotiate federal salaries.

3. **The applicant with the best connections usually gets the job. No!** The applicant who impresses hiring managers the most usually gets the job. This is the *only* book that provides application advice straight from federal hiring managers—the gatekeepers to federal jobs.

4. **Federal internships are voluntary and do not pay. No!** Tens of thousands of undergrads, grad students, law students, and recent grads currently enjoy well-paying federal jobs and internships. This book provides the *most* comprehensive list available anywhere of such opportunities.

5. **The federal workforce is not diverse. No!** Minorities are generally better represented in the federal workforce than elsewhere, and federal agencies are aggressively recruiting women, minorities, people with disabilities, and veterans. This book provides the *most* comprehensive advice available anywhere on special federal hiring programs for job hunters in these categories.

6. **The federal government is a monolithic mass. No!** Federal agencies are as different from one another as are private

"I had the dream about meaningful employment again last night."

organizations. This book provides the *most* comprehensive advice anywhere on how to get the inside scoop on your target agencies.

7. **The federal hiring system is a big, mysterious black hole. No!** The federal government has a straightforward hiring system, but you probably wouldn't know that from the way federal jobs are advertised. This book is the *only* book that clearly and concisely explains how the federal system *really* works and how to *really* work the system.

8. **It takes forever to get hired by the feds. No!** Applicants for federal jobs are frequently interviewed soon after applying. And many agencies have reduced the entire hiring process to 45 days, which is comparable to the private sector.

9. **You have to pass a civil service test to become a fed! No!** The civil service test is history. Today, only a few types of federal jobs require tests.

10. **Most feds are lazy and dim-witted. No!** Forget oddballs like Neuman on *Seinfeld* and Cliff Claven on *Cheers*. Most feds are smart, tech-savvy go-getters.

11. **Most federal jobs are in Washington, DC. No!** Almost 85 percent of federal jobs are located outside of DC in nationwide and overseas locations.

> The federal workforce is "an elite island of secure and highly paid workers," according to *The Washington Post*.

12. **Government work is dull and unimaginative. No!** Feds use creativity and judgment to carry out policies that significantly impact millions of people and precious resources.

13. **Only insiders can land federal overseas jobs—never outsiders. No!** Varied types of professionals from recent grads to midcareer professionals to stay-at-home parents returning to work are currently being recruited into exciting overseas jobs. This is the *only* book that provides advice straight from federal hiring managers on how to land these jobs.

14. **If your political party is not currently in power, you would have to abandon your principles to work for the federal government. No!** Federal agencies must fulfill their legally mandated missions no matter which party is in power and so most federal jobs are generally insulated from politics; federal staffers continue their work day in and day out, even after the political pendulum swings.

15. **Federal work schedules are rigid. No!** Most white-collar feds can, within reason, set their own daily arrival and departure times and work longer days in exchange for taking 3-day weekends every other week. In addition, a significant and growing percentage of white-collar feds work at home part of the week.

16. **If you have previously been rejected for a federal job, it's useless to apply for another. No!** Federal agencies hire more than 200,000 new employees and promote hundreds of thousands of others every year. Your standing in any particular job selection has absolutely no bearing on your standing in others.

17. **The federal government is being privatized and downsized. No!** The size of the federal workforce has remained fairly steady in recent years. And relatively few jobs have been privatized. Such losses are more than offset by a retirement wave that will open up about 40 percent of jobs in the next 10 years.

18. **All feds ascend the career ladder at the same pace—no matter what. No!** Feds can accelerate their career ascents by using the potentially pivotal career advancement strategies that are provided in this book (and nowhere else).

P A R T I

GEARING UP TO APPLY

And you're off . . . in hot pursuit of a new and better job. Part I explains why this is a great time to go federal, provides leads to hot openings, and presents simple, easy-to-follow instructions on landing domestic and overseas jobs—either by walking through the federal government's front door or by using little-known strategies to slip through its back doors. Part I also reveals how federal hiring managers *really* think—absolutely essential information for acing your applications and interviews.

In addition, the CD that accompanies this book features the most comprehensive directories available anywhere of: (1) well-paying federal internships, student jobs, and special recruitment programs for young professionals; and (2) fellowships for experienced professionals—including nonfeds and current feds.

Armed with this book's previously unavailable, behind-the-scenes guidance, you will easily and expertly navigate the federal system, whether you are seeking your first federal job or a promotion.

CHAPTER **1**

A Great Time to Go Federal

U.S. News & World Report *describes a government job as a terrific deal and includes "government manager" on its list of best careers.*

With about 2.7 million civilian employees, the federal government is the nation's largest employer. Every year, about 200,000 new hires join the federal workforce and hundreds of thousands of current feds are promoted.

Do you want to land an interesting job that pays a top salary, provides unbeatable, rock-solid job security, *and* will advance the public good in important ways? If so, you're probably primed to work for the federal government.

What does the federal government do? The federal government literally runs this country. To do so, it protects the strength and vitality of the U.S. economy; creates foreign policy; manages precious natural, cultural, and high-tech resources; predicts tornados and hurricanes; oversees the nation's planes, trains, and highways; secures our food and water supplies; protects the health and safety of workers; keeps unsafe products off the market; and funds most of the nation's scientific and medical research, to name just a few examples.

Why spend your career toiling in obscurity when you could be on your way to becoming a power broker? Feds contribute to the high-stakes, hot-button policy issues that cover the front pages of the nation's newspapers every day.

To run the country, feds do everything that private sector employees do—and more. So like the private sector, the federal government hires engineers, teachers, IT experts, scientists, business managers, lawyers, PR specialists, policy wonks, medical professionals, accountants, auto mechanics, electricians, property managers—and more.

Plus, the federal government has jobs that you won't find anywhere else. Feds work as spies, volcano watchers, park rangers, terrorist hunters, disease detectives, curators of precious historical documents, and diplomats. The possibilities are endless.

Feds work in every imaginable setting from offices, laboratories, museums, libraries, hospitals, parks, forests, and marine sanctuaries located throughout the United States to embassies located in far-flung countries. And they access and control resources—including huge budgets—that are unavailable to private-sector employees.

Another important advantage: the federal government provides one of the precious few workplaces where you can work exciting jobs, earn competitive salaries, and still have a life. Most feds stick to a 40-hour work week. The federal government also offers these first-rate perks:

> **Job security:** The federal government continuously hires for all types of jobs and internships—even when other organizations are laying off. And while nongovernmental employees may be "pink-slipped" when the economy falters, feds are rarely laid off. Also, it is generally much harder to fire federal employees than employees in other sectors.

> **Top salaries and advancement:** Studies and anecdotal evidence show that the average federal salary is significantly higher than that of the average private sector employee and that feds in many fields earn more than private sector professionals in the same fields. Plus, feds receive regularly scheduled promotions, merit-based promotions, and annual cost-of-living salary increases. For more information about federal salaries see Chapter 14.

➤ **Generous vacations:** Full-time federal employees enjoy 10 paid holidays and 9, 13, 20, or 26 days of vacation each year, depending on their seniority. They can take up to 12 weeks of unpaid leave to attend to a birth, adoption, or seriously ill family member.

➤ **Top-notch health insurance:** Feds choose from the nation's best health insurance, dental insurance, vision insurance, long-term care, and life insurance programs.

➤ **Stay close to the kids:** Many agencies have on-site childcare facilities.

➤ **Coverage for health care and dependent care costs:** Feds can pay up to $4,000 annually for childcare and up to $5,000 annually for adult dependent care expenses from tax-free accounts that are set aside from their paychecks. This option helps feds save up to 40 percent in out-of-pocket health care and dependent care expenses.

Forget stereotypes of sour-faced feds!

An average of 75 percent of government workers said they were happy at work from April 2006 to April 2007, compared to 71 percent of private sector employees, according to the Hudson Employment Index.

➤ **Excellent, secure retirement packages:** As corporate scandals and cutbacks erode private sector pensions, feds remain covered by generous, secure pensions that feature cost-of-living increases, a defined benefit based on length of service, and a 401(K)-like investment program with matching. Moreover, unlike most private sector employees, feds get another coveted benefit: lifetime health insurance coverage.

➤ **Flexible schedules:** Flexible work schedules and telecommuting options are freeing feds from the straight jacket of 9-to-5 schedules. Such programs, for example, currently enable about 20 percent of federal workers to work from home or from a nearby telework center at least 1 day per week—a figure that is increasing as telecommuting programs mature. In addition, many feds can opt to work 9 hours per day in exchange for taking off every other Friday.

➤ **Lose academic loans:** Some feds receive up to $60,000 in the student loan repayments. In addition, the College Cost Reduction and Access Act forgives the outstanding student loans of public service employees—including feds—after they have made 10 years of payments.

"True, the private sector has its benefits, but, then again, so does the public trough."

> ➤ **Be a do-gooder:** The ultimate aim of most federal jobs is—in one way or another—to better the world. In the words of a Peace Corps staffer, "I am doing what I love to do, and it's all for a very good cause." Moreover, even entry-level employees can wield tremendous responsibility in the government. "I have only been out of college for a year-and-a-half, and I am influencing huge budgets on environmental programs," observes a Program Analyst at the Environmental Protection Agency.

Ride the Hiring Wave

Linda Springer, the federal government's top personnel manager, says that the federal government is about to be hit by an unprecedented "retirement tsunami." During the next 10 years, about 60 percent of federal employees—including 90 percent of senior federal managers—will be eligible to retire and about 40 percent of employees are expected to retire, according to Springer.

To backfill for the impending retirement tsunami, the federal government is vigorously recruiting all types of professionals at all levels of their careers. Indeed, large percentages of new federal hires are now experienced professionals.

Moreover, every retirement at top grades is expected to trigger multiple staffing actions as lower level employees ascend to fill the resulting power vacuum. This means that the retirement tsunami will make it easier than ever to move up in the federal government.

New Blood

When you think of government employees, do you visualize dowdy, school-marmish women and frumpy, pocket protector–clad men toiling in musty offices? If so, your perceptions are due for an update.

Indeed, the Office of Personnel Management's statistics show that the federal workforce—which is already generally more educated than the private sector workforce—is steadily becoming more skilled and more educated. In addition, largely because of the approaching retirement wave and because of renewed interest in government service inspired by 9/11, "a potential for a quasi-youth movement in the government job sector" promises to infuse the federal government with new, revitalizing blood and fresh ideas, according to *Monster.com*. In other words, the feds are registering lower and lower on the stodgy-meter.

CHAPTER **2**

The Search Is On
Finding Openings

"The best way to predict your future is to create it."
— Unknown

Your job search is on and you have issued an All Points Bulletin (APB) for appealing openings. You can continue your quest online anytime, anywhere—at home dressed in your sweat pants while nursing your cappuccino, or between meetings at work while nursing your resentment for your current boss. This chapter explains how to find federal openings and provides leads to hot opportunities.

Where Do You Want to Work?

HOT TIP

Each federal organization and Congressional office has its own website that: (1) explains the who, what, where, when, and why of what it does; and (2) features a career section. To find opportunities in any particular agency, check the agency's own career website as well as the career website of the department in which it is housed. A hyperlinked A-to-Z directory of federal organizations is posted at http://www.usa.gov/Agencies/Federal/All_Agencies/index.shtml.

Contrary to popular belief, the federal government is not a single monolithic mass. Indeed, federal organizations differ from one another as much as do private organizations.

Some of these differences hinge on each organization's mission—from the National Science Foundation's collegial academic-like ambiance to the National Clandestine Service's cloak-and-dagger secrecy to the Security and Exchange Commission's "we're-the-good-guys" ethic. Other differences hinge on factors such as the agency's pay scales, willingness to reward producers with bonuses and promotions, workforce diversity and age demographics, level of office formality, hierarchy, and teamwork.

More tips on how to research federal organizations are provided at the end of this chapter and tips on Capitol Hill jobs are provided in Chapter 4.

What Credentials Do You Need?

Many types of professionals are hired by virtually every agency. These types of professionals include lawyers and specialists in human resources, information technology, accounting, communications, budget management, and administrative support. But the hiring of some types of specialized professionals is limited to certain agencies that address their specialties.

Some federal jobs require college degrees and some require graduate degrees. But many desirable federal jobs do not require college degrees and many others accept work experience as substitutes for degrees. The Office of Personnel Management, which is the federal government's human resources agency, explains, "The nature of your specialized experience is what really counts."

The requirements for each job opening are spelled out in its announcement. For more information about federal salaries and what salary range you should aim for, see Chapter 14.

The Federal Jobs Hotline

USAJOBS (http://usajobs.gov) is the official jobs website of the federal government. Clicking on USAJOBS is like hitting the mother lode of federal job openings; the site announces more than 15,000 jobs per day and is continuously updated throughout the day, every business day.

Included among USAJOBS's listings are jobs located all over the world and jobs that are at every level of almost every conceivable occupation. USAJOBS also announces some state, local, and private sector job openings and features links to the employment websites of many federal and state organizations.

An interactive phone version of USAJOBS operates 24/7 at 703-724-1850 and TDD 978-461-8404.

HOT TIP

Several commercial websites charge members to search lists of federal job openings and to be e-mailed customized lists of openings. USAJOBS provides the same service for free. Why pay for what you can get for free?

Vacancy Announcements

Federal job openings are advertised in vacancy announcements—the government's version of "Help Wanted" signs. You can search USAJOBS's collection of vacancy announcements by various criteria including keywords, salary, geographic location, job title, and hiring agency. See Chapter 5 for more info on vacancy announcements.

Wonder what government organizations are in your city? Check the blue government pages in your local phone book.

If you are unsure of which federal job titles best match your skills and interests, visit the *Career Exploration* pages under *Info Center* at USAJOBS, and do keyword searches on USAJOBS's job listings using common job titles in your field and words representing your areas of expertise.

The Window of Opportunity

The window of opportunity for applying for federal job openings varies. Some jobs are advertised for several weeks or longer. But others are advertised for the minimum amount of time required by law: 5 business days for jobs that are open to all applicants and 3 business days for jobs that are only open to current federal employees. So surf through USAJOBS every few days so that you don't miss out on any hot openings.

Which Jobs Are Not Posted on USAJOBS?

Federal agencies are required to advertise most job openings that are open to the public (not just to their own employees). They usually meet such advertising requirements by posting their announcements on USAJOBS. Nevertheless, some types of federal jobs are not necessarily posted on USAJOBS. These jobs include:

> ➤ Jobs that the hiring agency opts to advertise in other venues instead of USAJOBS, such as their own websites, newspaper classifieds, and online jobs boards.

> ➤ Most of the internships, recruitment programs, and fellowships that are covered in Chapter 3.

> ➤ Jobs in the legislative branch (Congress) and judicial branch (the courts).

> ➤ Jobs that are only open to the hiring agency's employees.

> ➤ Jobs that are filled exclusively by attendees of career fairs.

> ➤ Most contract and temporary jobs.

> ➤ Jobs that are in the excepted service rather than the competitive service. What is the difference between competitive service jobs and excepted service jobs? Competitive service jobs—which account for the majority of federal jobs—must be advertised and filled through open competitions. By contrast, excepted service jobs can be filled through relatively flexible procedures designed by the hiring agency that do not always involve advertising openings and holding open competitions for them.

> ➤ Most jobs in the foreign service.

> Excepted service jobs include: (1) all federal jobs such as attorneys, chaplains, doctors, dentists and nurses, and certain other professions; and (2) all jobs in certain agencies including the FBI, CIA, State Department, and various other agencies. For a list of excepted service agencies, look up *excepted service* in Wikipedia.

> To find excepted service openings, regularly check the website(s) of the appropriate agencies. (Though not required, some excepted service jobs are advertised on USAJOBS.)

Other Sources of Agency Openings

You may also find vacancy announcements for jobs in federal agencies via:

> ➤ **Federal Websites:** In addition to regularly checking USAJOBS, also regularly check the websites of your target agencies. Why? Because some agency openings appear on agency websites before appearing on USAJOBS while some never appear on USAJOBS.

> ➤ **The National Academies of Science (NAS) Website:** NAS is a quasi-government organization that employs scientists, policy experts, and administrative personnel. See http://www.nas.edu. (NAS openings are not posted on USAJOBS.)

➤ **Intelligence and Defense Websites:** The Defense Department (http://www.cpms.osd.mil/ and http://www.dodvets.com/vetinfo.asp) helps connect civilian job seekers to hiring agencies and provides application help. Live support at 888-DoD-4USA. See http://intelligence.gov for info on intelligence careers.

➤ **Job Fairs:** See this chapter's discussion of job fairs.

➤ **Newspapers:** Check the Sunday classifieds and papers that cover Capitol Hill, including *Roll Call* (http://www.RollCall.com) and *The Hill* (http://www.HillNews.com).

➤ **The Human Resources Offices of Federal Agencies:** These offices can tell you about unadvertised openings that will be filled through special streamlined procedures for special categories of applicants, including veterans and people with disabilities.

➤ **The Senior Environmental Employment Program (SEEP):** SEEP hires retired and unemployed Americans who are at least 55 years old for clerical, administrative, communications, and technical jobs that support Environmental Protection Agency programs throughout the United States. See http://www.EPA.gov/ohr.

➤ **Post Offices:** Find out about Postal Service jobs at local post offices and http://www.usps.gov.

Openings in Congress

Find openings on Congressional staffs at:

➤ **The Senate Employment Office:** Go to http://www.senate.gov; click *Visitors*.

➤ **The House of Representatives Employment Office:** Go to http://www.house.gov; click *Employment Opportunities*.

➤ **Publications That Cover Capitol Hill:** These include *Roll Call*, *The Hill*, and *Congressional Quarterly*. Also check http://www.politixgroup.com.

Chapter 4 discusses jobs on Congressional staffs and Chapter 14 discusses the salaries of those jobs.

Job Fairs

The federal government frequently participates in nationwide job fairs. At a single event, you may meet hiring managers from many agencies recruiting for jobs at all levels. Some agencies use these events to fill high-priority jobs or internships through fast-track procedures or even on-the-spot offers. Therefore, you may find openings at career fairs that are not advertised anywhere else.

HOT TIP

Gap Prevention Strategies

By volunteering or working temp jobs during your search, you will earn good references, generate contacts that could lead to permanent jobs, and avoid creating holes in your résumé that would turn off some employers. See Chapter 2 for leads on temp agencies.

NINE WAYS TO LAND A FEDERAL JOB

1. Anwer an announcement posted on USAJOBS or an agency or Congressional website.

2. Get hired at a federal job fair.

3. Get recruited into one of the internships, student jobs, or special recruitment programs for students, recent grads, and experienced professionals covered in Chapter 3 and on this book's CD.

4. Land one of the fellowships covered in Chapter 3 and on this book's CD.

5. Segue into a permanent job from a temp job or a contract job.

6. Use your networking and other professional activities to impress a federal manager enough to compel him/her to create a position for you or recruit you into an existing position.

7. Get accepted directly into the senior executive service (SES) by landing a place in the Federal Candidate Development Program (Fed CDP).

8. Join the foreign service.

9. Receive a political appointment.

ATTENTION WOMEN, MINORITIES, AND DISABLED JOB SEEKERS!

If you are a woman, a member of a minority or a job seeker with a disability, you may be eligible to participate in programs that promote diversity in the federal workforce:

- College students, grad students, and recent grads should consider the internships and recruitment programs for women, minorities, and people with disabilities that are covered in Chapter 3 and on this book's CD.

- Experienced professionals should consider applying for the senior executive service, which is discussed in Chapters 5 and 16.

In addition, special programs for veterans are discussed in Appendix 1 and special programs for people with disabilities are discussed in Appendix 2. Also, the SEEP program for retired professionals is covered in this chapter.

Agencies that are aggressively recruiting minorities and women for varied types of positions include the FBI, the Federal Deposit Insurance Corporation, foreign service agencies and some intelligence agencies. So check their websites for their openings and job fair schedules. Wonder which agencies are the best promoters of workforce diversity? Check out the rankings of federal agencies in workforce diversity at http://www.bestplacestowork.org.

Two more tips: (1) Many federal agencies regularly recruit professionals at conferences and other venues sponsored by minority organizations, such as the National Association for the Advancement of Colored People, the Society of Black Engineers, and the American Indian Science and Engineering Society. (2) Many federal agencies recruit at minority colleges and universities. So if you attend such a school, ask your career office for leads to federal jobs.

TEN TIPS FOR FARING WELL AT JOB FAIRS

1. Before the fair, check which agencies will attend. Then, troll through the websites of your target agencies so that you will be able to pepper each meet-and-greet conversation with evidence of your knowledge of the agency's goals and high-profile activities.

2. Practice introducing yourself with a 30-second, punchy opener that highlights your key qualifications and how they would benefit your target agency.

3. Present yourself as a decisive, goal-oriented job seeker who knows what type of job you want. Recruiters are universally turned off by job seekers who expect career guidance from them.

4. Prepare yourself for an on-the-spot job interview by reviewing Chapter 13.

5. Pack the following items in a professional briefcase: your ID, pens, pad, résumés, college transcripts, reference lists, business cards, your success portfolio as discussed in Chapter 13, documents verifying your eligibility for Veterans' Preference, if appropriate, and your most recent Notification of Personnel Action, if you are a current fed.

6. Dress as nicely as you would for a job interview. No eating or gum chewing, or sucking out of a water bottle in the interviewer's face.

7. Attend the fair alone, without bringing parents or friends with you. By doing so you will help prove that you're a sure-footed professional who doesn't lean on others or bring personal baggage to the office.

8. Collect the business cards of contacts so that you will have their names, titles, and contact info.

9. If a recruiter does not have openings that are suitable for you, ask him/her for other leads.

10. Immediately send thank-you letters to helpful contacts and follow up on promising leads.

Find federal job fairs by checking USAJOBS, the websites of your target agencies and target offices, the websites of your local newspapers, and online job boards. *Hint:* Some agencies in the intelligence and defense community, the State Department, the FBI, and some agencies that address banking and corporate finance are veritable job fair junkies.

Going Global in Government

Are you a globe-trotting adventurer longing for adventure in far-flung countries? If so, consider joining the tens of thousands of civilian feds who currently work overseas.

ON THE CD...

More Info on International jobs

For more information about overseas jobs, see the "Going Global in Government" chapter on this book's CD. Also see the directory of federal internships as well as my *Washington Post* articles on international careers and federal internships.

"To be completely frank, we have now discovered all your country's secrets, except how to make a million dollars in one's spare time at home with no personal investment."

What types of professionals does the federal government send overseas? Virtually all types of professionals. In fact, almost all professions have overseas applications. So no matter what you currently do or want to do for a living, you could probably do it overseas, if you want to.

What types of projects do feds work on overseas? They provide humanitarian and disaster relief; reduce world hunger; promote conflict resolution; train scientific researchers; conserve natural resources; fight diseases; identify and confront threats to the United States such as terrorism and other illegal activities; and hammer out international agreements on health, environmental problems, defense, trade, and immigration—to name just a few of their activities.

In addition, overseas feds provide all manner of administrative support and maintain the federal overseas infrastructure—by working on construction projects, running the administrative and accounting aspects of offices, procuring goods and services, protecting the security of diplomats and other Americans overseas, advancing IT projects, and contributing to other types of projects.

 The State Department consistently ranks as one of the best places to work in surveys of feds. Also, State ranked among the 10 best employers in a recent *Business Week* survey of undergrads and college recruiters.

Leads for Legal Eagles

The federal government is the U.S.'s largest employer of attorneys. Federal lawyers work throughout Capitol Hill and in virtually every federal agency—not just the Justice Department—and they are qualified for various types of jobs: They shape policy, write federal regulations that impact huge populations and important resources, liaison with Congress, advise political appointees, write Congressional testimony, enforce regulatory and administrative programs, work on ethics issues, and serve as trial lawyers and judges, to name just a few possibilities.

Many agencies hire legal interns and newly minted lawyers through their summer internship and Legal Honors Programs, which may or may not be advertised on USAJOBS. Find information on agency Legal Honors Programs by checking the careers websites of your target agencies and by "Googling" the names of agencies that interest you along with keywords such as *Legal Honors Program*.

In addition, many types of other legal jobs for lawyers of all levels are advertised on USAJOBS and agency websites, so check for them as well. And review the internships covered in Chapter 3 and on this book's CD. Also, if you want to clerk for a judge or explore other opportunities in the federal judiciary, go to the jobs section of the website of the U.S. Courts at http://www.uscourts.gov.

You may find unadvertised federal openings by networking with professional organizations, such as the Federal Bar Association (http://www.Fedbar.org) and the Public Service Law Network. In addition, do a "Google" search for the *NALP Legal Opportunities Guide*, which provides an excellent overview of federal attorney jobs and guidance on how to land them.

Leads for PhDs

With many excellent universities, a dynamic intellectual life, and employment possibilities for both halves of academic couples, Washington, DC, offers an attractive alternative to academia.

Although PhDs are hired by virtually all federal agencies and labs, several organizations are particularly popular among PhDs because they offer "think-tanky" environments and manage studies, reports, and programs on multidisciplinary topics involving foreign affairs, education, information technology, social issues, economics, public health, and the sciences. These organizations are: The Library of Congress, the Government Accountability Office, the Congressional Budget Office, the Office of Management and Budget, the National Academy of Sciences, and the National Science Foundation.

The Departments of Agriculture, Energy, and State; the CIA; FBI; NASA; and EPA are also popular destinations for PhDs. In addition, many Capitol Hill offices hire professionals with advanced degrees.

Also, many federal fellowships recruit PhDs. For more information about them, see Chapter 3 and the directory of fellowships featured on this book's CD.

Another lead: Many federal agencies, particularly science-based ones, have post-doc programs. EPA ranks third nationally as the best place to work for post-docs according to a survey by *The Scientist*.

Leads for Enviros and Public Health Advocates

Do you want to save the Earth or protect people against diseases and other public health threats? Federal environmental and public health advocates advise political appointees, write Congressional testimony, manage trail-blazing research and education programs, investigate industrial disasters, write and enforce national laws, manage precious natural resources, reduce the impacts of natural and unnatural disasters, and promote sustainable development.

Opportunities for enviros and public health advocates are offered by many agencies including: the Agriculture Department; Army Corps of Engineers; Chemical Safety Hazard and Investigation Board; Congressional Research Service; Consumer Product Safety Commission; Council on Environmental Quality; all agencies in the Department of Health and Human Services (particularly the Centers for Disease Control); the Departments of Defense, Energy, Justice, and Labor; EPA; Federal Energy Regulatory Commission; FEMA; Government Accountability Office; NASA; National Atmospheric and Oceanic Administration; Peace Corps; the Smithsonian; State Department; Transportation Department; USAID; the U.S. Public Health Service Commissioned Corps; Veterans Administration; U.S. Geological Survey; and the World Bank. Also consider the organizations listed under *Leads for PhDs*, and explore Congressional committees addressing natural resource and public health issues.

Leads for Medical Professionals

Common destinations for physicians, mental health professionals, nurses, physical therapists, and other medical practitioners include the Departments of Defense and State, USAID, FAA, the intelligence community, the U.S. Public Health Service Commissioned Corps, the VA, the FBI, and agencies in the Department of Health and Human Services, particularly the Centers for Disease Control.

Leads for Generalists

You may be a generalist if you have: (1) a liberal arts degree; (2) excellent research and communication skills; and (3) diverse interests rather than a passion for one esoteric issue that only about five people in the world really understand.

Find generalist jobs by searching USAJOBs on these keywords: *public affairs, communications, writer, Congressional affairs, policy analyst,* and *program analyst.* Also explore opportunities in the organizations discussed above under *Leads for PhDs.*

Base Realignment and Closure (BRAC)

BRAC is a Defense Department (DOD) program that is shutting down some military bases and expanding others. Because of BRAC, Maryland will receive up to 60,000 new federal jobs in the next few years—more than any other state in the United States—as well as thousands of contracting jobs. Get more information about BRAC locations at http://www.defenselink.mil/brac/faqs001.html.

Bases that are currently expanding because of BRAC are hiring many types of civilian professionals, including veterans with security clearances, specialists in high-tech disciplines, engineering and information assurance, project managers, contract managers, accountants, human resources managers, administrative assistants, and the list goes on. Find BRAC openings on the websites of your target bases, USAJOBS and http://www.cpms.osd.mil.

Follow the News: Find Hiring Blitzes

If you want to become a fed, become a news junkie. Why? Because current events and the priorities of the President and Congress influence the job market in general and help determine which agencies receive budget boosts that trigger hiring blitzes.

Without doubt, the news event that has most profoundly affected federal hiring in recent years was 9/11. Since the attacks, the Departments of Homeland Security and Defense, the FBI, and agencies in the intelligence community have been aggressively recruiting. But it is important to remember that such organizations hire varied types of professionals, not just security and intelligence experts. For example, the Drug Enforcement Administration has recently been snapping-up finance experts and accountants to track the money trails of drug cartels and terrorist organizations. Also, scientists are in demand by various agencies, including the Agriculture Department, to help fight bioterrorism.

> **INTERESTED IN INTELLIGENCE JOBS?**
>
> For insider accounts about intelligence careers, do keyword searches on bookseller sites on *CIA* and *intelligence*.

In addition to reflecting world events, federal hiring practices also reflect industry specific developments. For example, the recent corporate financing scandals compelled agencies that regulate corporate financing to staff up.

As you follow the news, look for organizations that receive budget increases and/or are assigned new legislation and programs to implement; new organizations, task forces, and commissions; and organizations that are reorganizing. Why? Because they are probably hiring.

High-Demand Professionals

The following types of professionals are in particularly high demand by the government.

> ➤ IT professionals, particular those skilled in cyber security, are being aggressively recruited throughout the government. (The salaries of IT experts are significantly higher in the federal government than in the private sector.)

> ➤ Intelligence analysts are wanted by intelligence and defense agencies. According to *The Washington Post*, "being an analyst is almost an academic profession—part taught, part absorbed, part intuition—that requires weighing volumes of information and boiling them down into reports for policymakers in the executive branch and in Congress."

> ➤ Professionals with language skills, particularly Middle-Eastern languages, Asian languages, and Russian, and professionals who are knowledgeable on intelligence issues, such as weapons of mass destruction.

> ➤ Contracting specialists are being snapped up throughout the government—which is the world's biggest buyer, spending more than $400 billion per year. Contract specialists manage and negotiate the purchasing of goods and services and oversee projects. See http://www.fai.gov.

> **HOT TIP**
>
> **Wanted: Intelligence, Security, and Language Experts**
>
> In the wake of 9/11, the Departments of Defense and Homeland Security have been offering recruitment bonuses to some new hires. In addition, several agencies are aggressively recruiting intelligence and language experts.
>
> - The National Security Agency (NSA), which offers signing bonuses worth up to $7,500, is seeking experts in languages, intelligence analysis, signals analysis, math, computer science, the physical sciences, and acquisition. Go to http://www.NSA.gov; then click *Careers*.
>
> - The National Geospatial-Intelligence Agency, which studies imagery from spy satellites and other systems, The Defense Intelligence Agency, and FBI, which offers recruitment bonuses to some types of professionals, will also hire large numbers of intelligence specialists and other professionals in the coming years.
>
> - The Central Intelligence Agency's Corporate Language Hiring Bonus Program offers some language specialists recruitment bonuses worth up to $35,000. Go to http://www.cia.gov; then click on *CIA Careers* and then *Language Positions*.
>
> - The Secret Service offers recruitment bonuses worth 25 percent of annual salary to language experts.
>
> For more leads on opportunities for language experts, go to http://www.makingthedifference.org and click *Foreign Language Programs in the Federal Government*.

➤ Auditors, budget specialists, and business mangers are also in high demand throughout the government. Accountants are also wanted, particularly by the IRS.

➤ Patent examiners are needed by the U.S. Patent and Trademark Office (USPTO) to help manage the technology revolution. (A Bachelor's degree in engineering or science is required.) Note that the USPTO is aggressively recruiting mid-career professionals with generous recruitment bonuses and that a large percentage of patent examiners work at home.

➤ Engineers are in high demand by the Defense Department, NASA, the Nuclear Regulatory Commission, and the Departments of Defense, Transportation, and Energy. Many of these agencies offer recruitment bonuses to some new hires.

➤ Thousands of tax examiners will be hired by the IRS over the next few years.

POLITICAL APPOINTMENTS

Granted, you probably won't be named Secretary of State if you don't already have serious inside pull and instant name recognition. But take heart: many of the 7,000 political jobs in the federal government are filled by ordinary, hard working professionals whose names have never graced *Time* magazine.

What They Are

Political appointees include ambassadors, Cabinet members, agency heads, members of regulatory commissions, judges, lawyers, and policy specialists. Many of the assistants and members of the immediate staffs of high-ranking officials are also political appointees.

All political jobs in the federal government are filled via nominations from the White House. (Some political jobs require Senate confirmation.) Professionals who have strong affiliations with the President, an administration staffer, or the President's political party have the best chances of landing political jobs. But many accomplished professionals who have no inside track land political jobs simply by applying for them.

Political appointees usually spend most of their time designing and advocating administrative policies and working closely with key officials. *READ*: power, influence, and prestige.

But the flip side to political positions is that they offer little job security and most appointees lose their jobs when the administration changes. And the stresses experienced by political appointees are reflected in memoir titles such as *Leaving Town Alive* by former National Endowment for the Arts Chairman John Frohnmayer and *Locked in the Cabinet* by former Labor Secretary Robert Reich.

Applying

If you apply for a political appointment, treat your quest like a campaign. The more endorsements you get from powerful advocates, the better. Exploit any White House connections—even distant ones—that you have. Perhaps, for example, your Congressman works closely with an administration official. Recommendations from associations, nonprofits, unions, academics, and business leaders will also help.

The best time to apply for political positions is right after a Presidential election. Nevertheless, many political positions turn over between elections.

Resources

A list of political positions is available in *The Plum Book*, which is published after each Presidential election. To find it, "Goggle" *The Plum Book*. *A Survivor's Guide for Presidential Nominees* is posted at http://www.brookings.edu/papers/2000/1115governance.aspx. Applications for political appointments are posted at http://www.whitehouse.gov/appointments/.

Follow the Money: Contract Jobs

Many federal contractors work on federal projects without being full-fledged federal employees. That is, these contractors do federal work, are supervised by federal managers, and are based in the offices of federal agencies. But such agency-based federal contractors are not employed or directly paid by the federal government. Instead, they are employed and paid by consulting firms that hold a contract with the federal government.

Because agency-based federal contractors work cheek-to-jowl with federal employees, agency-based contracting assignments provide ideal opportunities for networking, gaining government experience, and earning a salary while you job search. Indeed, many agency-based federal contractors are eventually hired into full-time federal positions.

Types of Federal Contractors

There are three major types of federal contractors:

1. Contractors who work for consulting firms that have contracted with a federal agency to provide specific services. The federal government is currently spinning off more and more projects into federal contracts that are awarded to these types of consulting firms.

    You can find job openings with federal contractors by checking job websites such as http://www.monster.com and http://www.hotjobs.yahoo.com, and the Sunday classified sections of newspapers, particularly *The Washington Post*, which occasionally includes a special section devoted to government contracting jobs.

2. Professionals who work for employment agencies that are contracted to help a federal agency fulfill its short-term staffing needs for various types of professionals, including lawyers, accountants, contract managers, writers, IT professionals, and administrative assistants. Note that temp jobs aren't just for receptionists anymore! Employment agencies (which may go by such names as temporary staffing or human resource agencies) advertise their contract openings on job websites and the classifieds sections of newspapers. Also, ask employment agencies listed in your local phone book if they help federal agencies staff up.

3. Personal service contractors—professionals who directly contract with an agency for a job for a specified time period. Many (but not all) personal service contracts are for overseas assignments. (See "Going Global in Government" on this book's CD.)

Finding Federal Temp Jobs

Tips for finding temp agencies that contract with the federal government:

➤ The State Department lists its temp firms at
   http://www.state.gov/m/dghr/flo/rsrcs/pubs/7248.htm.

➤ Temp firms that help federal agencies staff up include PoliTemps (http://www.politemps.com); Adecco (http://www.adecco.com/Channels/adecco/home/home1.asp); PRofessional Solutions, LLC (http://www.prstaffing.com); AmeriTemps (http://www.ameritemps.com);

CAREER TRANSITION SUCCESS STORY

By Barry Phelps, Supervisory Writer/Editor

A few weeks after I left my position as communications director for a small nonprofit organization, I decided to résumé my career with the federal government. An Internet employment website ad soon caught my eye. The ad, which had been placed by a temporary-placement firm, was for a temporary writer/editor at a federal Homeland Security agency.

I followed up and things moved quickly. I interviewed with the firm on a Friday and was working at the federal agency by the following Monday. When my initial 3-month stint ended, the agency offered me a full-time federal position as a senior writer-editor with its Office of Human Resources. The salary negotiations went well and I am now making more in compensation than at the nonprofit and at several other federal jobs I have previously held. Since starting my federal job, I've been transferred to the Office of Communications and Public Affairs as a supervisory writer-editor.

The type of seamless segue that I experienced from a temporary contract position to a permanent federal position is not unusual because the federal government has special, streamlined procedures for filling positions that address critical needs.

Snelling Personnel Services (http://www.snelling.com); Hire Standard Staffing (http://www.hirestandard.com); Answer Staffing Services (http://www.answerstaffing services.com); and Legal Personnel, Inc. (http://www.legalpersonnelinc.com).

➤ GCS (http://www.gcsinfo.com) specializes in helping government contactors staff up.

Treat your applications for temp jobs as seriously as your other applications. Most temp agencies look for the same qualities in applicants that other types of employers look for.

Finding Temp Jobs If You Have a Security Clearance

Professionals who have security clearances are in high-demand by federal agencies and federal contractors, and generally command significantly higher salaries than their noncleared counterparts. KellyFedSecure (http://www.kellyfedsecure.com) and http://www.ClearanceJobs.com place cleared professionals in security-related jobs throughout the United States. Also Tek Systems (http://www.teksystems.com) places professionals with and without security clearances in federal agencies and government contractors throughout the United States. If you currently or previously held a security clearance, cite this credential prominently on your résumé and other application documents.

Find Out Who Is in the Money

It is a good bet that a consulting firm that has *just* won a new federal contract will soon be staffing up. Therefore, such firms—flush with federal funds—provide strategic targets for searches for contracting jobs.

You can find companies that have just won federal contracts by checking your local papers and *The Washington Post's* lists of companies located in the DC area that have just won multimillion dollar federal contracts. These lists appear in the back of the Business section of *The Washington Post's* Monday editions under the heading *Federal Contracts*.

Once you identify the winner of a new federal contract that jives with your skills and interests, call the company's personnel office and ask for the manager of the new contract. Then, call the contract manager and explain why you would be an asset to the company's contracting team. If you act quickly, you may even reach contract managers before they start recruiting. You may thereby elbow out your potential competition.

Find More Leads: Research

By researching the federal community, you may identify managers and experts that you may want to contact for informational interviews, learn about promising networking events, and get tips on how to impress hiring managers. You may also identify agencies that:

> ➤ Promote an organizational culture that jives with your style.

> ➤ Are in the hiring mode because their budgets are increasing, are creating new programs, are reorganizing existing ones; or are leading special recruitment drives that feature recruitment bonuses or fast-track hiring procedures.

> ➤ Offer particularly enticing salaries. (For more information about federal pay scales, see Chapter 14.)

What's more, the knowledge you gain about agency-specific priorities through your research will help you gear your application to your target agency. Here are some free online resources that provide truckloads of information about federal agencies:

> ➤ *Federal Times*, which is a weekly publication available for free at http://www.FederalTimes.com.

> ➤ My *Career Matters* column which appears twice a month in *Federal Times*. (Go to http://www.FederalTimes.com; then click *Careers*.) In addition, my *Washington Post* articles and *WashingtonPost.com* online chats on federal jobs are linked to the *In The News* section of my website at http://wwww.IGotTheJob.net.

> ➤ *Washington Post.com*: (1) The site's *Jobs* section regularly features articles and live online chats with jobs experts. (2) Derrick Dortch, an expert on federal jobs, hosts an online chat once a month. To e-mail questions for upcoming chats or to read previous chats, go to http://www.WashingtonPost.com; then click *Jobs*, and *Get Advice*. (3) Sign of for the *Washington Post's* Federal Insider Newsletter at: http://www.washingtonpost.com/wp-dyn/content/politics/fedpage/index.html.

> ➤ Surveys of employee satisfaction in the federal workforce and information about the culture of federal agencies are posted on http://www.BestPlacestoWork.org.

➤ *GovLoop.com*: a popular social networking site for government professionals, students, and job hunters seeking government jobs.

➤ *FedSmith.com*: an information portal for feds (http://www.FedSmith.com).

➤ Every other year (usually in October or November), *Washingtonian Magazine* ranks the best places to work in Washington, DC, including the best federal agencies.

➤ *GovernmentExecutive.com*. Also peruse monthly issues of *Government Executive* magazine. *Federal Computer Week* (http://www.FCW.com) and *Government Computer News* (http://www.GNC.com) cover trends in federal IT hiring and management.

Resources for Young Professionals

➤ The Partnership for Public Service's site at http://www.makingthedifference.org is overflowing with practical information about landing federal jobs, including a directory of opportunities for young professionals.

➤ Young Government Leaders, a very active group of under-40 feds, sponsors professional development and social activities. See http://www.YoungGovernment Leaders.org.

➤ http://www.YoungFeds.org.

Rolodex-Stuffing Activities

You certainly don't *need* to have friends in the federal government to land a federal job, but it never hurts to have friends in high places. They can advance your job search by:

➤ Hiring you into a current opening or creating a job for you. Yes, a hiring manager can tailor a job opening to the credentials of a particularly desirable applicant, and thereby ensure that the applicant will be a shoo-in for the position.

➤ Pulling strings for you with other hiring managers.

➤ Informing you of job openings as they develop.

➤ Referring you to other promising contacts.

Make a Rolodex Connection

Remember the rule about six degrees of separation? It says that every person on Earth is connected to every other person through six contacts or fewer. Well, you're probably connected to a promising lead through only one or two degrees of separation. I know this because I have met many feds who were steered toward their current jobs from people in their orbits.

For example, I know a federal writer who learned about her current position through a conversation with a stranger in an elevator; a marketing manager who was invited to apply for her current position after one of her clients, a government contractor, put in a good word for her at her current job; and a public affairs specialist who landed her position after a family friend had greased the skids for her.

What worked for these feds could work for you, too. Increase your chances of hitting employment paydirt by working your Rolodex. Tell everyone you know about your job search and ask everyone you know to tell everyone they know . . . and so on.

Create a Networking Card

Make it easy for your contacts to sing your praises by arming them with your networking cards, i.e., business cards that provide a concise list of your credentials and your contact info. You can professionally print hundreds of business cards for less than $20.

Hand out your networking card to friends, family, colleagues, the parents of your children's friends, your spouse's colleagues, friends of your parents, neighbors, and fellow residents of your apartment building. Don't hold back. Shyness is the enemy of the job seeker: hand out your card with wild abandon. Give them to fellow travelers on trains, planes, and buses. Pass them out at family gatherings and parties. Promote yourself at meetings of:

> ➤ Professional organizations: If you are a student or a career-changer, join professional organizations in your target field.

> ➤ Informal networking groups, such as meet-ups.

> ➤ Alumni organizations

> ➤ Community and PTA groups

> ➤ Political groups

Break Out of Your Cubicle

If you're a current fed, stuff your networking Rolodex by joining workgroups, committees, and task forces and by signing on to detail assignments that will expose you to colleagues from other offices within your agency or from other agencies. Enhance your chances of being appointed to such groups by informing your supervisor of your interest in them.

Also attend meetings of professional organizations in your field that are frequented by members of your target community. (For more on this, see Part IV.) Stay in touch with new contacts by inviting them to lunch or other social outings and via e-mail.

If you want to branch out into a new field, look for opportunities within your current job that may provide pivotal experience. For example, I know of a human resources specialist who volunteered to write articles about his office's activities for his agency's newsletter and Intranet site. By doing so, he eventually qualified for a position as a writer in his agency's public affairs office.

You may also gain pivotal experience by volunteering with professional organizations and advocacy groups. As Janet Hanson, the founder of a billion-dollar investment firm and a networking guru, told *ELLE* magazine: "Volunteering is one thing you don't have to ask permission to do. You can go beyond your job description—there are no boundaries, road-blocks, or glass ceilings."

For more ideas of how to raise your profile and amass résumé-stuffing experience, see Part IV.

Run a Cyber Campaign

Use a scorched-earth approach to publicizing your job search. One option for doing so is to announce your availability to your network via a concise group e-mail with a relevant subject line. This e-mail should summarize your credentials, mention that you are looking for job leads related to your expertise, and link to your professional website, if you have one. Also, attach your résumé in a PDF format as opposed to a Word file. (For more on PDF files, see Chapter 9.) Also announce your job search on the list serves of professional organizations.

Cold Calling

Another method for making important contacts is to call and send your résumé to federal agencies that do the type of work that interests you. But be aware that cold calling may be a more productive strategy for landing jobs in agencies that belong to the excepted service than those that belong to the competitive service. Why? Because the relatively flexible hiring procedures followed by excepted service agencies enables them to snap-up applicants on a spontaneous, ad hoc basis more easily than competitive service agencies can.

If you make cold calls or send out snail-mail queries, aim your efforts at a specific person. This is important because if you send your résumé to a nameless recipient, such as "To Whom It May Concern," it is unlikely to concern anyone. You can get a copy of your target agency's employee directory from its website or Public Affairs Office.

**HOT TIP
Essential Ammo For Your Networking Campaign**

One savvy networking method is to send your résumé and/or request informational interviews with managers at your target organizations. Get the names and contact info (including email addresses) of federal managers from the Federal Yellow Book and Congressional Yellow Book, which may be available at your public, college or government library.

CHAPTER **3**

Oodles of Internships, Student Jobs, and Fellowships for Experienced Professionals

"That summer pretty much settled things. I think I knew from that point on that I was going to be a physicist."

—DEBORAH JIN, WINNER OF THE MACARTHUR GENIUS AWARD, DISCUSSING IN *THE WASHINGTON POST* HER COLLEGE SUMMER JOB INVOLVING CONDUCTING RESEARCH AT THE GODDARD SPACE FLIGHT CENTER

"I'm tying to avoid the missteps of early success."

The best way to learn about a field is through a total immersion experience—like those provided by summer and year-round internships and student jobs for undergrads, grad students, recent grads and lawyers and by fellowships for experienced professionals.

Federal internships, student jobs and fellowships are available in virtually every discipline. So whether your passion is space exploration or more earthly concerns like information technology, economics, international relations, ecology, law, art, or history, the federal government runs a career-boosting internship or fellowship for you.

Internships and Student Jobs

More than 60,000 students and undergrads, grad students, law students, and recent grads currently work summer and year-round federal internships. These internships are based all over the United States and overseas. Many internship programs specially recruit women, minorities, and people with disabilities.

Although many Congressional and White House internships are voluntary, dozens and dozens of federal internship programs offer excellent salaries. **That's right, you don't have to slave for free even if you're just starting your career!**

Fellowships for PhDs and Experienced Professionals

Federal agencies and Congressional organizations also offer dozens of well-paying fellowship programs for newly minted PhDs and seasoned medical researchers, journalists, economists, policy experts, teachers, and other professionals. These programs feature training, mentoring, lectures, career-building seminars, and social outings. (Fellows range in age from their 20s to 70s.) Some federal fellowships exclusively recruit nonfeds, but others are open to current feds. Some programs favor minorities.

One of the best kept secrets in government is that there are tens of thousands of well-paying—not volunteer—internships available in the federal government.

While contributing to hot-button policy issues or conducting cutting edge research, fellows gain top-level experience and generate powerful networking contacts. Therefore, fellowship programs offer fantastic opportunities to pivot into new careers: after completing their programs, many fellows land permanent jobs on the staffs of federal agencies, Congressional organizations, think tanks, lobbying groups, or consulting groups. Alternatively, after completing federal fellowships during sabbaticals, some academics and industry professionals return to their home organizations.

ON THE CD...

This book's CD features program descriptions and links to the websites of over 100 well-paying, dynamic federal internship programs, student jobs, and special recruitment programs for young professionals. The CD also features program descriptions and links to the websites of dozens of fellowship programs for PhDs, experienced professionals, and current feds. Programs that specially recruit for minorities, women, and people with disabilities are flagged.

Benefits of Internships, Student Jobs, and Fellowships

Through an internship, student job, or fellowship you can:

> **Earn a competitive salary.** Some internships and fellowships even provide housing, round-trip travel expenses to assignment locations, and tuition money during the school year.

> **Have eye-opening experiences.** Meet people and learn about issues that are entirely new to you. These exposures may steer you onto fascinating career paths that you would otherwise have bypassed.

> **Get the real deal.** The best way to learn about an occupation is to work it. An internship or fellowship may show you whether your target career is all that it's cracked up to be, or whether you want to detour onto a different track.

> **Expand your mind.** Many internships and fellowships offer training.

> **Enhance your marketability.** Internships and fellowships provide expertise that is highly valued in private industry, nonprofits, and government. In addition, many programs segue into permanent federal jobs—like "rental with an option to buy" contracts—and/or provide fast tracks into management.

> ➤ **Change the world.** Interns and fellows weigh in on important issues, such as environmental problems, medical research, international relations, and corporate finance.

> ➤ **Rub elbows.** Interns and fellows work shoulder-to-shoulder with distinguished scientists, economists, diplomats, business experts, writers, and other professionals who provide mentoring and references. In addition, many programs feature professional and social activities that introduce participants to like-minded peers.

> ➤ **Escape the cubicle farm.** Internships and fellowships are based in some of the world's most magnificent parks, forests, and marine sanctuaries and most dynamic museums, libraries, labs, and embassies.

> ➤ **Satisfy your itch for a career switch.** Many experienced professionals use internships and fellowships to launch entirely new careers. For example, I know a New York City police officer who used the Government Accountability Program's Professional Development Program to launch a policy career. I also know a school teacher who used an internship program at a defense agency to start a career as a federal contract manager. He says he landed his position "by emphasizing my experience in front of a classroom as evidence of my leadership skills."

Types of Programs

Each internship, student job, and fellowship program has a unique design. For example, some programs operate year-round, some programs only operate during the summer, and some programs are part-time. Other factors that vary among programs include salaries, types of assignments, training opportunities, opportunities for advancement, program duration, eligibility, and application requirements. Also, some programs are based in Washington, DC, while others are located throughout the United States or overseas. So consider all appropriate programs described on this book's CD before focusing on particular program(s).

Housing for Out-of-Towners

If you're moving to a new location for a new professional opportunity, ask your employer for housing leads. Also check the housing listings posted at local colleges and on online boards. In addition, the University Career Action Network has an online listing of subletting opportunities throughout the nation. See http://www.cdc.richmond.edu:591/ucan/. And "Google" phrases such as *temporary housing in [name of your city]*.

If your internship is in Washington, DC, Washington Intern Student Housing may help you find housing. See http://www.internsdc.com/.

Tips from Hiring Managers on How to Write a Winning Internship or Fellowship Application

❑ **Be an early bird.** Avoid the manic panic of last-minute scrambles for opportunities by scoping them out many months before your desired start date. Start searching for summer programs in the fall. Hiring managers have told me that many applicants have been rejected for internships and fellowships because—probably in a last-minute crunch to make a deadline—they mindlessly cut-and-pasted the name of the wrong programs onto applications. Oops!

❑ **Target your application.** Hiring managers warn against using the same application for multiple programs and merely repeating your résumé in answers to essay questions. Why? Because, when reviewing your application, hiring managers will primarily look for evidence that you want to participate in their program, and would contribute to it and benefit from it. To provide this evidence, your application must address the requirements, emphases, and activities that distinguish each program.

To do so, your application should: (1) open with a purposeful statement, such as, "I am eager to contribute to this program because . . . "; (2) describe what types of projects you would like to work on as an intern or fellow (but also describe your flexibility); and (3) explain how your academic or professional experience, team-friendly approaches, and other credentials would enhance the program.

Another tip: interview veterans of your target program. Then, explain in your application how your resulting understanding of the program enhanced its appeal to you.

❑ **Explain sharp turns.** If participating in your target program would require you to make a major career switch or follow a nontraditional career path, explain why you are angling to take such an alternative route.

❑ **Address major application weaknesses.** If there is an obvious important weakness in your background, explain it. For example, a hiring manager in the federal fellowship program sponsored by the American Association for the Advancement of Science advises, "If you are a scientist with a weak publication record, address this issue; don't let us just wonder about it because we probably won't give you the benefit of the doubt without being given a reason to do so."

❑ **Prepare your references.** Help your references advance your case by explaining to them why you want to participate in your target program, how participating in the program would advance your career and why your background fits the program.

❑ **Be persistent.** If you are rejected from your target program, apply again.

The article on the following page is about special recruitment programs for young professionals appeared in the April 30, 2006, issue of **The Washington Post**. It was written by Lily Whiteman, author of this book. More of Lily's **Washington Post** articles are included on this book's CD.

SUMMER WORK CAN BE A LAUNCHING PAD

Federal Internships Offer Experiences Beyond Filing and Phone Duties

By Lily Whiteman
Special to The Washington Post
Sunday, April 30, 2006; Page K01

If Shirley Murillo had settled for flipping burgers during her college summers, she probably would not be what she is today: a hurricane hunter at the National Oceanic and Atmospheric Administration who flies straight into the earth's deadliest storms to collect life-saving information.

So what did Murillo do during her summers to catapult her career into the clouds? She interned in the federal Significant Opportunities in Atmospheric Research and Science (SOARS) program in Boulder, Colo. She worked shoulder-to-shoulder with leading scientists in state-of-the-art labs analyzing real-time data on hurricanes as they plowed across the United States—experiences that "helped me realize that hurricanes were my passion," Murillo said.

The program, she said, also featured mentoring, networking with prominent scientists, and training in giving conference presentations that introduced her to the scientific culture. And because SOARS houses interns together in rent-free townhouses, pays generous stipends and covers travel costs, the program offers an all-expenses-paid, around-the-clock immersion that interns describe as the scientific community's version of MTV's "Real World."

SOARS is just one of dozens of well-paying internship programs that are based in federal offices, labs, museums, courts and parks around the country. In preparation for a huge retirement wave, federal agencies are currently rolling out these entry-level programs almost as fast as Starbucks is opening new cafes.

Like SOARS, most new internship programs feature advanced training and substantive project work. "Interns aren't here to fetch coffee or Xerox," said Raul Quintero, who spent a summer during his master's in public administration program interning at the Government Accountability Office, a watchdog agency. "We were given important projects, and we ran with them."

His projects included attending congressional hearings on border controls and reporting on them to agency executives, and writing chapters of a published report on flood control policies.

Quintero compares internships such as his to rent-with-option-to-buy leases because they can help interns and the agency decide whether to seal long-term deals with one another. His summer job led to his admittance into the agency's two-year professional development program, which grooms staffers for advancement.

But even internships that don't segue into permanent jobs can provide pivotal credentials, said Tomas Rivas, who will soon complete a year-long internship at the National Gallery of Art. He interned there after earning a master's in fine arts "because it's the best place to learn about exhibit design."

Now, he's confident that his experiences—which included single-handedly designing a house-sized, three-dimensional collage for the gallery's popular Dada exhibition—will help him land another job.

Another benefit of federal internships is their networking opportunities, said Scott Douglas, who completed the Health and Human Services Department's two-year Emerging Leaders Program. "I met people in many offices through the program's rotational assignments," he said. "The contacts—that was where the program had its magic."

Douglas is now a program analyst at the agency, and those contacts are still valuable. "If I haven't addressed an important issue before, one of my Emerging Leaders friends has. And I call them and get their take on it," he said.

Similarly, Tamara Singleton, a SOARS alumnus who is now a PhD student at the University of Maryland, still sometimes benefits from SOARS guidance, even though her internship ended in 2004. "SOARS offers an ongoing relationship. Those scientific conferences can be big and intimidating. So I might e-mail my presentation to my SOARS advisers beforehand to get their feedback on it," she said.

If you want to become an intern, Singleton offers advice for writing successful applications: Study your target organization's Web site. Ask the program director how to contact previous interns, and interview those interns about their experiences. Then, convey in your application your program knowledge, enthusiasm, credentials and commitment to taking advantage of opportunities offered.

CHAPTER 4

Into the Capitol Hill Power Vortex

Working for Congress

"If you want a front row seat to history, you want to work for Congress."

—SENATE STAFFER

"But how do you know for sure you've got power unless you abuse it?"

If your pulse quickens the closer you get to power, if you're a political junkie, if you enjoy political horse races, consider working for Congress.

What Does Congress Do?

While federal agencies carry out and enforce laws, Congress writes them. Congress also researches and holds hearings on issues it legislates, oversees federal agencies, confirms the political appointees who run those agencies, and establishes foreign policy. In addition, Congress investigates various governmental activities, as in *What did you know and when did you know it?*

Ka-ching! Congress holds the nation's purse strings: It doles out foreign aid and approves the federal budget. Congress decides, for example, how much money goes to scientific and medical research and how much goes to defense every year. And generally, only Congress, not the President, can declare war.

What Do Congressional Staffers Do?

Congressional staffers help the members of Congress do their jobs: they write and track legislation, research and strategize policy alternatives, plan the appearances of members of Congress, write their speeches, negotiate compromises, communicate with the press, meet with lobbyists, and respond to constituents' concerns.

Congressional staffers also organize hearings on hot-button issues. In fact, the next time you see footage of Congressional hearings on the news, look for the people who occasionally whisper in the ears of members of Congress and pass them notes: they are Congressional staffers.

Congressional Versus Agency Jobs

Congressional staffers (also known as "Hill staffers") work in the nation's power vortex. Indeed, many Hill jobs provide prime opportunities to influence members of Congress and thereby influence history. One Senate staffer remembers: "After having one conversation with my boss—a Senator—I convinced him to insert a line into a bill that for the first time declared Tibet an occupied territory, which was a major historical milestone. That's all it took—one conversation. No bureaucracy."

But despite the power that may accompany Hill jobs, Hill careers involve some relative disadvantages. For one thing, only about 24,000 staffers work on the Hill, so Hill jobs account for only a very small percentage of the federal workforce.

Another disadvantage of Hill jobs is their lack of job security. Instead of following civil service or uniform personnel regulations, each House Representative, Senator, and Congressional Committee hires and fires based on its own criteria. In addition, whenever members of Congress voluntarily or involuntarily leave their jobs, their staffs usually lose their jobs as well. This means that networking and maintaining contacts are very important for survival on Capitol Hill. But the high turnover on the Hill also means that there are frequent openings.

In addition, because the activities of Hill staffers revolve around Congress's legislative sessions, work schedules are relatively rigid and workdays are long. Also, Hill offices tend to be more cramped and require more formal dress than agency offices.

Other differences between Congressional and agency jobs are summarized in Table 4-1.

Types of Congressional Jobs

Congress hires lawyers, economists, communications experts, experts on various policy issues, IT professionals, procurement managers, administrative assistants, and many other types of professionals. To see a list of some common job descriptions in Congressional offices, go to: http://www.politixgroup.com; then click on this series of links: *Politics 101 Resources*; *U.S. Congressional Resources*; *Jobs in the U.S. Congress*.

There are basically three types of Congressional employers: (1) members of the House of Representatives; (2) members of the Senate; and (3) Congressional Committees that address specific issues.

For links to the websites of all members of Congress and all Congressional committees, go to http://www.thomas.loc.gov/links. See Table 4-2 for a comparison of the pros and cons of working for the three types of Congressional employers.

(text continues on page 38)

TABLE 4-1 Working for Congress Versus Federal Agencies		
	Congressional Staffers	**Agency Staffers**
Proximity to Power	Almost all staffers have some interaction with members of Congress. They may also enjoy occasional power perks, like a ride on Air Force One.	The farther up the agency career ladder staffers climb, the more likely they are to work directly with political appointees.
Involvement with Politics	Congressional staffers impact politics and are greatly impacted by it.	Most agency staffers are insulated from politics and are not significantly impacted by it.
Impact on National Issues	Congressional aides help determine what national laws say and how members vote on them. They may do so by working directly with Members without confronting multiple layers of bureaucracy.	Staffers manage large budgets, enforcement and research programs, high-profile events, reports, investigations, and other decision-making tools. But to impact national policy, agency staffers must usually work through multiple layers of bureaucracy.
Salaries	Significantly less than agency salaries. And most Congressional internships are volunteer. (Nevertheless many organizations place salaried interns in Congressional offices via internship programs that are listed in Chapter 3.)	Significantly higher than Hill salaries. And almost all agency internships are salaried. See Chapter 3 for agency internships.
Work Hours	Many Hill staffers work long hours with relatively inflexible schedules.	Most feds work a 40-hour week. Many have flexible schedules and/or telecommute part of the week.
Job Security	Very little. Congressional staffers can easily be fired. When Members leave their jobs, their staffers frequently do also. When the majority party shifts, Committee staffers may lose their jobs.	Unbeatable. Layoffs and firings are rare.
Location	Almost all jobs are based in DC. (Although members of Congress do have small staffs in their districts.)	Jobs are based throughout the United States and overseas.
Importance of Political Experience to Your Application	Everything is partisan on the Hill. So only apply for jobs that jive with your beliefs. Also, emphasize your political passions and experience. If, for example, you worked for the Democratic or Republican National Committee, say so.	Federal agencies are supposed to be partisan-free zones. So if you brandish your politics, you risk alienating hiring managers who have opposing beliefs. If, for example, you worked for the Democratic or Republican National Committee, don't mention it, if possible.

TABLE 4-2	Comparison of Capital Hill Employers		
	House	**Senate**	**Congressional Committees**
Size of Staff	Smaller than Senate staffs	Larger than House staffs. Senators from states that have bigger populations have larger staffs	Depends on the Committee
Prospects for Finding Openings	There are more House offices than Senate offices. So it may be generally easier to find House openings than Senate openings.	Senate staffs are generally larger than House staffs and so any particular office may have openings at any time.	Depends on the Committee
Focus of Office	Offices answer the requests of constituents and interest groups, manage member's activities, research policy issues, and contribute to legislation. Committee and Subcommittee Chairs have the most influence.	Offices answer the requests of constituents and interest groups, manage members' activities, research policy issues, and contribute to legislation. Generally, the typical Senator has more influence than the typical House member.	Little grunt work and constituent work. Each Congressional Committee researchs, holds hearings, and reports on a particular issue. Therefore, Committees tend to hire subject matter experts with advanced degrees.
Type of Experience Offered by Jobs	Because House staffs are relatively small, they are generally more stretched than Senate staffs. Therefore, assignments tend to be less compartmentalized and less rigid, and tend to offer more opportunities for gaining diverse and high-level experience than jobs on Senate staffs.	Jobs in Senate offices tend to be more specialized and so tend to offer narrower areas of experience than jobs on House staffs.	Each Committee offers experience in the particular topics that it addresses.
Salaries	Usually lower than Senate salaries.	Usually higher than House salaries but lower than Committee salaries.	Usually higher than House and Senate salaries. See Chapter 14 for more info on Congressional salaries.

How to Land Capitol Hill Jobs
Finding Openings

Capitol Hill jobs are not posted on USAJOBS. You can find them by using the Congressional resources listed in Chapter 2. Some additional strategies recommended by Capitol Hill hiring managers:

1. **Be a campaigner.** When you work on political campaigns, you will probably cultivate key Capitol Hill contacts. And if your candidate wins, you will have an excellent chance of getting hired onto his/her staff. Find openings on campaign and Hill staffs by contacting the Democratic and Republican National Committees, the Democratic and Republican Congressional Campaign Committees, or the Democratic and Republican Senatorial Campaign Committees. ("Google" these organizations to find their websites.)

2. **Do internships.** Hill internships for students and recent graduates of graduate-level programs and law school provide valuable experience and references, and frequently segue into permanent jobs. For information on well-paying internships, see Chapter 3 and the list of internships included in the CD accompanying this book.

3. **Do fellowships.** Hill fellowships for recent graduates of PhD programs and experienced researchers, academics, policy wonks, and teachers provide many of the same advantages as internships but are designed for senior-level professionals. For information on well-paying fellowships, see Chapter 3 and the list of fellowships included in the CD accompanying this book .

4. **Go with the home team.** Many members of Congress give priority treatment to applicants from their own states. So contact the Senators and Representatives from your home state and the state(s) where you went to school. If such offices are not currently hiring, ask them for leads.

5. **Work your issues.** Contact members of Congress and Congressional Committees that take a strong stand on issues that you have studied or worked on before.

6. **Network.** Participate in alumni events and contact fellow alumni who work on Capitol Hill. Also, attend DC happy hours and meetings of professional associations and advocacy groups because you will almost certainly meet Hill staffers at these events. Before each event, practice describing your credentials and interests concisely and energetically. Then when you arrive, work the room—don't just hang with your friends.

7. **Find mentors.** Milk you Rolodex for direct or indirect Hill connections and seek them out. When you consult mentors, make it easy for them to help you; provide them with your résumé and concisely explain to them your interests and goals. Send a thank-you note and/or gift to anyone who extends themselves for you and keep them posted on your progress.

8. **Leap frog.** Look for jobs with DC associations, nonprofits, and lobbying groups; such positions will arm you with pivotal Hill contacts.

Application Tips

1. **Do the reading.** Subscribe to *The Hill* and *Roll Call* or read these publications on-line. For an excellent article on Hill jobs, "Google" *The Washington Post* with *Help Wanted on the Hill.*

    Also read the *National Journal*'s "The Hill People" issue, which is published every 4 years. This issue features profiles of key Congressional aides that will provide important background information on key players in your target offices, help you prepare for interviews, and enlighten you about Capitol Hill culture and various potential career tracks.

2. **Do the research.** Before applying and interviewing for jobs with members of Congress or Congressional Committees, review their websites, hearings in which they participated, and look them up in *The Almanac of American Politics.* Also, review their voting record and read about the legislation they sponsored. You can access a database of every Congressional vote since 1991 by "Googling" these terms: *The Washington Post* and *U.S. Congress Votes Database.* Also, be prepared to explain to interviewer(s) why you want to work on the Hill.

3. **Target the right people.** Address your application to your target office's top manager; in many offices, this is the Staff Director or Chief of Staff. Get the names and titles of top managers in Congressional offices by calling these offices or by retrieving them from the *Congressional Yellow Book,* which provides the names, titles, and contact info (including e-mail addresses) of staffers in each Congressional office.

4. **Target your applications.** In your applications and interviews, emphasize any previous Hill experience you have, including internships, or campaign or advocacy experience. Also explain why you want to work in public service in general and in your target office in particular. In addition, emphasize your leadership skills, coursework in politics or government, substantive knowledge of issues addressed by your target office (such as economic, public health, or defense issues), skill in conveying such issues to laymen, ability to meet deadlines in high-pressure environments, and multi-tasking skills.

5. **Use good timing.** The months following an election are particularly promising because that's when new members of Congress create their staffs. In addition, turnover is also high in the fall after summer interns leave. Nevertheless, there is regular turnover throughout terms. Also keep in mind that during Congressional recesses and days surrounding weekends, votes are usually not held. Therefore, during these periods, Congressional offices are usually relatively relaxed and would therefore probably be particularly inclined to give your bid for employment attention.

6. **Do walk-ins.** If you visit or live in DC, personally visit your target offices. If possible, make an appointment before your visit with the office's hiring manager. But if this is not possible, drop into your target office(s) without an appointment(s). When you arrive at each office, ask to speak to the hiring manager, inquire about job openings in his/her office, ask for other leads, and give the hiring manager your cover letter (addressed to him/her) and your résumé. Dress in business attire for such visits.

7.   **Persevere.** Follow up and follow through on all your applications and leads. Brad Fitch, a former Hill Chief of Staff, told *Roll Call* that job hunting on Capitol Hill is mostly about "polite persistence . . . and don't take it personally."

Stand Out from the Pack

1.   **Use connections.** Work your Rolodex to find any Hill connections that may be lurking within your circle of family friends, neighbors, professors, colleagues, and others. Ask your Hill contacts to alert your target Hill employers of your impending applications and/or to write a short letter introducing you accompanied by your résumé.

     To survive mail screens and reach the desk of a senior staffer, an introductory letter should identify the writer's personal connection with the senior staffer it addresses by saying something like the following:

> *Dear* [Name of senior staffer goes here]*:*
> *How are Alice and the kids? I am sure that you are very busy because I read in the news that you are doing X, Y, and Z.*
>
> *I'm enclosing the résumé of* [your name goes here]*. She/he has an impressive background in X, and I wanted to give you a heads-up that she/he will contact you soon about her/his search for a* [titles of your target jobs go here] *position. I would greatly appreciate if you would give her/his application your personal consideration.*

2.   **Stand out for the right reasons.** Forget gimmicks like résumés printed on pink paper rimmed by blinking disco lights. Why? Because such gimmicks may get you noticed but probably won't get you hired in government

     Instead, stand out from the pack by doing more than the pack. How? By, for example, including in your applications writing samples and glowing written references from previous employers or professors, even if they're not requested.

     Also, craft your cover letter to convey zest. For example, I know a 13-year veteran of senior Hill jobs who landed his first Hill job with the help of a cover letter that opened with this text:

> *If you want to communicate your message in new and different ways, I would be eager to develop innovative communications strategies for your office. (However, if you're looking for a Press Secretary who will just track press clippings and write standard press releases, please don't consider me.)*

3. **Make an offer they can't refuse.** At the beginning of an election year, write to a member of Congress who is running for reelection and say something like:

> *Dear Senator X:*
> *I understand that you're running for reelection, and so some members of your office staff may currently be detailed to your campaign. If your Senate office is now short-staffed, I would like to offer my assistance. I am available to join your Senate staff on a very cost-effective basis. I offer expertise in X, Y, and Z.*
> *Please note that I would not request a commitment to continue working for you after the election. (But I would hope that if you are satisfied with my work, you would want to keep me on.)*

Moving Up

If you're a recent grad, set realistic goals; don't expect to instantly become a Capitol Hill power broker. In the Hill's highly competitive and political environment, you will probably have to prove your loyalty and diligence by working your way up through the ranks.

As Fitch told *Roll Call*, "I spent a lot of time in the basement of Rayburn [a Congressional office building] with an autopen." The key to getting past this phase is to stay aggressive, he said, and not miss any opportunities that may present themselves.

More tips from veteran Hill staffers on how to move up from the basement:

HOT TIP
Communicating with Congress

Snail mail to Congressional offices is often severely delayed and damaged by security screens. Therefore, it is generally better to communicate with Congressional offices through e-mail than snail mail, when possible.

➤ Show humility and deference to senior staffers and use every Hill job to learn how Congress works.

➤ Stay on good terms with all of your managers and colleagues, particularly your office's Staff Director. If you don't regularly interact with him/her, occasionally submit to him/her progress reports on your projects, even if they are not requested.

➤ Approach one of your office's Legislative Assistants who addresses your areas of interest and volunteer to help him/her out with some of his projects.

➤ When you start looking for your next Hill job, remember that many positions are filled via connections. So maximize your chances of landing such inside jobs by regularly reminding your Hill contacts about your search.

➤ Read *The Hill's* "Onward and Upward" columns at http://www.thehill.com, which features profiles of successful Hill staffers; reviewing descriptions of their experiences may give you ideas about how you may similarly succeed on the Hill.

CHAPTER 5

Those !@#! Vacancy Announcements

"*Adventure isn't hanging on a rope off the side of a mountain. Adventure is an ATTITUDE that we must apply to the day to day obstacles of life-facing new challenges, seizing new opportunities, testing our resources against the unknown and in the process, discovering our own unique potential.*"

—JOHN AMATT, MOUNT EVEREST CLIMBER AND WILDERNESS EXPEDITION LEADER

So you've found a juicy job opening(s), and you're rarin' to throw your hat into the ring and apply, right? Well, not so quick. First, you've got to figure out if you can and should apply to the opening. And to do that, you must decipher those dense announcements of federal jobs called vacancy announcements; this task is commonly associated with a syndrome called *docutrauma*.

You can prevent docutrauma by reading this chapter. This chapter explains everything you need to know in order to understand and use vacancy announcements, including:

➤ How to find the information you really need from them

➤ How to decide which openings to pursue

➤ The various hiring mechanisms used by federal agencies

➤ The basic components of federal job applications

➤ How to apply for executive jobs

How to Read Vacancy Announcements

Vacancy announcements are flat-out confusing, boring, and long-winded. And those are the user-friendly ones!

But even many of the most dynamic federal jobs are announced in seemingly impenetrable announcements. So you shouldn't judge a job by its vacancy announcement. In other words, don't abandon a juicy job opening that meets your salary and geographic requirements just because its announcement was written in verbose bureaucratese.

And don't be intimidated by the length of vacancy announcements. Much of their hulk and bulk is generated by legal filler satisfying regulations that probably don't concern you.

CAUTION
Sometimes a single federal opening is advertised with two vacancy announcements: (1) one vacancy announcement that is open to all applicants, including non-feds as well as current and former feds; and (2) another vacancy announcement that is open only to current and former feds. If you are a current or former fed without veterans' preference, be sure to apply to the announcement that is for current and former feds. (See Chapter 8 for more on this.)

Steps for Reading a Vacancy Announcement

Once you find a vacancy announcement that piques your interest and meets your salary and location criteria, decide whether you should apply by:

1. Checking the location of the job.

2. Checking whether you fulfill the "Who May Apply" criteria. Some openings are open to *all* U.S. citizens. But others are restricted to current and former feds or the hiring agency's current employees. (Most current feds have what is known in government lingo as "status," or "competitive status"; most former feds have what is known as "reinstatement eligibility.") Most federal jobs are only open to U.S. citizens.

3. Ensuring that you can meet the application deadline, known as the "closing date." A few caveats about closing dates:

   ➤ Applications submitted via online application systems are usually due by midnight Eastern Standard Time of the closing date. To meet such deadlines, you must hit the "submit" key of your electronic application by midnight of the closing date.

   ➤ If paper applications are accepted for your target opening, the closing date may identify the deadline for postmarking or the deadline for the agency's receipt of the application. Check with your target opening's contact person if you are unsure which deadline your closing date identifies.

   ➤ Under some limited circumstances, late applications from active military or veterans accepted. For more info, type *filing late applications* and *veterans* into the search window at *www.opm.gov*.

4. Evaluating the "Salary" section of the vacancy announcement. (See Chapter 14 for salary guidance.)

5. Checking the "Series and Grade" section of the vacancy announcement to evaluate the position's promotion potential. Note that when you reach the top of a position's series and grade, you can only move up by landing a more senior position or by convincing your boss to upgrade your current job—a lengthy process.

6. Checking whether you want the job and meet its requirements. Do so by evaluating its job description and essay questions (known as KSAs or ECQs); these essay questions usually appear in the "Qualifications and Evaluations" section of its announcement. (More guidance about essay questions appears later in this chapter and in Chapter 10.)

   If you don't meet almost all of the job's KSAs or ECQS via your education and/or work experience, your time would be better spent applying to other openings. Why? Because the raw reality is that most federal openings draw dozens of applications, or more. And so if you don't meet all of your target job's requirements, somebody else(s) probably will—and that somebody else will likely get hired.

7. Reading the vacancy announcement and crossing out any information that is irrelevant to you.

8. Verifying that you meet any background, licensing, physical or medical requirements, or other conditions of employment specified for the job.

9. Listing everything you have to do and submit in order to apply for the job. Gather this information from the "How to Apply" section of the vacancy announcement, as well as from other sections of the vacancy announcement that specify additional requirements.

10. If you have questions about an opening and/or are unsure about whether to apply for it, get the contact info for the job's hiring manager from the Human Resources contact person identified on the job's vacancy announcement. Then call the hiring manager and discuss your concerns with him/her (and ask him/her for additional leads).

Ways That Federal Jobs Are Filled

There are two major ways that the federal government fills jobs: through competitive appointments and noncompetitive appointments. (In government lingo, an "appointment" is a job.) It may be helpful for you to quickly familiarize yourself with the basics of how competitive and noncompetitive appointments work so that you will understand the associated terminology included in most vacancy announcements.

THE REAL DEAL ON PRESELECTED JOBS

Granted, some federal jobs are initially targeted to selected candidates, though no stats are available on this phenomenon. But I know that a large percentage of desirable jobs at all levels, even executive positions, are NOT preselected because: (1) I have coached hundreds of professionals into them, and (2) along the way, I have landed a few such jobs myself.

And even if you do apply for a preselected job, you may land it anyway. This may happen if: (1) the preselected applicant accidentally misses their application deadline or, for one reason or another, does not apply for the preselected job after all; or (2) preselection attempts are thwarted by the checks and balances built into federal selection processes as well as by the weight given to veterans' preference. Both of these types of situations happen more often that you would think!

Many job seekers wrongly believe that any federal job that is only open for 2 weeks or less is preselected. According to this myth, the short window of opportunity for applying reflects the hiring agency's effort minimize its processing of doomed applications. But the presumed 2-week red flag is really a red herring. In fact, many agencies keep *all* of their vacancy announcements open for only 2 weeks so that they can fill openings quickly. (Too bad that the federal government's reputation for sluggishness is so entrenched that its quick response policies are apparently almost enough to spawn conspiracy theories!)

The truth is that there is simply no sure way to identify preselected jobs from their vacancy announcements. (A vacancy announcement will not surrender its secrets easily!) Nevertheless, a vacancy announcement that describes responsibilities that are so specific that they could only be fulfilled by one or two people in the world is more likely to be preselected than one that describes reasonably broad responsibilities. And because agencies are unlikely to pay to advertise preselected jobs, it is safe to assume that those advertised in fee-based publications are not preselected. In addition, any opening that has been filled without any interviews is suspect.

Conversely, a vacancy announcement that advertises multiple openings is less likely to be preselected than one that announces a single opening. But the chances of being thwarted by preselections are too remote and vacancy announcements for multiple openings are too few for either of these phenomena to provide the sole basis for any sensible job search. **Bottom line: You should apply for every opening that would be a good fit for you.**

Competitive Appointments

A competitive appointment is a federal job that is filled through an open competition that is designed to identify best qualified applicants. In an open competition, applicants are rated and ranked based upon their qualifications and veterans' preference. Then, based on interviews or other criteria, the selecting official selects one of the best qualified applicants. For more info on competitive appointments see Chapter 6.

Noncompetitive Appointments

Some federal jobs are filled through noncompetitive appointments. When an agency fills a job through a noncompetitive appointment, it bypasses requirements to hold an open competition and to award the job to the most qualified candidate.

Instead, the agency uses special, streamlined procedures to hire an applicant who meets or exceeds the job's basic qualifications *and* meets certain, other specified criteria that allows them to bypass competitions. In other words, to qualify for a noncompetitive appointment, an applicant does not have to beat the best qualified applicant; s/he only has to meet the minimum qualifications and fall into one of these categories:

> **Veterans.** Veterans are eligible for noncompetitive appointments to federal jobs under the Veterans' Employment Opportunities Act of 1998 (VEOA), the 30 Percent or More Disabled Program, or the Veterans Recruitment Appointment. For more information about these and other special hiring opportunities for veterans see Appendix 1.

> **People with Disabilities.** People who have severe physical, cognitive or emotional disabilities may receive noncompetitive appointments to certain positions under Schedule A Appointments. For more info on this topic see Appendix 2.

> **Displaced Federal Employees.** Federal employees who have been laid-off or whose jobs have moved are eligible for noncompetitive appointments to some federal jobs through the Career Transition Assistance Program (CTAP) and Interagency Career Transition Program (ITAP). (A federal lay-off is called a RIF—short for reduction-in-force.)

> **Returned Peace Corps Volunteers (RPCVs).** RPCVs receive noncompetitive appointments during the first year after completion of their tour of duty. See *Resources for Returned Volunteers* at http://www.peacecorps.gov/index.cfm?.

> **Bilingual/Bicultural Program.** The Bilingual/Bicultural Program gives preference to applicants who are fluent in English and Spanish or other languages or who are knowledgeable about the Hispanic culture or another underrepresented culture. This program is used to recruit for some entry-level jobs that require bilingual skills or special cultural knowledge.

Also note that because Hispanics are particularly underrepresented in the federal government, many federal agencies are particularly eager to recruit Hispanics. In addition, many security agencies are particularly eager to hire applicants who are fluent in Arabic or other languages, or who are familiar with Muslim, Mid-East, and other cultures. So if your target job requires language or cultural skills but its announcement does not specify the Bilingual/Bicultural program, ask if the hiring agency would consider hiring you under this program.

➤ **Applicants to Internships and Student Jobs Programs.** Participants in many internships and student jobs programs covered in Chapter 3 are hired noncompetitively.

➤ **Current and Former Feds.** Current feds can be transferred to other federal jobs at their current grade without competition. Former feds that have reinstatement eligibility can be noncompetitively hired into jobs that are of equal or lower grades than their previous jobs.

Why do federal agencies frequently opt to fill some jobs through noncompetitive appointments rather than through competitive appointments? In order to help them meet their obligations to hire certain numbers of the types of employees that are listed above. In addition, noncompetitive appointments are much faster and easier for the hiring agency to process than competitive appointments.

Finding Noncompetitive Openings

Each vacancy announcement posted on USAJOBS lists the types of noncompetitive appointments that can be used to fill the opening. Therefore, you can use the name of a noncompetitive appointment in a keyword search of vacancy announcements posted on USAJOBS to find those that meet your requirements.

Some federal jobs that can be filled through noncompetitive appointments are not advertised. To find them, contact your target agency's Selective Placement Coordinator. These Coordinators stay current on noncompetitive hiring and match eligible applicants with openings. To find these coordinators, type *Selective Placement Coordinators* into the search window at http://www.opm.gov/. You can also find Selective Placement Coordinators by "Googling" that phrase along with the name of each of your target agencies.

If You Apply for a Noncompetitive Appointment

1. Specifically state your request for a noncompetitive appointment in the cover letters of paper applications and carefully answer the short-answer questions about noncompetitive appointments in online applications.

2. Answer all application questions just as carefully and completely as you would if were requesting a competitive appointment. Even though you don't necessarily have to be the most qualified candidate to land a noncompetitive appointment, the hiring agency is not required to hire applicants who qualify for noncompetitive appointments. But the better your application is, the better your chances of receiving an offer.

> ### CAUTION
> ### Follow Directions
>
> Believe it or not, most federal job applications are rejected simply because they're late or omit required information. This means that just by making your application deadlines and following all application instructions, you will beat out most of your competition. Apparently, the saying that "90 percent of life is just showing up" is as true in federal job applications as in life.
>
> Unfortunately, if your application is problematic, the hiring agency won't notify you of the problem or give you a second chance. So keep your application out of the circular file by following all directions in the "How to Apply" section of vacancy announcements and by conquering potential online glitches described in Chapter 8.

The Meat of Most Applications

The vacancy applications of most white-collar federal jobs require applicants to submit some combination of the following components:

> ➤ **A federal résumé.** As covered in Chapter 9, résumés for federal jobs must include more types of information than résumés for other sectors. Alternatively, instead of submitting a résumé, you may submit a form called an OF-612. But these long-winded, stodgy forms are a rarely-used, hard-to-read anachronism. So avoid them if possible.

> ➤ **Short answer questions about your credentials.** These questions are usually formatted as yes/no, check-the-box, or tiered response questions that ask for self-ratings on your skills. For example, a short answer question about oral communication might ask you to rate your experience presenting information to others from five multiple-choice ratings ranging from "I have not had any education, training, or experience performing this task" to "I am regularly consulted by others as an expert in this task."

The more types of experience and the more high-level experience you claim on short-answer questions, the higher your rating in the competition will be and the more likely you will be to get an interview. (See Chapters 6, 8, and 10 for more guidance on short-answer questions in online systems.)

OPP'Y OF A LIFETIME

Fast-growing midtown corp needs bright, articulate M/F to reorganize 760,000 files from top to bottom, fire four people nobody else will, and take care of children aged three and one. Must be certified in UNEX, GOM, SYSCO, CREM, LEM, ZOT, FENIX, JOD, and FRON. Own car a necessity, also up-to-date trucking license. Knowledge of quantum physics, short-order cookery helpful. Can you type? Even better. If you have $250,000 cash and are not afraid of large dogs, we're looking for YOU. At least twelve years' experience required. Personable, attractive college grads only call 555-2121 for appt. Starting salary 9K. Great benefits.

R. Chast

> ➤ **Essay questions.** These questions—known as KSAs—usually identify the primary requirements of the job. The more proof you provide in your KSA answers that you have mastered the primary requirements of the job, the better your application will do. See Chapter 10 for more guidance on writing winning KSAs.

Note that the civil service no longer exists, and that very few types of federal jobs are now screened with tests.

Applications for Senior Appointments

The senior executive service (SES) is the federal government's corps of big enchiladas, top brass, and muckety mucks. There are about 6,000 career, nonpolitical executives in the SES.

You need two things to land an SES job:

1. An offer for an SES job from a federal agency

2. Certification for membership in the SES from the Office of Personnel Management (OPM)—the federal government's main personnel office

Avenues into the SES

There are two ways to fulfill the two SES prerequisites:

1. **The Direct Route.** You can apply for an SES job just like other jobs—by submitting an application in response to an opening advertised on USAJOBS or an agency website. But there's one extra step: once selected for an SES job, you must apply to OPM for SES certification.

   OPM will evaluate your application for SES certification based on your résumé and essays explaining your experience in five executive core qualifications (ECQs): (1) leading change; (2) leading people; (3) results driven; (4) business acumen; and (5) building coalitions. As soon as you received this SES certification from OPM, you would be permitted to start your new SES job.

2. **The Indirect Route.** You could apply to a federal SES prep program, known as a Candidate Development Programs (CDP). A CDP would give you experience in the ECQ areas. At the end of the program, you would submit your application for SES certification to OPM. Once you receive this certification, you could land an SES job by (1) being selected straight into an SES job without competing against other applicants, or (2) by winning a competition involving the same type of rating and ranking of applications that are used to fill other federal jobs.

Types of CDP Programs

CDPs last anywhere from 14 months to 2 years and provide classroom training, mentoring rotations, seminars, and experience in group projects.

There are two main types of CDP programs: One type of program is OPM's CDP. (See http://www.opm.gov.fedcdp.) This is a small program that only accepts a few dozen participants at a time.

Other CDP programs are run by federal departments. These programs are open only to their own employees. Most departments post information about their CDC programs on their websites.

A Few Pointers for Applying to the SES

1. CDC programs and SES jobs are *very* competitive and applying for them can be very time-consuming. Only apply if you truly have advanced credentials and are willing to devote a considerable amount of time to your pursuit.

2. Federal agencies are currently working to increase the diversity of the SES. This means that if you are a member of a minority or are a woman, this is a great time to apply for the SES.

3. When preparing your applications, use the résumé preparation guidance in Chapter 9 and the essay writing guidance in Chapter 10.

4. If you are a current fed, your agency's SES training specialist can provide you with strategic advice and advice on preparing winning SES applications.

5. CDP programs only accept applications during limited windows of opportunity. So check these dates on program websites and plan accordingly.

6. SES pay varies by agency. Agencies whose performance appraisal systems have been approved by OPM pay better than agencies whose systems have not been certified. Check the SES site for details. Also, SES bonuses vary by agency. You can look up your target agency's bonus history in OPM's *Fact Book*. Find it by "Googling" OPM together with *The Fact Book*.

7. More info about the SES is provided in Chapter 16 and posted online at http://www.opm.gov/ses/.

CHAPTER 6

Think Like a Hiring Manager

How Applications Are Screened

"I want to hire someone who really wants the job. If an applicant doesn't want the job enough to spend some time tailoring their application to the opening, then they don't want it enough to deserve to be hired."

—A FEDERAL HIRING MANAGER

Many job seekers use the mass-mailing approach to apply for jobs: they send out the same, generic application to every federal job and private sector job that they can get their hands (or mouse) on. Although the mass-mailing approach is the easiest method, it's also the least productive method. **Don't be a mass mailer!**

Why not? Because many federal job openings draw dozens or even more than 100 applications. If you fail to tailor your application to your target job, there is bound to be a gap between what the job requires and what your generic application says you offer—a gap big enough for an army of competing applications to fill. And if your application fails to cater to the federal government's unique hiring process, it will almost certainly be overshadowed by more accommodating applications.

Here's another way to think about it: your application for a job is a really a letter to hiring managers explaining why they should hire you. Just as you give more attention to incoming letters that are personally addressed to you than to your junk mail that is addressed to the entire world, hiring managers pay more attention to applications that are addressed or targeted to *them* than to generic employment pleas addressed to the entire world.

Yes, it does take more time and effort to tailor applications to job openings than to send out mass mailings. But your chances of hitting employment paydirt will be much better if you devote your limited time to targeting fewer applications than to carpet bombing the federal airwaves with large numbers of generic applications that will all miss their mark.

Take a moment to think about all of the blood, sweat, and tears that you've already devoted to your career. Isn't your career worth a few more make-or-break hours of work? Don't scrimp on the last few hours of labor required to tailor each application—hours that could keep it out of the circular file and guarantee its place in the contender file.

In order to tailor your applications to your target jobs and the federal selection process, you must understand how the federal selection process works and its special demands—as explained in this chapter.

Selection the Old-Fashioned Way: Peer-Review Panels

Agencies that have not automated their screening processes rate applications through these steps:

1. **Screen for Basic Qualifications.** During the screen for basic qualifications, a human resources staffer compares each application to the "basic qualifications" defined in the job's vacancy announcement. Applications that meet basic qualifications survive; those that don't are kicked out of the competition.

   Think of the basic screen as almost a laugh test: if you can't imagine a hiring manager saying that you're qualified for the opening with a straight face, your application won't survive this hurdle.

2. **Rating via a Panel Screen.** All applications that meet basic qualifications are rated by a panel of subject matter experts—usually agency employees whose jobs are similar to the opening. Nevertheless, because every federal job is somewhat unique, panelists are not always thoroughly versed in the ins and outs of jobs that they screen.

Most panelists don't volunteer to serve on panels. Rather, they are usually drafted onto panels by superiors. (I have frequently been told by hiring managers that I may be the only person in Western civilization to ever volunteer to serve on selection panels; I frequently do so to gain insights into how to impress hiring managers.)

How do panelists rate applications? Each panelist usually receives a thick stack of applications—so thick it makes a huge THUD when dropped. Panelists rush through this application stack because of:

➤ The tediousness of the task: most job applications are remarkably similar to one another and are well . . . um… er… boring. After all, the typical opening draws umpteen vague, faceless applications from applicants who are looking for "a challenging and rewarding position that provides opportunities for growth" and are "convinced that I am a perfect fit for the opening." They also generate gazillions of application essays formatted with minuscule margins, tiny, eye-squinting fonts and monotonous mile-long paragraphs that would dwarf the Empire State Building. Panelists are supposed to read all of them. Some fun.

➤ The time crunch: a single federal application, including a long-winded résumé and pages and pages of essays, may exceed 10 pages. So 10 times the number of applicants for the job equals the number of pages that each panelist must review—usually by the day before yesterday. So how much time does each page get? Please—you do the math. (I don't want to be the bearer of bad news.)

➤ The heavy workloads of panelists: panelists are good people. They take their panel assignments seriously. But they are busy—always. And like most jurors, they regard their stints on peer review panels as unwelcome interruptions from their "real work," which is piling up in their absence.

During the panel screen, each application is rated by each panelist. As shown on the sample rating sheet in Figure 6-1, each panelist rates each applicant's answers to essay question (KSAs or ECQs). Then, all panelists' ratings are tallied to give each applicant a total rating on a scale from 1 to 100 points.

3. **Rating and Ranking Applications.** After being rating by panelists, applicants are divided onto two tracks depending on whether they are currently or ever have been a fed. The rules governing the ranking of applicants in each track differ. Here's how:

➤ One track is for all applicants, including outside applicants without any federal experience. Applicants on this track are, as warranted, given points for veterans' preference—a system of points awarded to certain types of veterans based on their military service. (Note that the sample rating sheet in Figure 6-1 has a column for veterans' preference.) When rated and ranked against other applicants, veterans with veterans' preference frequently "float to the top" because of their extra points. Therefore, veterans' preference can be a deciding factor in hiring competitions.

NAME	KSA #1	KSA #2	KSA #3	KSA #4	Veterans' preference	TOTAL POINTS
Applicant #1						
Applicant #2						
Applicant #3						
Applicant #4						
Applicant #5						
Applicant #6						
Applicant #7						
Applicant #8						
Applicant #9						
Applicant #10						
Applicant #11						
Applicant #12						
Applicant #13						
Applicant #15						

NAME OF PANEL MEMBER _____

Figure 6-1. Sample panel rating sheet. Each panelist grades each applicant on each of his/her responses to application essays—known as KSAs or ECQs—identified in the vacancy announcement and scores them on a sheet like this one. Notice that scores are based on essays and veterans preference; résumés are not specifically scored. Hence, the importance of application essays.

> Another track is for current and former feds who are said to have "status." Applicants on this track cannot count their veterans' preference. Therefore, when applicants on this track are rated and ranked, feds without veterans' preference cannot be outranked by applicants with veterans' preference.

4. **Generating the Certs.** After applicants on each track are rated and ranked, top scorers on each track are added onto a certification list of "best qualified candidates." In government lingo, these surviving applications have "made the cert." Applications that don't make the cert are (sniffle, sniffle) rejected.

   The number of applications that makes each cert varies according to the hiring agency's rules. But anywhere from 3 to 10 applications are included on most certs.

5. **The Final Cut.** The certs are submitted to the selecting official—usually the future supervisor of the new employee (or a member of his/her staff). But note that the selecting official for any particular job is not necessarily in the same profession as the applicants s/he is screening. For example, a department head who is an accountant could serve as the selecting official for an opening in his/her department for a communications expert.

   The selecting official reviews all applications on the certs and, depending on agency policy, may decide to interview all, some, or none of them. (Phone interviews are allowed.) What types of applications tend to do best in this type of contest? Applications that cater to a rushed, distracted, and not necessarily expert manager by concisely conveying impressive, relevant credentials in reader-friendly language that does not assume specialized knowledge.

Once the selecting official finishes interviewing applicants and checking references, she/he picks the winner of the competition who is offered the job. If the winner rejects the offer, another qualified candidate is usually offered the job.

If an outside applicant with no federal experience is picked, she/he usually must serve a probationary or trial period, which usually lasts one year. If a current or former fed with status is hired, she/he does not have to serve a probationary period.

Taking the Human Out of Human Resources: Machine Screens

Online Versus Paper Applications

Some agencies still only accept paper applications. But more and more federal agencies have automated their selection processes—and some federal agencies allow applicants to choose for themselves whether to submit a paper or online application.

If your target agency gives you a choice between submitting a paper application or an online application, choose the paper option. Why? Because:

> Most online applications don't recognize and accept modern text formatting features, like bold and bullets. Therefore, applications created on these systems invariably print out as dense slabs of tiny, featureless text. Reading page after page of such texts is about as much fun as reading page after page of the phone book. By contrast, well-formatted paper applications are considerably more eye-catching and memorable. Therefore, hiring managers tend to give paper applications more attention than online applications.

> Some online applications do not have spellcheckers and so are prone to errors and typos that can—by themselves—doom an application. By contrast, spellchecked paper applications that can easily be printed for proofreading are more likely to be error free.

The raw reality is that, in most cases, when time-pressured hiring managers confront piles of applications that include concise, well-formatted paper applications as well as dense, hard-to-read online applications, the online applications sink to the bottom of the pile— perhaps never to be exhumed again. Such burial does not bode well for the hiring prospects of their authors.

As one hiring manager said (with rolling eyes), "PEEE-UUUU! I hate those online applications. Page after page of long, unbroken paragraphs in tiny print remind me of the warning inserts that come with prescriptions. Nobody reads them because they are unreadable!"

How Online Applications Are Screened

Online applications usually feature the following components: résumés, essay questions, and short-answer questions that ask applicants to describe their experience via true/false, check-the-boxes, and tiered-response answers.

Each potential response to each short-answer question is worth a certain number of points; the more types of experience and the more senior-level experience it reflects, the more points it earns. **So interpret your experience liberally and give yourself the highest rating you possibly can on each short-answer question.**

Here's how online applications are screened by electronic hiring systems:

1. **Generating the Certs.** Computers—instead of people—rate each application based on their responses to short-answer questions and veterans' preference, and then list top scorers on the certs.

2. **Checking the Certs.** Human resources staffers verify that the short-answer questions in each application on the certs are supported by the applicant's résumé and essays. Unsupported applications are rejected. Applications on each cert that pass this screen are forwarded to the selecting official.

3. **The Final Cut.** The selecting official reviews top-scoring applications on the certs (usually quickly), interviews his/her top picks, and then makes the selection decision, just as selecting officials do in traditional hiring processes.

Does the speed and superficiality of this system seem brutally harsh to you? If so, that's because it is. But selections in the private sector are even more brutal than federal ones. Why? Because federal agencies are required to review all complete applications that make the deadline. They are also required to fill positions based on the qualifications of applicants, not on their own personal preferences or nepotism.

This is not true in the private sector where applications can be filed directly in the circular file without ever being reviewed by a person or machine, and where hiring managers are free to base their hiring machines solely on nepotism or other subjective criteria.

What Makes a Successful Application

Whether you're applying for an entry-level job or an executive job, your hiring manager's main goal is to hire the zero-risk applicant who will solve their problems, not create problems. And because it's relatively difficult to fire feds, your hiring manager is probably particularly scared of hiring a bait-and-switch applicant—one who looks great on paper but fritzes out once hired.

Proving That You're the Zero-Risk Applicant

How can you prove that you're the zero-risk applicant who will solve problems, not create them? The first principle of application preparation is that your essays (KSAs and ECQs) and short-answer self-rating questions are critical to your success. If you don't give yourself top scores on all the short-answer questions and answer all of the essay questions in ways that prove you're a qualified producer, you almost certainly won't earn enough points to make the cert. So skipping any of these questions because of your understandable desire to save time or because of carelessness is like hitting the third rail of the application process. Don't even *think* about doing it.

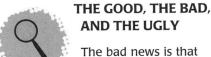

THE GOOD, THE BAD, AND THE UGLY

The bad news is that most job openings draw dozens of applications. But the good news is that most applications present irrelevant qualifications in rambling, typo-filled texts. So if you submit a targeted, concise, polished application, you will almost certainly stand out from the pack.

Also, even if you're applying to an agency that screens applications electronically, to be successful (that is, to make the cert and win over interviewers), your application must still impress harried, time-pressured human resource officials and interviewers who want a quick, easy, impressive read.

Remember: hiring managers don't read applications like they read suspense novels—savoring every word, while sipping wine cuddled up by a cozy fire. Instead, they race through applications solely to get through the pile, dismiss applications, and whittle down the pile to a few choice candidates so they can get back to their "real work." And believe me, they use any plausible reason to eliminate applications, down to grammatical errors and typos. So make your application an easy, instantly impressive read by formatting and phrasing your application to:

> **Be eye-catching.** Your application should be concise, formatted to support skimming, and crafted to make your key credentials leap off the page.

> **Present yourself as an experienced veteran of your target position.** Prove that you've already done your target job and done it well by describing your credentials and success stories that parallel the requirements of your target job and by providing objective validation of your successes, as explained in Chapter 7.

> **Be understood by nonspecialists who are not familiar with your field and know nothing about your current organization or projects.** You can make sure that your application will be understood by hiring managers by soliciting feedback on it from friends, colleagues, and relatives before you submit it. Remember that hiring managers are plucked from the masses to serve on hiring panels. This means that today's cube neighbor is tomorrow's hiring manager; yesterday's hiring manager is today's cube neighbor. Therefore, today's cube neighbor can help you preview what tomorrow's hiring manager will think of your application.

> **Wake up hiring managers by showing your enthusiasm and zest.**

> **Be polished and error-free.**

Part II of this book—*Cranking Out Your Application*—will teach you how to craft applications that meet all of these requirements.

WHAT HIRING MANAGERS WANT

By Kathy Alejandro, Federal Manager and Supervisor

Throughout my career, I have helped hire and promote many federal employees. What do federal hiring managers, like me, usually look for in job applicants?

The three qualities that impress me most in job applications are *experience*, *experience*, and more *experience*. That's because if I have a staffing need, I want to fill it NOW. So I want to hire someone who can hit the ground running with minimal supervision and training. And applicants who are experienced in the same types of projects demanded by the job opening are most likely to be able to quickly and independently deliver. I also want to hire professionals who:

*   are hard-working and conscientious.

*   *really* want the job, and go the extra mile to prove it.

*   are professionally reliable. (Yes, when you are screening strangers, the possibility of hiring an axe murderer is, shall we say, less than appealing.)

How can you, as a job applicant, show hiring mangers that you have these winning qualities? First and foremost, by loading your KSAs with specific examples of successes that relate to the opening. You will thereby prove that you would produce similar successes if you were hired for the job.

But if, on the other hand, you submit an application that omits required KSAs, you are virtually guaranteed to be rejected. Likewise, if you pump up your KSAs with generic or irrelevant information that lacks specifics, you will probably strike out. After all, you can't expect hiring managers to fill in the gaps and make sense out of *your* past. That's your job.

Among my pet peeves are KSAs that are filled with conclusionary statements about how qualified the applicant is and what the applicant can do without providing any examples of accomplishments that support these statements. I am similarly turned off by KSAs whose irrelevance to the vacancy announcement suggests that they were originally written for another purpose.

As someone who has written many KSAs for my own job applications, I sympathize with applicants who would rather not have to write KSAs. But by the same token, as a hiring manager, I weigh KSAs even more heavily than résumés. That's because KSAs invite applicants to provide thorough but concise descriptions of their relevant qualifications. By contrast, résumés are usually diluted by jobs, projects, and training that have, in no way, prepared the applicant for the opening. Why should I sift through that if I can get exactly what I need from KSAs? Moreover, any applicant who squanders the opportunity to sell themselves and show how they are qualified for the job probably doesn't want it very much.

Here are some other pointers for preparing winning federal job applications:

*   **Write for Nonspecialists.** Let me give you an example of why this is important: By training, I am an attorney. But I have served as the selecting official for jobs such as a contract specialist and safety/health specialist in which I have no background. So it is hard for me to understand, let alone be impressed by applications for such positions that are filled with abbreviations, acronyms, and technical or agency-specific jargon. But I am likely to be bowled over by applications for such positions that cite success stories and other credentials that are free of such impenetrable obstacles.

*   **Research Your Target Agency.** Surf through your target agency's website, read recent articles about the agency in newspapers and magazines, and research your target agency through the online resources provided in Chapter 2 and Chapter 11 of this book. Reflect your resulting knowledge in your application. In interviews, mention how you have researched the agency, and then mention specific, relevant news items about the agency to prove it.

*   **Proofread and Edit.** Typos, grammatical errors, missing words, and misspellings on job applications are absolute no-nos. One of my favorite bloopers involved an applicant who mentioned that he had brought a project "to fruitarian" (instead of "to fruition"). On first blush, I

though the applicant had brought the project to someone who studied fruit or was a vegan! Other applications have included sentences such as "I have letters of accommodation" (instead of "commendation"), and ironically, "I am an excellent profreader" (instead of "proofreader").

Though such mistakes provide comic relief to hiring panels, they reflect poorly on the applicant's communication skills. But even worse, an error-filled or incomplete application that incorporates a sloppy, half-hearted approach bodes poorly for an applicant's future performance.

Here is a tip that will be the gift that will keep on giving: run each of your applications by at least one critical, articulate editor. Your editor will help you eliminate bloopers and sharpen the organization and clarity of your descriptions of your experience.

- **Use Inside Contacts.** Do you have inside contacts who will vouch for your professional reputation and reliability? An inside contact may be an employee of the hiring agency or a personal or professional associate of a hiring manager. If so, encourage your inside contact to sing your praises to the powers-that-be as soon as you submit your application.

- **Infuse Your Application and Interview with LIFE!** Unfortunately, many job seekers wrongly believe that just because they are applying for a federal job, their application should read as dryly as the *Federal Register*. NOT! An application or interview that reflects a high-energy individual who enjoys their job, whose personality fits their profession, and who considers their job important and respects the mission of the agency will almost always stand out from the pack.

HOT TIP
Become an Insider

As the saying goes, "It takes one to know one." So if you really want to understand how hiring managers think, become one. To do so, tell your boss, Human Resources Office, or managers who are currently hiring that you would like to serve on hiring or interviewing panels. They will probably welcome your help. And, in return for your efforts, you will be paid in spades with career-boosting insights on how job applications are evaluated and how job seekers present themselves to prospective employers.

PART II

CRANKING OUT YOUR APPLICATION

"Hiring managers don't hire people; they hire applications."

Your application represents you to hiring managers . . . It is you on paper . . . It is your brain on paper . . . It is the *only* version of you that hiring managers will see when they decide whether to invite you to an interview or deposit your application in the circular file.

This means that in the selection process, it doesn't really matter how qualified you are for your target job. It only matters how qualified your application "*says*" you are, and how clearly and persuasively it says so. In other words, if you don't include all of your relevant qualifications and describe them in clear and persuasive terms, you will risk getting beaten out by less qualified applicants who convey their qualifications more skillfully.

With advice straight from federal hiring managers, Part II will teach you how to identify your key qualifications and format and phrase them for a quick, clear, and persuasive read—whether you are preparing a hard-copy or online application.

CHAPTER 7

Your Bragging Writes

"You can't sit around and wait for inspiration. You have to go after it with a club."

—JACK LONDON, AUTHOR OF *THE CALL OF THE WILD*

Many job seekers short-sell themselves: They omit from their applications many potentially pivotal credentials. Then when they do describe their credentials, they use forgettable, ho-hum terms instead of terms that convey the importance of their contributions. Other job seekers fill their applications with vague, self-serving puffery unsupported by specifics.

These kinds of problems are caused by common tendencies. For example, most of us:

> ➤ Forget some of our important achievements. No matter how devoted we were to previous projects, we forget key aspects of them once they are eclipsed by new projects.

> ➤ Cannot be objective about ourselves. We have been applying our skills for so long and so intensely that we don't even know which ones are extraordinary anymore. And we have trouble distinguishing which accomplishments would be most important to hiring managers vs. which ones are most important to us because of sentimental or other reasons.

> ➤ Were never taught how to express achievements in terms that capture their true value.

> ➤ Fear that inventorying our successes will make us sound like conceited blowhards.

This chapter will help you avoid these tendencies and teach you how to craft applications and answers to interview questions that will prove to hiring managers that you are qualified for your target job. It will do so by walking you through a step-by-step process for mining your qualifications for golden selling points and describing them in winning, memorable terms without sounding egocentric.

You will be able to incorporate your selling points developed through this chapter into your cover letters, résumés, application essays, and interviews. In other words, this chapter will help you create a reservoir of selling points that will help you impress hiring managers during every step of the application process.

Selling Yourself

Guess what: If you are looking for a job, you are in sales—even if you have never in your life asked a shopper, "Would you like that in paper or plastic?" Huh? Yes, if you are a job seeker, you are a salesperson. The big ticket product that you are selling is *you*, and your potential buyers are your target employers.

As a salesperson, you would be wise to consider some basic sales principles:

1. **A winning sales pitch addresses the *buyer's needs*, not the seller's *needs*.** After all, you wouldn't buy a car from a seller whose sales pitch focused on *his* potential profits from the sale rather than how the car would fit *your* needs. Likewise, an employer is unlikely to hire you if you harp on how getting hired would improve your life and how the target opening represents the perfect next step for you, instead of how *you* would improve *the employer's* operations.

Put another way: On your job application and in your interview, you should ask not what your hiring manager can do for you . . . but what you can do for your hiring manager.

2. **Just as a sensible shopper wouldn't buy any big-ticket item, such as a car, without understanding its virtues, an employer won't hire you without understanding your qualifications.** And the only way to make an employer understand your qualifications is by describing them in your applications and interviews. After all, if you don't persuasively sell the product—*you*, no one else will, and so you will probably be passed over for another product (i.e., one of your competitors who gives a more persuasive sales pitch).

3. **A subtle sales pitch is a losing sales pitch.** Unfortunately, you can't expect hiring managers to read between the lines, or sleuth-out hidden messages in applications, or interpret the hints of reticent interviewees. In most cases, it takes nothing less than a verbal two-by-four to get and keep the attention of harried, time-pressured hiring managers as they whip through piles and piles of applications. In other words, if you don't explain your credentials loud and clear to hiring managers, they won't notice or be persuaded by them.

But do not mistake an aggressive sales pitch for an egocentric sales pitch; you *can* toot your own horn without sounding brassy, self-serving, or cocky. To do so, you must describe what you have accomplished and why it was important and how it improved your employer's operations—without asserting how wonderful or valuable you are, predicting how impressed hiring managers will be by you, or describing yourself in unqualified grandiose statements. Remember: bombast usually bombs.

HOT TIP
What Does Your Online Identity Say About You?

Google yourself through the eyes of a cold-hearted, humorless, and judgmental employer. Will your online identity increase or dash your chances for landing your target job?

Instead, support descriptions of your results with concrete examples, hard data, and objective validation of your results. In short, present yourself in factual, specific terms. By doing so, you will provide evidence of your high value that will compel employers to conclude that you are a prize. That is a more persuasive strategy than directly proclaiming yourself as such or promising what others will think of you.

What follows is a step-by-step approach for developing factual, validated descriptions of your achievements.

Step #1: The Paper Chase

Collect all documents that can help you identify your golden selling points, including:

➤ The vacancy announcement for your target job.

➤ A recent résumé. If you don't have one, list your jobs from the last 15 years, describe your main successes at each one, list your promotions and what you did to earn them. Include special assignments, detail assignments, task forces, workgroups, and committees on which you served.

➤ List of your academic degrees.

➤ List of professional training courses that you have taken.

➤ Copies of your performance evaluations from the last 10 to 15 years.

➤ Any academic/professional awards, professional honors, or letters of commendation you have received. For current feds, this includes the write-ups accompanying performance awards and Quality Step Increases (QSIs). If you have won any fellowships or awards from professional societies, cite statistics or descriptive info that conveys their selectivity.

➤ Complimentary letters or e-mails from superiors, stakeholders, clients, customers, trainees, contractors, or conference participants. (Don't restrict yourself to positive feedback that you received from your supervisor.) And don't restrict yourself to written positive feedback. Any positive feedback given to you—whether delivered orally or in writing—is yours to keep and quote as you please, including in your application or interviews.

➤ Positive evaluations from attendees of training classes or events that you organized.

➤ Work products from your projects, such as documents or websites, and positive feedback that you received from people who used them.

➤ List of teams or other work groups that you were specially selected for.

➤ List of your presentations, speeches, and other public-speaking engagements, including conference presentations and poster presentations.

➤ List of your publications.

➤ List of websites that you contributed to.

➤ List of awards, honors, or positive press pieces that you helped your organization earn.

➤ Clips in your organization's newsletters, popular press, or trade publications that you wrote or that covered your projects.

➤ Record of military service.

➤ List of computer hardware and software systems that you can use.

➤ Languages in which you are proficient or fluent.

Students and Recent Graduates

Collect these documents:

➤ Your academic transcripts. Compute your overall GPA and your GPA in your major, and use whichever makes you look better.

➤ List of your major papers, class projects, independent study projects, your grades on these projects, and any positive verbal praise that they earned.

➤ List of merit-based scholarships, fellowships, and grants. Cite statistics or descriptive info that conveys their selectivity.

➤ List of your honors and awards. Of course, if you were valedictorian and/or gave a commencement speech, note this stellar achievement.

➤ List of your class and conference presentations, major speeches, public speaking engagements, and any associated positive feedback that you received.

➤ Copies of your articles or articles that covered your activities in school papers, academic publications, or the popular press.

➤ List of your student jobs, teaching assistantships, tutoring jobs, summer jobs, internships, and positive feedback that you received in these positions, such as praising evaluations, promotions, and invitations to return to summer jobs.

➤ Extracurricular activities, including clubs, newspapers, athletic activities, artistic and theater activities, and volunteer jobs. Emphasize your leadership positions, such as positions in student government and any study groups, organizations, or events you organized.

➤ Document demands on your time that reflect your multitasking ability (i.e., number of hours per week spent on classes, lab assignments, sports, jobs, and other scheduled activities).

Step #2: Brainstorm Your Achievements

It may be helpful to you to jog your memory about your work history and coax your creative juices before inventorying your credentials. To do so, review the documents that you collected in Step #1, as well as the Idea Generator on page 72 and Table 7-1. Then experiment with the five brainstorming methods for identifying your achievements suggested here.

One caveat: Avoid incorporating into your descriptions of your achievements vague statements from job descriptions that begin with phrases like "My responsibilities include..." or "My duties include..." Why? Because such stale, actionless assertions will bore hiring managers; reading or listening to them is about as exciting as reviewing someone else's "to do" list. Moreover, job descriptions only define general areas of responsibility that you did not necessarily fulfill. And most importantly, they do not capture your most important selling points—your specific successes, achievements, and results.

Method #1: Ask Yourself What Makes You ... You

We each have our own professional bents, biases, and personalities that are reflected in almost everything we do.

A case in point: If two professionals of equal stature were assigned the same project, they would probably produce two totally different results. Both results might be good, but they would certainly be different. For example, suppose two different web designers each produced a website showcasing the same government project. One designer might design a website full of multimedia features and lots of color. Another designer might produce a classic website in striking black and white that did not feature any moving graphics. Both sites might be eye-catching, informative, and impressive, but they would certainly convey different looks.

Our uniqueness is reflected right down to the way we complete simple, everyday tasks. Even two receptionists handle calls differently. One might answer calls with a more cheerful, friendly greeting; the other might be more likely to connect callers to the correct contact.

Apply the uniqueness principle to yourself by defining what makes you ... *you*. What do you do better than your peers and junior colleagues? How does your work reflect your special stamp? In what ways would your employer's operations be different if you had never been born?

Method #2: Get Interviewed

Ask colleagues, friends, or relatives to interview you about your professional achievements. Include among your interviewers those who are familiar with your job history as well as those who are not. Encourage your interviewers to ask you probing questions. If you feel comfortable doing so, show the documents that you collected in Step #1 to your interviewers.

This brainstorming method may sound like a "Mickey Mouse" kind of exercise. But it works. Why? For one thing, the dynamic give-and-take of conversation may fire your brain and revive memories of important achievements better than will the solitary experience of sitting in front of an intimidating blank piece of paper. In addition, colleagues, friends, and relatives who are familiar with your work may remind you of achievements and associated positive feedback that you may have forgotten. And those who are unfamiliar with your work will help you recognize extraordinary aspects of your achievements that you take for granted.

Method #3: Do You Deserve a Promotion?

When I lead "how-to-land-a-government-job" seminars, I frequently ask attendees whether they deserve promotions on their current jobs. Almost all of them invariably answer "yes." Then, I ask attendees to explain why. In response, long lists of stellar achievements invariably roll off their tongues; they usually cite achievements such as their:

➤ High productivity levels and recent increases in their responsibilities.

➤ Creation of important programs from scratch with little supervision.

➤ Experience in simultaneously managing multiple projects that had tough deadlines.

➤ Record of improving audits, investigations, publications, regulations, or other work products.

Several minutes after asking my attendees why they deserve promotions, I ask them to name their most important achievements. They invariably respond to my request with tongue-tied silence and heads bowed in "please-don't-call-on-me" postures—not realizing that they had already answered that question when it had been phrased differently.

My classroom observations suggest that the easiest way for you to identify your best credentials may be to simply ask yourself why you deserve a promotion. Then, write down all of your skills and achievements that pour forth.

Method #4: Pretend You're Someone Else

Are you one of those professionals who freely praises everyone but yourself? If so, it may be helpful to try to see yourself through someone else's eyes instead of through your own modest eyes. You can do so by pretending, for a few minutes, that you are the President of the Official [your names goes here] Fan Club. Then, through this alternative identity, review your documents from Step #1 and explain to an employer why they should hire you. This kind of detached, out-of-body-experience may free you to abandon your inhibitions, and give yourself the glowing sales pitch that you deserve.

Method #5: Take Someone Else's Lead

Ask a colleague, friend, or relative to describe their achievements to you. Listening to their descriptions will help psyche you into describing your own achievements.

Method #6: Use the Cheat Sheets on This Book's CD

Use the "Application and Interview Cheat Sheets" in this book's CD to help jog your memory and stimulate your creative juices.

Method #7: Seek a Second Opinion

No matter what initial brainstorming method you use, show your list of accomplishments to colleagues, relatives, or friends. Likewise, always solicit feedback on your application and practice interviewing with your trusted advisors. **Remember: the only way to really gauge how your descriptions of your achievements come across to other people is to ask other people how they come across.** The more advisors you consult, the better; each of them will give you different and usually valid advice on when, where, and how you can deliver your messages more clearly and persuasively and modulate your tone for maximum impact.

THE IDEA GENERATOR: IDENTIFY YOUR ACHIEVEMENTS

- Which of my academic or professional achievements mirror those demanded by my target job, and/or address the issues and stakeholders addressed by my target job?

- What would I like to be asked about in a job interview?

- Which achievements am I most proud of and/or have I worked mightily to accomplish?

- Which of my achievements have drawn recognition, such as high grades, awards, promotions, bonuses, or verbal praise?

- How do I do my work better/differently from peers or more junior professionals? What do I offer that no one else does?

- How would my employer's services, employee resources, morale, or any other aspect of my organization be different if I had never worked for it?

- What did I do to earn an excellent reputation among my professors or employers and how can I prove that I have done so?

- How have I shown initiative, gone the extra mile, and taken on more than the minimum?

- How have I made other peoples' work easier or improved their productivity?

- When have I wisely used my judgment, discretion, or creativity?

- In what contexts have I communicated my knowledge to other students, professors, colleagues, supervisors, and trainees?

- How have my projects become more advanced/increased in responsibility in recent years?

- What special knowledge/skills do I have? What is unique about my education, training, or experience?

- What am I an expert or fanatic about?

- What makes my job or field interesting or important?

- When have I contributed to high-pressure, high-profile, high-dollar, or high-priority projects?

- Which of my achievements helped or impacted the most people?

- Which of my achievements benefited or involved high-ranking executives?

- Have I managed sensitive situations or confidential or top secret information?

- How have I helped save time or money for my organization or streamlined a process?

- Do any of my accomplishments warrant superlatives like the first, the only, the best, the fastest, the highest-rated, the most, the strongest, or in the top tier? You don't have to be the first climber up Mt. Everest to have an important superlative under your belt. You should, for example, brandish your role in automating a process, creating a new website, developing new trainings, creating a first-of-its kind, trail-blazing document, or completing a report in record time

- Have I helped pioneer a new approach?

- Am I the only employee, or one of the only employees, qualified/entrusted to conduct an important activity?

- How have I demonstrated my multitasking abilities and ability to meet tight deadlines.

TABLE 7-1	Using the Idea Generator: Achievements Go From Fizzle to Sizzle
Before	**After**
1. My project went well.	1. Created agency's new website on deadline and under budget; website received special praise from Chief Financial Officer.
2. Write reports.	2. I am an expert in translating technical information into easy-to-read language. Played pivotal role in agency's release of annual report in record time.
3. I am interested in International Relations	3. Took six courses on the Middle-East crisis and earned a GPA of 3.7 in them.
4. Develop contracts.	4. Developed company's first incentives-based supply contracts that give contractors financial incentives for beating deadlines.
5. Manage the books.	5. Closed company's books within three days of end of month for first time in company's history, and earned more than seven unqualified opinions in a row.
6. Deal with customer complaints.	6. Use tact, diplomacy, and programmatic knowledge to transform dissatisfied customers—whose hard-to-resolve complaints were not solved by junior staffers—into satisfied, repeat customers.
7. File documents.	7. Developed company's first electronic filing system giving company's 200 employees quick access to commonly used forms.
8. Created information security program.	8. Created from scratch the agency's first information security program, which protects the personal data of agency's 5,000 employees and top secret information on the production and transportation of 11 billion coins per year.
9. Run Alternative Dispute Resolution Program.	9. Created company's Alternative Dispute Resolution program that now saves my agency $2 million annually in legal costs.
10. Manage internship program.	10. Developed internship program employing 50 high school students per year. Program has significantly reduced drop-out rates of participants and improved company's image in the community.

Step #3: Quantify Your Achievements

Statements supported by statistics, measurements, counts, and other metrics sound scientific, indisputable, and objective (whether or not they really are). So by supporting descriptions of your activities with statistics, measurements, counts, and other metrics, you will make them sound scientific, indisputable, and objective (whether or not they really are) and thereby avoid sounding like a self-serving braggart. In addition, by quantifying your activities and results you will underscore the massiveness of your achievements; numbers give your achievements weight and heft.

When you consider how to quantify your activities and results, think in terms of time, the number of people/organizations impacted by your work, money, productivity, geography, and any other types of metrics that apply. The Number Generator on page 76 and Table 7-2 can give you some ideas on how to do so. A few more tips on quantifying:

> ➤ You may get more ideas for metrics that can help you quantify your achievements by reviewing your current office's annual report, strategic plan, or newsletter/Intranet articles.

> ➤ When you can't cite an exact number, estimate figures and use phrases, such as "dozens of . . . ," "a significant increase in . . . ," or "more than 100 . . . "

> ➤ Use creative (but honest) accounting. For example, a federal attorney was recently asked about her supervisory experience in her application for a managerial position. But because she had only been supervising three professionals at the time, she did not cite that relatively small figure. Instead, she stated that during her 15 years as a supervisor, she had supervised dozens of professionals. Plus, she also quoted some of the praise she had received from her staffers in their thank-you cards to her. Her strategy worked: She got the job.

> ➤ Also, even if you supervised, led, or trained employees only on an informal basis, count it as supervisory experience (but don't volunteer that your interaction was informal).

> ➤ If you missed a target, quota, or deadline, don't mention it, but cite whatever stats reflect how much you *did* accomplish in a short time.

> ➤ Managers: See "Metrics for Managers" in the "Application and Interview Warm-Up Tip Sheets" folder in this book's CD.

Step #4: Name-Drop and Title-Drop

Applicants who are perched on the highest rungs of the career ladder usually impress hiring managers the most. How can you prove to hiring managers that you occupy a lofty position in your current organization's hierarchy? By mentioning in your résumé, application essays, and interviews the titles of the highest-level managers who have blessed or benefited from your work, the organizations you have interacted with, and the most important projects that you worked on. The common name for this practice is name-dropping.

Although name-dropping is generally a *faux pas* in social situations, professional name-dropping, or better yet title-dropping, is an invaluable tool for job seekers. How does citing your high-level associations help your case? By helping you prove that you can operate successfully in high-pressure environments, and that you are adept at the care and feeding of muckety mucks—important skills in government.

By showing that you have earned the trust of senior officials, you will reassure potential employers that it is also safe for them to trust you. By the same principle, you will win the trust of your hiring managers by citing in your applications and interviews any staffers in your target organizations who will vouch for you as references.

When you cite your high-level associations, don't restrict yourself to title-dropping your immediate supervisor(s). Go as high up the food chain as you can by mentioning the titles of senior staffers who reviewed, approved, or used your work products, praised you orally or in writing, attended events that you organized, interacted with you, belonged to the target audience of your documents or other work products, or in any way benefited from your toil. Whether your highest-level contact is an assistant or the President of the United States, it doesn't matter: drop their title. Also mention the names of high-profile documents or other work products that you contributed to.

In addition, format and phrase your résumé and KSAs to brandish your own job titles as well as the names of your employers—particularly if they are large companies, influential think tanks, Congressional committees, and important nonprofits.

If you are reluctant to name-drop because it feels forced, remember that in the job-searching realm, the squeaky wheel principle applies; the more you tell your potential employers about your high-level successes, the more likely they will be to hire you.

Moreover, you've worked hard to help make your bosses look good: you've hauled and carried, you've endured the boring meetings, you've knocked yourself out to meet the impossible deadlines, you've trouble-shot the last-minute emergencies—now it's payback time. It is time for your muckety mucks to help make you look good. Go ahead: bask in their reflected glow by dropping their titles.

THE NUMBER GENERATOR (#$%)

Time

- Number of years of experience you have.
- Number of hours of training you took on a subject (or number of classes or papers you wrote on a subject).
- Tight deadlines you met.
- Your productivity in a specified time period (i.e., number of a certain type of work product you produce per year, or number of articles, reports, or other documents you produced or published within a specified period of time).
- Time-savings in producing a work product with streamlining procedures.

Number of People/Groups Impacted by Your Work

- Number of employees or contractors you supervised, led, recruited, or trained in formal or informal trainings.
- Number of people attending your presentations, conferences, or other events that you manage.
- Circulation of publication or website that you work on or increase in circulation that you helped bring about.
- Number of people or organizations that must comply with a regulation you produced or enforce.
- Reductions in the number or rate of deaths, injuries, accidents, or illnesses within a specified time.
- Number of customers/clients/calls that you serve within a specified time period.
- Number of managers you support.
- Number of people using a network or other system you manage.
- Number of people using a product that you designed, produced, or marketed.
- Number of stakeholder groups you interacted with.

Money

- Size of budget you manage and/or budget increases you helped generate.
- Annual revenue of company that you manage.
- Dollar value of contracts that you approve or manage.
- Dollar value of cost savings you produced by streamlining or automating processes or by negotiating contracts.
- Dollar value of accounts, legal cases, property, or equipment you manage or protect.
- Dollar value of merchandise you sell per day, week, or month.
- Increase in production or sales (dollar value or percentage) you produced.
- Sales of product that you helped design or sales generated by catalogue or advertising campaign you helped produce.
- Size of bonuses or number of bonuses you received.

Geography

- Number of square feet of building space or number of acres of land that you manage.
- Number of facilities, states, or countries in your jurisdiction.

Other

- Number of your suggestions or regulations you implemented.
- Size of database you manage.
- Number of cases you manage/have won.
- Improvements in product quality or survey results you helped bring about.
- Stats that reflect the selectivity of a scholarship, grant, or another honor that you received.

TABLE 7-2	Using the Number Generator: Achievements Go From Fizzle to Sizzle
Before	**After**
Received a graduate fellowship.	Was one of 50 nationwide students out of 1,500 applicants awarded the Homeland Security Graduate Fellowship.
Manage graphic artists.	Supervise 10 graphic artists and manage office's $4 million annual budget.
Solve IT problems.	Solve hundreds of technical support calls per month about problems on network used by 500 staffers. Specialize in troubleshooting "impossible to solve" problems.
Reorganized office.	Saved agency millions of dollars per year by managing the transfer of hundreds of jobs to a shared service provider.
Helped with office moves.	Managed office consolidation involving 700 employees and their office equipment that reduced space needs by 20 percent and saves $5 million in office rent per year.
Answer the telephone and word process.	Screen calls for five department chiefs, and format and finalize 15 controlled letters per week.
Directed the transportation of equipment during Gulf War.	Directed transportation of 500,000 pounds of explosive weapons, 5,000 troops and 50,000 pounds of perishable food from Kentucky to Kuwait during Gulf War.
Manage important accounts.	Manage five bulk corporate accounts that are worth more than $25 million per year.
Serve as time-keeper.	Manage all payroll and time-keeping records of 200 employees. Accurately perform bi-weekly updates. Answer dozens of time and attendance questions from managers monthly.
Help produce website.	Research and write content of agency's Internet site, which is accessible to all of the agency's 3,000 employees, and receives 100,000 hits per week. Typically write three 800-word articles per month under tight deadlines.
Implemented IT system.	Managed the purchase and implementation of agency's $10 million online hiring system that tripled the number of applications to agency jobs, increased the quality of the applicant pool, and helped the agency meet its diversity goals.
Run trainings.	Deliver anti-sexual harassment trainings to 500 employees per year. Over 95 percent of attendees rated trainings as excellent.

TABLE 7-3	Title-Dropping Makeovers: Achievements Go From Fizzle to Sizzle
Before	**After**
1. Gave presentation.	1. Delivered presentation on my summer research project to dozens of graduate students and six professors. Department Chair described project as a "tour-de-force."
2. Arrange travel.	2. Arrange international and domestic travel for five senior attorneys and director of sales and marketing. In a typical month, arrange 10 trips.
3. Serve as Chief Financial Officer for No-Name Inc.	3. Serve as Chief Financial Officer of No-Name Inc.—a start-up fiber-optics company that doubled its revenues in the last 2 years to $15 million annually.
4. Work as paralegal.	4. Serve as sole paralegal for eight senior attorneys in high-pressure, deadline-driven environment.
5. Led trainings.	5. Designed and delivered trainings on communication skills that were attended by hundreds of senior scientists.
6. Create presentations.	6. Design PowerPoint presentations delivered by Chief Financial Officer at department's monthly "all hands meetings" which are typically attended by dozens of employees and executives.
7. Helped plan conferences.	7. Served as co-organizer of two international conferences that drew more than 300 attendees, including members of Congress, and received glowing reviews in national trade publications.
8. Write reports.	8. Wrote 15 quarterly reports to Congress that were scrutinized by agency Director and approved with few edits.
9. Arrange stakeholder meetings.	9. Arranged annual meetings of the Laboratory Directors Conference attended by 75 directors of national research facilities, including the director of Lawrence Livermore National Laboratory.
10. Pitched stories to the press.	10. Successfully pitched stories to dozens of national publications, including X, Y, and Z.

Step #5: Validate Your Success

How many times have you done this? You receive positive feedback, such as verbal compliments, exemplary performance evaluations, praising e-mails, awards, or excellent evaluations on events or trainings you ran. You tell only a few select members of your inner circle about your positive feedback, if anyone, and perhaps enjoy a few fleeting hours of glee that ends as soon as your next personal or professional *crisis du jour* arises.

The next time you clean up your desk, you throw away your praising document, or bury it in a cramped, out-of-the-way drawer instead of storing it an organized, easily accessible file; it is about as likely to ever be dug out again as your second-grade report card. It never even occurs to you to write down whatever verbal praise you received.

The result: your verbal praise is gone with the wind and you quickly forget about your written praise. In other words, you've needlessly wasted your ammunition for advancement!

And so the decision makers who hold the keys to your future—your hiring managers—will never learn about your successes. (Unfortunately, your friends and relatives who may know about your success probably can't promote or hire you.)

The pity of it all! Why work like a harnessed beast to earn accolades without using them to help catapult your career to the next level? Remember: The praise and recognition that you receive from your toil is part of the pay you receive for your work. You shouldn't carelessly throw it away any more than you should throw away your paycheck!

Record Your Success

Whether or not you are job searching now, create an easy-to-find file for documents that validate your success—your success file. Store in this file:

> ➤ A running list of your projects that describes how they improved your organization's effectiveness, efficiency, budget, public image morale, or any other aspect of its management. Title-drop and quantify in your achievement descriptions.

> ➤ Copies of your work products. These may include printouts from PowerPoint presentations you gave; your academic papers; copies of press releases, articles or reports you wrote, articles that quote you or cover your projects; explanatory photos, maps, or charts; your artwork; results of surveys, investigations, or audits you contributed to; agendas from events you organized or gave presentations at; printouts of websites you helped create; and consumer products or catalogues you helped design.

> Transcribed versions of positive feedback you have earned and copies of any written or e-mailed positive feedback from your managers, colleagues, clients, trainees, stakeholder groups, professors, or other associates. These may include annual evaluations, thank-you e-mails, evaluations from trainings you gave, or events you organized, and awards you earned or helped your organization earn.

> Other evidence of success cited in The Validation Generator.

For more guidance on creating a success portfolio and using it to impress interviewers, see my *Washington Post* article, Make Every Interview a Show and Tell, which is included in this book's CD—and also online on the book's website.

Cite Your Success

Use objective feedback from your success portfolio to crown descriptions of your achievements in your cover letters, résumés, KSAs, and interviews. By doing so, you will go a long way toward proving that you are an action-oriented producer by objective standards—not a self-promoting talker.

One way to cite your praise in your application is to copy a technique used by movie ads that string together excerpts of reviews with phrases like, *FEEL-GOOD MOVIE OF THE YEAR . . . WHITE-KNUCKLE THRILLER! . . . AN OSCAR CONTENDER . . .*

You can similarly brandish your good reviews by excerpting quotes from your oral and written praise and including them in your application documents. For example, here are excerpts of written and oral praise featured in a résumé that generated four interviews for senior-level jobs:

> Sample Feedback From Executives: *Joe is a vital asset . . . his contributions are multifaceted . . . has gone the extra mile time and time again . . . always provides clients with expert advice and guidance . . . provides exceptional writing/editing services . . . an excellent team member . . . works independent of supervision . . . one of the most pleasant, if not the most pleasant, person to work with at this agency.*

Use the Validation Generator on page 82 to help you identify positive feedback you have received that you can quote to validate your success.

THE VALIDATION GENERATOR: PROVING THAT YOU ARE A PRODUCER

Formal Recognition of Your Performance/Trustworthiness:

- Superior performance evaluations. For example, say: *Consistently receive very positive annual reviews.*
- Your record serving effectively in high-level "acting" positions.
- Performance bonuses and awards, including team awards.
- Security clearances.
- Letters of commendation.
- Patents.
- Grants and fellowships.
- Your publications.

Advancement:

- Hired from contract or temporary position into permanent position.
- Rapid advancement. For example:
  - *Accepted into senior executive service after only 2 years as a federal employee.*
  - *Advanced from a Clerk to Program Manager in 6 years.*
  - *Received two merit-based promotions in 4 years.*

Oral and Written Praise:

- Oral comments or praising e-mails from a supervisor, senior official, stakeholder, client, contractor, customer, or your staff members.
- Favorable comments on performance evaluations. For example:
  - *Please note these comments from my supervisor on my annual evaluation: "Whenever there is a problem here, John comes up with a foolproof solution. He is an expert problem-solver."*

Feedback from Training, Conference, or Other Event:

- Drawing a large crowd to event or organizing events that receive standing ovations.
- Favorable evaluations, or oral or written praise from attendees or favorable coverage by the press.

Special Requests for Your Contributions:

- Requests by customers, clients, or stakeholders groups from your participation in projects.
- Specially selected to serve on detail assignments, workgroups, committees, or task forces. For example:
  - *Recruited to serve on EPA's Communication Task Force due to my problem-solving and writing skills.*
  - *Personally selected by CFO to write annual report.*

Your Enviable Reputation:

- How your work products or advice are incorporated into organization-wide programs or procedures.
- How your projects have served as a model or template or set the standard for subsequent projects.
- Your ability to gain approval of your work from managers without requiring significant revisions.
- Your record of completing projects under budget and on-time—or even beating budgets or deadlines.
- Your record for accuracy, which eliminates the need for redundant efforts.
- Your record of completing of increasingly responsible, complicated, or specialized projects.
- Your record of being consulted by other professionals as an expert.
- The numbers and types of publications that have quoted you or covered your projects.
- Your experience providing training.
- Your organization-wide reputation. For example:
  - *Because of my expertise in using Excel, I serve as my organization's spreadsheet troubleshooter.*

Evidence of Your Trustworthiness:

- Authority to award contracts or allocate grants.
- Authority to manage, disburse cash or checks.
- Your management of confidential information.

Students and Recent Grads:

- Overall GPA, GPA in your major, or grades in relevant classes on assignments.
- Honors, awards, merit-based scholarships, fellowships, and grants.
- Written and oral praise from professors in response to a thesis defense, exams, papers, independent projects, oral presentations, and other projects.
- Ability to simultaneously multitask school, student jobs, sports, or other commitments.
- Leadership role in student government, teams, contributions to teams or events, experience advising or teaching other students, and associated positive feedback.
- Your selection for particularly competitive summer jobs or internships.

Step #6: Add Power Words and Phrases

These power phrases and words may help you convey your work's importance and value:

➤ I am an award-winning…

➤ I am an expert in…

➤ Multimillion dollar

➤ High-dollar

➤ High-pressure

➤ High-priority

➤ High-energy

➤ High-volume

➤ High-profile

➤ High-visibility

➤ High-traffic, fast-paced, or fast-track

➤ Precedent-setting or trailblazing

➤ Record-breaking

➤ Front-line

➤ Deadline-driven

➤ I played a pivotal role in…

➤ I single-handedly…

➤ I produced glitch-free…

➤ I created from scratch…

➤ On time and within budget

Step #7: Match Your Skills and Achievements to the Opening

Once you've created a list of your credentials, tailor them to your target job. How? By winnowing down your list to those that parallel the demands of your target job and reflect your substantive knowledge of the issues addressed by your target organization. (Don't serve-up brain dumps of *all* of your credentials.) You can do so by analyzing the skills demanded by the opening, and then matching your experience to them as explained below.

A SAMPLE JOB DESCRIPTION

Here is a job description for a policy analyst opening followed by a skills analysis for the job.

The incumbent will be policy analyst in the Department of *Transportation's* Office of External Communications. This involves a broad spectrum of specialized and complex *analytic, communications, and project management duties* related to the mission of the Office of Communications. *Develops strategies and plans for a communications program* to respond to *public and Congressional inquiries. Researches, identifies, and establishes viable communications methods* and tools to inform the *public and internal department organizations* of the Office's policies, programs, services, and activities. *Independently writes, edits, creates, and updates* materials intended to be definitive *descriptions of the Office's programs, accomplishments, and policies. Serves as a liaison with stakeholder groups and regional offices, advises them* of communications strategies, and *solicits updates* on *program progress* from them. *Updates HQ officials on regional progress. Ensures communications comply with Agency policies,* standards, and formats and content is accurate. *Synthesizes summarizes and translates complex legislative materials into easy-to-understand documents for varied audiences.* Analyzes, synthesizes, and *integrates a variety of inputs to produce* an optimum written communication approach for designated audiences. *Interfaces with headquarters offices to* analyze, recommend, and create Agency written materials, products and web page designs. *Resolves conflicts with internal experts creating and maintaining standard reply information. Helps organize stakeholder meetings and conferences. There will be time periods when priority deadlines must be met and overtime required. Must distribute Information and report on legislative tracking to senior officials.*

SKILLS REQUIRED BY JOB

Strategic Planning

*   Develops communication strategies and plans for informing Congress, the public, and other internal and external audiences, and for responding to their information requests.

Research

*   Collects, synthesizes, and summarizes technical information from varied sources.
*   Tracks legislation.
*   Collects progress reports on program implementation from regional offices.

Analysis and Writing

*   Writes, edits, and updates documents and ensures their compliance with agency standards.
*   Describes programs, accomplishments, and procedures.
*   Integrates information from various sources.
*   Translates complex information into easy-to-understand language for varied audiences.
*   Creates hardcopy and web documents

Oral Communication/Project Management

*   Interfaces with various HQ offices to resolve conflicts in development of standards.
*   Advises regional offices; serve as a liaison with stakeholder groups.
*   Reports to senior officials on legislation, regional progress on program implementation, and other developments.
*   Helps organize meetings and conferences.
*   Works independently and works extra hours to meet tight deadlines on document production.

Analyze the Opening

The skills demanded by each opening are defined in its application questions and job description. Granted: job descriptions are frequently dense, rambling, and repetitive. But you can extract their essence by:

1. Underlining each important phrase/task only once, not every time it appears.

2. Grouping similar skills under categories.

3. Consolidating similar skills and eliminating redundancies.

4. Listing remaining categories and skills.

Provided below is a typical federal job description followed by a skills analysis of the job.

Match Your Skills

To match your skills to those demanded by the opening, review your credentials that you identified through this chapter. Then, select those that fit the demands of your target job, and eliminate irrelevant ones.

Repeat keywords: Your application documents should repeat keywords from the opening's job description. Suppose, for example, that you were applying for the writer/editor opening discussed above, which involves: *Develop[ing] communication strategies for responding to information requests from Congress, the public, and other internal and external audiences.*

If you have previously demonstrated this skill, you would be wise to say something like this in your résumé and essays: *Developed communication strategies for responding to information requests from Congress, the public, and other internal and external audiences.*

HOT TIP
Interpret the description of your target job as a question that asks, "Do you have this experience?" The more ways you can answer this question with, "Yes, I have this experience," the higher you'll score in the selection process.

Some applicants wrongly believe that such parroting is perceived by hiring managers as contrived or cheating in some way. *Au contraire!* (Purge your memory of images of your grade-school teacher wagging her index finger at you while warning of the evils of plagiarism.) Rather, by repeating key words in your descriptions of your achievements, you will help affirm, in no uncertain terms that cannot possibly be misunderstood, that your experience exactly matches the job's demands. In other words, the best way to prove to hiring managers that you would do an excellent job on your target job is to show that you have already done it and done it well.

If your credentials don't exactly match the job description of your target job, just include as many keywords as you can in your application. Also, cite your relevant academic experiences. For example, here is an excerpt from a KSA about communication skills that could be submitted by a new grad applying for the writer/editor opening with keywords from the job description underlined:

I wrote and edited a paper on transportation policy for an urban planning class. For this paper, I researched transportation policies, tracked transportation legislation throughout 2007, synthesized, summarized, and translated legislation into easy-to-understand language, and communicated results orally to my class. I received a B+ on the paper and an A- in the class.

Strengthen your descriptions: Don't just mechanically regurgitate keywords without adapting them to *your* background; remember to strengthen your descriptions by quantifying, title-dropping, and providing objective evidence of your success. For example, here is an excerpt from an application for the writer/editor position that embeds keywords within strengthened descriptions:

I developed communication strategies for responding to five Congressional requests for information about multimillion dollar federal transportation grants to the states. Such projects involved meeting with representatives of Ways and Means Committee every month for 5 months and meeting tight deadlines by working many weekends.

CHAPTER **8**

Mastering Online Applications

"There have been times when I encountered so many maddening problems on online application systems that by the time I could finally submit my application, I was so wigged out that I bore a scary resemblance to Nick Nolte in his infamous mug shot."

—A FRUSTRATED (BUT ULTIMATELY SUCCESSFUL) FEDERAL JOB APPLICANT

"On the Internet, nobody knows you're a dog."

Like private sector organizations, many federal organizations are automating their hiring processes through USAJOBS, QuickHire, Avue, and other systems. The good news is that online systems are speeding hiring processes.

But the bad news is that each federal online application system is separate and unique; the registration, résumé, and application information that you enter into any of these systems does not carry over into any others. This means that you must input your info into as many systems as you use. (Ugh!)

What's more, there is no such thing as a glitch-free online application system. Virtually all online application systems (including private sector ones) have annoying constraints, snags, and potentially fatal traps that can thwart the unwary. **This chapter is a must-read for anyone using online application systems because it explains how to easily defeat exasperating, application-busting problems.**

Inputting Your Application

Problem 1: Some federal jobs are announced via two vacancy announcements with different announcement numbers. Unfortunately, it's easy to confuse multiple announcements for the same job. Here is how they differ:

> ➤ One type of vacancy announcement is open to all applicants, including current and former feds and nonfeds. Applicants who apply to this type of announcement can count their veterans' preference. If hired, they must serve a 1-year probationary period. This probationary requirement applies even to experienced feds who have previously completed probation.
>
> If you are a nonfed, you should always apply only to this type of announcement. If you are a current or former fed, you should apply to this type of announcement only if you want your veterans' preference to count and if you're willing to complete a probationary period. Be aware that if you are a current or former fed without veterans' preference and you apply to this type of announcement, you may be outscored by an applicant with veterans' preference.

> ➤ Another type of vacancy announcement is open only to current and former feds (applicants with "status"). Applicants who apply to this type of announcement cannot count their veterans' preference but, if hired, will skip probation.
>
> If you are a current or former fed, you should always apply to this type of announcement when it is an option in order to avoid competing against veterans' preference applicants and to skip probation. But if you want to count your veterans' preference and are willing to serve probation, you should also apply to announcements that are open to the public. (For more info on this topic, see the definition of Merit Promotion Procedures in the Glossary.)

Solution 1: When you start your application, double-check all of its identifying information—particularly its "who may apply" section—to ensure that you are working on the correct announcement. Then, if you receive an electronic acknowledgement of your application after submitting it, carefully check the announcement number cited in your acknowledgement to confirm that you applied to the correct announcement.

Problem 2: Many online applications won't let you view each application question until you have answered all previous questions. This constraint may prevent you from quickly previewing all of an application's questions when you are deciding whether to apply to the job, and when you are strategizing your answers to essay questions.

Solution 2: In most online applications, you can provide dummy answers to questions (including essay questions) so that the system will let you advance to the end of the application. Then—at any time before the job closes—you can replace your dummy answers with genuine ones.

Problem 3: Like all online systems, online application systems can inexplicably develop vexing, perplexing electronic glitches—the kind that make you want to grab a sledge-hammer, smash your computer, ditch your professional career altogether, and join a traveling road show.

Solution 3: The "human" hasn't been totally removed from "human resources" yet; most online application systems still employ tech support specialists to help applicants troubleshoot technical glitches. So before grabbing your sledgehammer, contact them. See this chapter's Mayday box.

Problem 4: Most online applications ask applicants to rate their professional experience via a series of short-answer questions. Though these applications never say so, in most cases, an applicant must receive the highest rating on most questions in order to be seriously considered for the job.

Solution 4: Scrutinize the answers to each short-answer question on your online application to identify the one that represents the most senior experience level; that is the answer that is worth the most points. Then, comb your credentials and interpret them liberally, and give yourself the highest rating you honestly can for each question. Also, make sure that your high self-ratings are corroborated by the descriptions of your achievements in your résumé and any required essays.

Warning: If you can't give yourself the highest rating for most questions on an application, redirect your efforts to another application.

MAYDAY! MAYDAY!

If you need help troubleshooting technical snags on an online application, contact the application system's technical support staff. Some systems only provide e-mail support; some also have phone support.

The contact info for tech support is probably on your online application or on the main log-in page of the online application system. I have personally issued Maydays on many online systems, and technical support usually responded in 24 hours.

CAUTION
Do Not Leave Your Application to the Last Minute!

The window of opportunity for applying for each federal job usually slams shut on midnight EST of its closing date.

Online application systems can present time-consuming technical glitches at any time. So the only way you can be sure to make your deadline is to finish your application way ahead of time.

IS ALL OF YOUR ONLINE DATA CURRENT?

Every time you apply for another job via an online application system that you have previously used, check the currency of all information stored in the system about you—particularly your contact info and your description of your current job.

Problem 5: An online application system can crash or go down for maintenance at any time without warning. If it does so while you're inputting your application, all of your unsaved work will probably be wiped out. (Gulp!)

Solution 5: Create and save each application in a word processing file before cutting and pasting it into the online system. Also, as you enter or change text in your online application, save your changes frequently. One more thing: beware that the "save" buttons in online résumés and after essay questions in many online application systems are easy to miss, so look out for them and use them with wild abandon.

Formatting Text

Problem 6: Online application systems can make you look bad without even trying. Why? For several reasons:

> Modern formatting text features—such as bold, bullets, various font types and sizes, and shading—are not recognized by most online application systems and so do not transfer to these systems. Therefore, résumés and application essays print out from these systems as dense featureless slabs of text. So if you're not careful on online application systems, your best credentials—instead of leaping off the page—may get buried by textural overburden, never to be exhumed by harried hiring managers quickly plowing through dozens of applications.

> Many online application systems either don't have spellcheckers or have defective ones. Therefore, many applications are studded with typos and other errors that, by themselves, can, and frequently do, doom applications.

Solution 6:

> Don't write your application directly into an online system. Instead, create, edit, and spell-check your application in a word processing program, print it out, and repeatedly proofread it before copying and pasting it into its online application system. **Such quality controls are essential because typos and grammatical errors are among the most common causes for rejections of federal applications.**

> As you write your application, restrict yourself to basic formatting features from the ASCII format; that way, all of your formatting will be accepted by the online system. To do so:

>> Use capital letters to create headings and emphasize important information, such as job titles in résumés.

>> Emphasize headings by skipping lines and creating horizontal lines before and after headings. Create horizontal lines by repeating a keyboard character, such as a tilde (~), plus sign, minus sign, equal sign, or period.

>> Instead of a bullet, use an asterisk followed by a space (not a tab), or a number followed by a right parenthesis and a space (not a tab)

>> Don't use centered or right justified text tabs, quotation marks, or hyphens because these features change the text or format of your application in odd ways that you would probably not anticipate. (See the next problem for more on this topic.)

>> Write in short sentences and short paragraphs and use white space liberally.

The use of these basic formatting features is demonstrated by (1) a sample résumé featured in Figure 8-1; (2) a sample USAJOBS résumé featured in the résumé part of this book's CD; and (3) sample application essays found in the KSA-ECQ Prep part of this book's CD.

```
========================================================

JANE SMITH

========================================================

1234 Yellow Brick Road; City, State, ZIP Code
Work: (123) 123-567
Home: (123) 123-4567
E-Mail: Jsmith@E-mail.com
Social Security Number:  000-00-0000
U.S. Citizen

++++++++++++++++++++++++++++++
SUMMARY OF QUALIFICATIONS
++++++++++++++++++++++++++++++

  *  AWARD-WINNING CONTRACT MANAGER:  Seven years of
experience in managing multi-year, multi-million dollar contracts for
large federal agencies.

  *  REGULATORY EXPERT

  *  POLISHED COMMUNICATOR

  *  B.A. in ECONOMICS

++++++++++++++++++++++++++++++
PROFESSIONAL EXPERIENCE
++++++++++++++++++++++++++++++

SENIOR CONTRACT SPECIALIST: May 2000 to Present
ENVIRONMENTAL PROTECTION AGENCY (EPA) Office of the Chief
Information Officer
1200 Pennsylvania Avenue, NW Washington DC  20460
Salary:  $66,229 (GS-13/Step 1) (1102 Series)
40 hours per week
Supervisor: Mike Jones (You may contact at 101-111-1111)

  *  Authorized to award contracts for goods and services worth up to
$5 million without additional approvals.

  *  Serve as technical advisor to senior EPA officials, including the
Chief Financial Officer, on developing streamlined procedures for
conducting pre-award cost analyses; planning, negotiating and
soliciting contracts; and managing and closing out contracts.

  *  Advise program managers on cradle-to-grave acquisition
planning, including preparing Statement of Works (SOW); conducting
market research of vendors; and researching contractors' capabilities
for handling government contracts.

  *  Lead team of six EPA Contract Specialists who procure
Information Technology (IT) support and services worth approximately
$6 million annually
```

Figure 8.1. Sample of ASCII résumé.

Problem 7: The application that you send hiring managers is probably different in some significant ways from the one they will receive. In other words, what you see isn't what they get. Why? Because online application systems change the text and layout of applications in odd ways that you would probably not anticipate. For example, before delivering applications to hiring managers, some online systems automatically—believe it or not—convert all quotation marks into upside question marks, or move around text that has invalid characters

"I've seen online applications that were peppered with upside-down question marks or chunks of misplaced text because the applicant had inadvertently used invalid characters," laments one hiring manager. "It's a shame, because those applications might have been from qualified applicants, and they will never know why they were rejected." What's more, these types of quirks vary from system to system in unpredictable ways.

Solution 7: Here's how to view and edit exactly the same version of your applications that hiring managers will view:

> Start your application with plenty of time to spare before your deadline. When you reach the very end of your application, put a check in the box (if there is one) that asks whether you want to receive an e-mailed copy of your application.

> Submit your application. Immediately thereafter, a copy of your completed application should either be e-mailed to you or posted on your password-protected space on the online application system. These submitted versions of your applications should be identical to the ones delivered to your target organization. So double-check their formatting and proofread them well.

> Print and carefully review your application.

> If you identify problems in your application, reenter your application. (In some systems, you must go to the page that lists your previous submissions to reenter, change or delete your previous applications.)

> Revise your application as necessary. Then, submit your application again. In most systems, your latest submission will override your previous one, until the job closes.

> Repeat these steps as many times as necessary until your target job closes.

Problem 8: After you hit the "save" button for an essay or résumé on an online application system, it may, without warning, automatically delete any characters that exceed the essay's character limit.

Solution 8: Create and save your résumé and essays in a word processing file. Always do a character count before you cut-and-paste these documents into your online application and check that they will not exceed the system's character limits.

HOT TIP
Less is More

Harried, time-pressured hiring managers appreciate brevity and conciseness. So don't feel obliged to max out the generous character limits on most online résumés and application essays. Only use as much space as you need to prove you're qualified for the job. Omit any irrelevant or dated information that—no matter how personally important it may be to you—would not be important enough to help convince a hiring manager to hire you.

Making Deadlines

Problem 9: Unfortunately, many applicants believe that as long as they log onto the application system and start working on their online application before their deadlines, they'll be able to slip their application in under the wire and make their deadlines. But under most circumstances, only applications that are submitted—not just started—by their deadlines are accepted. As a result, many late-starters miss their deadlines and so are rejected.

Solution 9: Hit the "submit" button of each online application before its deadline.

Problem 10: Some online applications require applicants to fax, e-mail, or upload to the application various documents, such as transcripts and performance reviews. But if you are unexpectedly stumped by last-minute fax busy signals, uploading glitches, or difficulties accessing necessary computers, faxes, or scanners, you may miss your deadline.

Solution 10: Long before your target job's due date, identify everything you must submit to apply to the job, and how you will access all necessary hardware to do so. Also, label all documents so that the hiring agency will correctly match them to your main application. After you submit these documents, confirm with your target job's agency contact person that he or she received them.

Problem 11: Many applicants unfortunately assume that all they have to do to submit an online application is input their résumé and answer all application questions. Unfortunately, they either don't understand or forget that in order to submit their application, they must hit its "submit" button.

Solution 11: When you're ready to submit your online application, hit its "submit" button. After you do so, the system should almost immediately e-mail you or post a confirmation of your submission on a password-protected website. If the system does not provide such confirmation, you probably haven't applied to your target job.

Problem 12: Believe it or not, confirmation that your application has been electronically sent does not guarantee that your target agency has received it. After you hit your application's "submit" button, your application can mysteriously disappear into the electronic ether before reaching the hiring agency, even if you have received an e-mail confirming its delivery. I know a number of applicants who missed out on federal jobs because they only learned after their target job's closing date that their application had never reached the hiring agency—even though they had received e-mails confirming their submissions.

Solution 12: After you submit your online (or paper) application, call the hiring agency to confirm its delivery. Also keep a copy of the application system's electronic confirmation of your submission as well as confirmation of any faxes you sent to your hiring agency so that you will be able to prove that you made the deadline, if necessary.

> **HOT TIP**
> **Oh, That Sinking Feeling!**
>
> What should you do if you realize that your online application contains a mistake or should be revised in some way after you've already hit the "submit" button? In most systems, your latest online application will override your previous one as long as the job is still open. So just re-enter your application, and then correct and resubmit it. Alternatively, if you discover the problem after your target job has closed, call the agency contact person for your target job to ask how or whether your problem can be fixed.

Checking Your Application Status

Problem: Although some agencies update applicants on the status of their applications via e-mail or updates on a password-protected website, others do not. What's more, online status updates may contain mistakes or outdated information.

Solution: If more than 45 days have elapsed since your target job closed, find the contact info for the agency contact person for your target job, call that person, and ask whether the job has been filled and/or when the agency expects to make a decision.

Retrieving Online Applications

"He isn't feeling well today and won't be able to make it to his keyboard."

Problem 13: Many applicants create more than one account on the same online application system, but then only remember creating one account. Therefore they lose résumés and other information stored on forgotten accounts.

Solution 13: Limit yourself to just one account on each online application system, and record your password information in an easily accessible place.

Problem 14: When each job closes, its vacancy announcement is removed from USAJOBS and the hiring agency's website. Nevertheless, after your target job closes, you may need its vacancy announcement to, for example, find the phone number of its agency contact person or to review its job description as part of your interview preparation.

Solution 14: Print out and keep a copy of the vacancy announcement of any job you apply for.

Problem 15: You may want to access one of your previously submitted online applications in order to: (1) prepare for an interview or (2) recycle passages of it into applications for similar jobs. But online application systems do not provide reliable data storage. What's more, in recent years, tens of thousands of stored online applications have been accidentally lost.

Solution 15: Save printed and electronic versions of all of your applications.

CHAPTER **9**

Crafting Irresistible Résumés

"I'll read a concise, neat, deftly formatted résumé immediately. Long, difficult-to-read clunkers or résumés that have mistakes immediately get buried in the bottom of the résumé pile— perhaps never to be exhumed again."

—A FEDERAL HIRING MANAGER

ON THE CD...

This book's CD features templates for online and hard-copy résumés that you can quickly customize to your own background.

"*I see you've flown around the world in a plane, and settled revolutions in Spain. Around a golf course you're under par. Metro-Goldwyn has asked you to star. Very impressive, I must admit, but we're looking for someone with marketing experience.*"

When I recently asked a hiring manager how long he spends reading the typical résumé, he answered: "20 seconds at most." I chuckled in response. So he emphasized, "*No really*; I'm busy and impatient, so that is all the time I can give. Plus, I can tell almost instantly whether or not a person has what I am looking for."

My interviews with dozens and dozens of hiring managers about their job-screening techniques indicate that, believe it or not, the pace of "the 20-second hiring manager" is, if anything, leisurely. This means that, to be effective, your résumé—your personal marketing document—must serve as a verbal two-by-four that instantly knocks out hiring mangers.

To score an instant knock-out, your résumé must be: (1) formatted to be eye-catching, skimmable, and error-free; and (2) phrased to immediately peg you as the zero-risk applicant who would solve the hiring agency's problems, not create them. Your résumé should meet these two requirements whether it is a hard-copy or online document, and whether it is targeting a specific opening or submitted as part of your networking campaign.

This chapter, along with the CD accompanying this book, provides guidance and templates to help you craft résumés that meet these requirements AND meet the special information required of federal résumés.

The Test of Time

Compare the two résumés on the following pages (Figures 9-1 and 9-2) . . . Which one would pass the 20-second test?

Sam Eastman

1234 Yellow Brick Road
Any Town, Any City 12345

Objective
To achieve my personal and professional goals by working on a management team where my education and experience in the graphic arts can be best utilized. Specifically, I can contribute in the areas of planning and achieving short and long range goals, team building, staff planning and development process improvement and profitability. My education, dedication, focus and diverse business experience provide the foundation for achieving these goals.

Education
M.A.S. Business - 1985
Johns Hopkins University, Baltimore, MD
B.S., A.S. Printing Management & Technology - 1975

Rochester Institute of
Technology, Rochester, NY
A.A.S. Liberal Arts - 1973
Mitchell College, New London, CT

Experience
1999-Present
Desktop Operator-Jones Integrated Graphics, Silver Spring, MD
I joined Wallace while in the process of ceasing operations at the pre-press business I owned and operated until Dec. 1999. I provide Macintosh, PC and Scitex-based electronic pre-press services including scanning preflight file preparation, RIPing, trapping, imposition, film output and digital proofing. Additional duties include conventional proofing and platemaking. I have continued to build my knowledge of electronic pre-press, network and digital asset management, which I feel are the key areas for me to stay abreast of in order to return to a formal management position.

1995-1999
Founder/Owner-Incredible Designs, Inc., Jessup, MD
Founded a pre-press service bureau based on my cumulative experience and education in the Baltimore/Washington graphic arts market. The business was targeted at providing more sophisticated Scitex-based pre-press services to the smaller design, publishing and printing buyers in the market, which was being contested by newly formed conglomerates and low-end service bureaus. Built the sales up to $250,000 with only several part-time employees and myself. I was responsible for all business operations.

1993-1995
Vice President Sales-Eagle Color, Forestville, MD
I joined the firm to try to revitalize falling sales, and have the opportunity to purchase an interest in the firm, which was privately owned. Developed and serviced new accounts, provided strategic planning and equipment upgrading plans. The owner's unexpected death forced the closing of operations and the return of leased equipment. My efforts to purchase the name and assets of the firm broke off when a closer inspection of the firm's financial and contract labor (union) obligations made it more logical to start with new equipment at a different location.

1980-1993
Vice President/Director-Harry W. King Co., Baltimore, MD
Originally joined the firm as a CSR/Planner. Promoted to Production Manager in four years; a shareholder and Vice-President of Production Operations in another two years, and elected to the Board of Directors in 1990. I reported directly to the President and the Board of Directors. Responsible for all printing operations including estimating, customer service, production planning, inventory control and contract labor relations.

Personal
Married 25 years, three children age 8, 17 and 20. My spouse owns and operates a successful music studio in Columbia, MD. My primary interests include motor sports and outdoor activities, although much of my spare time is devoted to assisting in the operation of the music studio and supporting our children's activities.

Figure 9-1. Can you identify Sam Eastman's profession in 5 seconds? If not, hiring managers won't be able to do so either. And a résumé that doesn't serve up even that basic information instantly will not pass the 20-second test, and is destined for the circular file.

The most important principle of formatting is that **what stands out on the page is what stands out in the reader's mind**. But because nothing—not even Sam Eastman's job titles—is formatted to stand out, nothing stands out to the reader. Notice, for example, that Eastman's job titles are no more prominent than his ZIP code! Moreover, Eastman's job summaries are lackluster because they are wordy and not achievement-oriented. What's more, this résumé, which is based upon a real-life résumé that was submitted for a public affairs job, provides no qualifications that fit the target job. No wonder the federal government rejected this résumé's real-life counterpart.

JOE TINMAN
Expert in Federal Contract Management

1111 Yellow Brick Road ◆ Anywhere, Kansas 01234
Work: (111) 123-4567 ◆ Home: (111) 234-1234 ◆ E-Mail:JT@E-mail.com

Social Security Number: 012-34-5678   U.S. Citizen

OBJECTIVE

SENIOR CONTRACT SPECIALIST   Position Number: 123456

SUMMARY OF QUALIFICATIONS

• Ten years of experience managing all phases of multimillion dollar contracts.

• Warrant: Award contracts worth up to $10 million without additional approvals.

• First-Rate Reputation: Consistently earn very positive annual evaluations.

• B.A. in Economics from Georgetown University.

FEDERAL EXPERIENCE

US MINT
801 9th Street; Washington DC 20220

CONTRACT SPECIALIST (1102 Series)   April 2004 to Present
Office of the Chief Financial Officer
Supervisor: John Doe (You may contact at 202-234-4467)
Salary: $107,770 (GS-14/Step 3): 40 hours per week

Management Achievements:

• Currently manage 15 contracts for IT services worth a total of $100 million.

• Designed the Mint's first multi-million dollar performance-based contract for IT services. My techniques have served as a model for all performance-based contracts that followed.

• Supervise all work of five contract managers.

Figure 9-2. Can you identify Joe Tinman's profession from the first page of his résumé within 5 seconds? It is easy because this résumé heeds the principle that *"what stands out on the page is what stands out in the reader's mind."* It emphasizes important information and is uncluttered even though it includes extra info required for federal résumés. Its other virtues include its Summary of Qualifications and concise, achievement-oriented bullets. A template for this résumé, which I have provided to countless numbers of successful job seekers, is featured on this book's CD and website.

Requirements for Federal Résumés

Federal agencies require résumés to include some persnickety details that are not required by other employers. Wonder if you *really* have to include all of these details in your résumé? The truth is that many federal hiring managers wouldn't ding you for submitting a standard, nongovernment résumé instead of a federal résumé.

But, on the other hand, some federal hiring managers automatically reject all applications that omit required information. And because you can't predict whether your résumé will be judged by a tolerant or a nit-picking hiring manager, the safest strategy is to meet all federal requirements. (But keep in mind that most Capitol Hill offices prefer regular nonfederal résumés.)

Listed here are the types of information required by federal agencies:

Information About the Opening

➤ Announcement number, title, and grade

Your Personal Information

➤ Name, address, and day and evening phone numbers

➤ Country of citizenship

➤ Social Security number

➤ Veterans' preference, if you have it

➤ Reinstatement eligibility, if you are using it

➤ Highest federal civilian grade held, including job series

Education

➤ Names of each college or university you currently or previously attended.

➤ Address of each college or university

➤ Degree and date; if no degree, state total number of credits and expected date of completion.

➤ Name of high school

  ➤ Address of high school

  ➤ Date of diploma or GED

Work Experience

For each paying or volunteer job you worked during the last 10 years and for relevant earlier jobs, state the following:

➢ Job title

➢ Employer's name and address

➢ Supervisor's name and phone number: say whether current supervisor may be contacted

➢ Starting and ending dates (month and year)

➢ Number of hours worked per week

➢ Salary

➢ Accomplishments

Other Qualifications

➢ Current job-related certificates and licenses

➢ Job-related training courses, including the title and year

➢ Job-related skills, including languages, computer software/hardware, and special equipment

➢ Honors, awards, and special accomplishments, including publications, public speaking credentials, performance awards (including dates), leadership activities, and memberships in professional or honor societies

Your Caché of Resumés

Depending on your job-search strategy and your target organizations' requirements, you may create some or all of the following types of résumés during your job-search:

➢ Federal résumés for various online application systems.

➢ Hard-copy federal résumés for agencies that still accept paper applications.

➢ A nonfederal hard-copy résumé that omits the extra federal information. You will need this type of résumé to: (1) submit your résumé to networking contacts, either by hand delivery, snail mail, or e-mail; and (2) bring your résumé with you to interviews.

Options for Creating Résumés

Here are options for designing eye-catching, reader-friendly formats for online and hard-copy résumés:

➤ Create résumés for online application systems using the formatting and editing tips provided in Chapter 8.

➤ Customize to your own background the hard-copy federal and nonfederal résumé templates that are contained in this book's CD.

➤ Create résumés using résumé templates and the résumé wizard that comes with Microsoft Word. These tools would be particularly helpful for creating nonfederal hard-copy résumés. To find them, open a Word file. Then:

➢ Click *New* under *File*.

➢ Under the Templates window, click *On my computer*.

➢ Click the *Other Documents* Tab.

➤ To access more résumé templates from Microsoft's website, open a Word file, and then:

➢ Click *New* under *File*.

➢ Under the Templates window, click *Templates on Office Online*

➢ When you arrive at the site, click *Résumés and CVs* under *Browse by Category*.

➤ Design your own format for federal or nonfederal résumés. See the formatting tips provided in Appendix 3.

Formatting

Your résumé should stand out—but not for the wrong reasons. A résumé that is longer than Princess Diana's wedding train, has tiny margins, is hand-written in Victorian calligraphy, printed on paper that is colored brightly enough to cause snow-blindness, and packaged in a big honkin' binder will generate attention without drawing an invitation for an interview.

What will impress hiring managers is an inviting, neat, organized document that has: (1) wide margins; (2) clean, conservative, good-sized fonts; (3) prominently formatted headings, job titles, and employer names; and (4) bullets that send a hiring manager's eyes flying down the page. You will also impress hiring managers by:

> **HOT TIP**
> Run "Google" searches on terms like *sample résumés* and *example résumés* together with your job title to see résumés that will help you craft your résumé. Also, see Chapter 7 for tips on describing your achievements in impressive terms.

➤ Heeding the most important formatting principle: *What stands out on the page is what will stand out in the reader's mind.* To make important information stand out on the page, use capital letters, various font sizes, various font types, indents, and bolding. Check, for example, that your job title stands out more than your zip code.

➤ Following instructions for formatting online résumés (including creating online bullets) that are provided in Chapter 8, and instructions for formatting hard-copy résumés (including creating bullets) that are provided in Appendix 3.

➤ Expressing subordination through formatting. That is, headings should be bolded and positioned to stand out, and information that follows headings should be formatted to reflect its subordinate status.

➤ Using white space to break up text and enhance its readability.

➤ Creating a balanced layout that sensibly distributes information throughout the page. Remember that your résumé, and particularly the first page of your résumé, represents valuable acreage. Don't short sell yourself by wasting this prized real estate on empty space or unimportant information.

➤ Formatting your résumé consistently. This means that once you pick a format, stick to it throughout your résumé. For example, margin size, alignments, justifications, the size of the gap between each bullet and accompanying text, and the amount of space following headings and lines should be identical throughout the document. In addition, headings of comparable weight should be formatted identically.

➤ Printing out your résumé, repeatedly proofreading its content, and eyeballing its format for eye-appeal and consistency. Also, subject your résumés to the editing techniques recommended in Chapter 10 for application essays. When you're satisfied with your résumé's content and format, check it again, and then show it to an objective advisor.

Target Practice

No matter which résumé format you use, target your résumé (as well as the rest of your application) to the skills sought by your hiring agency by:

➤ Phrasing your job summaries to reflect the demands of the opening; use keywords from your target job's vacancy announcement when possible. Also, use Chapter 7 and the Application and Interview Cheat Sheets' in this book's CD to identify your best, most relevant selling points.

➤ Using the principles of primacy and "recency" to emphasize your best credentials. In other words, position your most important credentials as early in each section of your résumé as possible and format them to leap off the page when possible.

➤ Tailoring your objective to match the opening.

➤ Using a summary of qualifications to hit hiring managers with your best shot up top. (But unfortunately, some online systems do not provide space for this feature.)

➤ Eliminating irrelevant information.

Résumé Components

Provided below are some additional tips on crafting each section of your résumé. Many of the tips discussed below are incorporated into the résumés in this book's CD.

The Header

➤ Create a header that has a balanced design and does not create holes in the center of the page. Your header should include your name, address, phone numbers, and e-mail address.

➤ Emphasize your name by formatting it in large, bold letters. (You're the star of your show, so highlight your name as if it were posted on a movie marquee.) If you have advanced degrees or certifications, position the abbreviations for them after your name.

➤ Quickly tell hiring managers what you do by positioning a title right after your name on the top of the page. If your current job title is not flattering, or if you're currently unemployed, use the phrase "Expert in . . ." or "Specialize in . . ." instead of a title. Alternatively, if you have won prestigious awards, give yourself the title of Award-Winning . . ."

➤ See Appendix 3 for guidance on how to insert a horizontal black line below your header and insert special characters into your contact info.

Objective

An "Objective" is not required in federal résumés. However, you may include an objective in your federal résumés, unless your formatting is constrained by an online application system that does not accommodate this feature. To be effective, your objective—like all other résumé features—should brandish what you *offer* rather than what you *want* from your target job. This principle is violated by many résumé objectives, which itemize everything that the applicant would need from a job to reach a state of professional Nirvana. (Such objectives might as well be relabeled as "the gimme section.")

Other objectives pile on meaningless info. For example, the objective on page 99 describes Eastman's desire to achieve his personal goals. Whaaat?!?!? (Is Eastman looking for a job or a date?) And when Eastman's objective finally does get around (at last!) to identifying what he offers, he cites—ironically after promising to get specific—everything but the kitchen sink. Sorry pal, the credibility meter just hit zero.

By contrast, Tinman's objective on page 100 cites his target job. Wow—What a concept! Tinman's objective is specific, succinct, informative, AND has the added advantage of being true!

Another way to craft an objective is to concisely define how you would add value to the agency. Some examples:

➤ An administrative position using my 6 years of experience organizing meetings and arranging travel for senior executives.

➤ A position on an IT Help Desk where my knowledge of large networks and trouble-shooting expertise will improve network efficiency.

Summary of Qualifications

Federal résumés are not required to include a "Summary of Qualifications." But if you're an experienced professional, consider positioning several quick-read summary bullets near the beginning of your résumé (as does Joe Tinman's résumé on page 100) to:

➤ Broadcast your best-selling points to hiring managers who will only skim your résumé or neglect to read the entire document. These selling points may, for example, include your degrees, security clearances, licenses, and certifications—particularly a certification by the Qualifications Review Board for the senior executive service.

➤ Summarize your most relevant credentials. For example, if you were applying for a job requiring communication skills, you could emphasize your communication skills by including a bullet about your communication skills in your summary of qualifications. For example:

  ➤ Polished Communicator: Experienced in delivering presentations to executives and representing my organization at industry meetings.

➤ Emphasize older, but relevant and important, qualifications from earlier jobs that would probably otherwise be overlooked because of their positioning deep in the document.

Work Experience

➤ Position your "Work Experience" section before your "Education" section—unless you're currently a student or a recent grad, or your degree(s) relate more to your target job than does your work experience.

➤ What you offer today is more important than what you offered yesteryear. So sequence your jobs in reverse chronological order (most recent to earliest job), and devote more space to recent than to earlier jobs, unless your earlier jobs are more relevant to your target job. (Because federal agencies don't accept functional résumés, they are not an option for applicants for agency jobs.)

➤ Either omit information about jobs that ended more than 10 or 15 years ago or list them under an "Early Experience" or "Other Experience" heading unless they are directly relevant to your target job. Include only very brief descriptions of early irrelevant jobs, or list only the titles of such jobs without providing any descriptions of them at all.

➤ If you have worked more than one job for the same employer, identify the name of that employer only once—by citing it as a bolded heading in the center of the page. Then list each title underneath that employer's heading; position these titles flush with the left margin, bold them, and cite the starting and ending date of each job and other required information. Under each job title, cite your achievements in a bulleted list. By doing so, you will avoid wasting space by repeatedly citing your employer, and you will emphasize your ascent up the career ladder.

➤ Present each job summary on your résumé as a list of snappy bullets.

➤ Don't waste space by starting bullets with the pronoun "I"; hiring managers already know that *your* résumé describes your work without your telling them so. And puh-lease omit job description-like phrases such as *I was responsible for* . . . or *My duties* included . . . Why? Because such phrases invariably introduce long laundry lists of responsibilities and day-to-day activities that could apply to hundreds of other employees. Instead, use each bullet to convey your achievements and home run triumphs.

➤ Begin each bullet with a different action verb. (To find lists of action verbs, "google" *action verbs for résumés*.) And put each verb following a bullet in the first person. Note that the first person is the verb form that would accompany the pronoun "I" if "I" were present. You can test for the first person by silently inserting the pronoun "I" in front of each verb (Table 9-1).

TABLE 9-1 Action Verbs	
Wrong Verb Form for Bullet	**Correct Verb Form for Bullet**
manages website.	Manage website.
tracks correspondence.	Track correspondence.

➤ The order in which your résumé presents information is almost as important as the information itself. Why? Because hiring managers are most likely to read and re-member what they read first. So sequence bullets for each job summary according to their relevance to your target job—not according to how much time you spent on the activities they describe; your most relevant bullets should precede your less relevant bullets, even if you spent little time on them. For example, suppose you currently spend 20 percent of your time on project management and 80 percent of your time running trainings, and you're applying for a project management job. Then your project management bullets should precede your training bullets.

➤ Break up long lists of job summary bullets into categories, such as "Management Achievements," "Communication Achievements," and "Strategic Planning Achievements." Some of the résumés included in this book's CD use this method.

➤ Write for laymen who are unfamiliar with your field and current organization, and the projects, computer systems, databases, regulations, and programs you manage. Eliminate acronyms and eliminate or explain technical terms. (See the explana-tion on how to communicate clearly in Chapter 10.)

➤ Briefly explain any significant gaps between employment dates, such as: *returned to school* or *became care-taker for seriously ill family member.*

➤ Briefly describe the mission of any obscure employers you name.

Education

➤ List academic credentials in reverse chronological order.

➤ If you're currently a student, indicate degree, university, and expected graduation date.

➤ If you're working towards a degree while working a job, say so. For example:

> ➢ Concurrent with full-time employment: working toward JD, Howard University Law School, Washington, DC (Degree expected in 2009).

➤ If you're a student or a recent grad, include your grade point average if it is B-plus or better.

Other Headings

Include in your résumé a heading titled "Leadership Experience," if possible. Why? Because every employer values leadership experience. Even if you never led the cavalry into battle, organized a mutiny against a Captain Bligh-like rogue, or negotiated a billion-dollar deal on Wall Street, you probably still have sought-after leadership credentials. These credentials may, for sample, include experience orienting freshman at your college, serving in student government, tutoring, or organizing campus events. So scour your record for your experience supervising, orienting, advising, coaching, organizing, training, negotiating, and mentoring—and then brandish it in your leadership section.

Other potential headings include the following:

> ➤ Awards and Honors
>
> ➤ Licenses and Certificates
>
> ➤ Public Speaking
>
> ➤ Consulting Experience
>
> ➤ Publications
>
> ➤ Systems and Software
>
> ➤ Training Courses
>
> ➤ Professional Associations
>
> ➤ Foreign Languages
>
> ➤ Military Experience
>
> ➤ Volunteer Experience
>
> ➤ Community Service

Excluded Information

Your résumé should not mention anything about your marital status, children, religion, or irrelevant hobbies because such information should not influence hiring decisions, and may compel hiring managers to (illegally) discriminate against you. Also don't waste space by stating that your references are available upon request; that is assumed.

Résumé Length

I recently heard a résumé expert being interviewed on a radio show. During the interview, the résumé expert was asked about résumé lengths. In response, the expert listed expected résumé lengths for various types of professionals. Four pages for this type of professional . . . five pages for that type of professional . . . and so on.

Less Is More

To me, that kind of advice is just crazy talk! It makes no sense! The real deal is that all federal and nonfederal hiring managers are very busy; they have neither the time nor desire to hack through dense biographies. In fact, they want to read long-winded tomes about as much as you want to do a line-by-line reading of the phone book right now. So no matter where you are in your career or what your target job is, the correct length of your résumé is the minimum length you need to prove that you're qualified for your target job.

So rather than aiming for a specific résumé length, aim to: (1) Format your best credentials prominently and position them as close to the top of the document as possible; (2) keep your résumé as short as possible; and (3) ruthlessly edit redundancies, dated information, and credentials that don't relate to your target job.

When you evaluate whether to include a certain credential, ask yourself: (1) if that info could realistically help you get the job; and (2) if you were reviewing this résumé as a hiring manager, would that credential really matter to you? If not, purge it.

Break the One-Page Rule

But don't eliminate important information or create a cluttered résumé in order to cater to the "one-page" myth. It's much wiser to create an attractively formatted multiple-page résumé with good-sized headings and copious white space than to jam your relevant experience onto a cramped one-pager that will alienate hiring managers; the one-page rule simply does not apply to anyone who has been working for any significant amount of time.

WILL YOU PASS THE 20-SECOND TEST?

Show your résumé to a trusted advisor for 20 seconds, and then ask them to describe your best credentials. If they can't do so, keep working on your résumé.

The one-page rule is particularly irrelevant to applicants to federal agencies. How come? Because the extra informational requirements of federal agencies inevitably add length to résumés. Moreover, hiring managers always cross-check answers to short-answer questions and essays questions against résumés, and penalize applicants for discrepancies. So craft your résumé to validate all achievements described in the body of your application, even if doing so extends your résumé.

HOT TIP
Whenever e-mailing your résumé, send it as a PDF attachment. That way, its formatting won't be fouled up during its electronic journey. You can quickly convert any document into a PDF at http://pdfonline.com/convert_pdf.asp.

Quality Controls

Don't send off your résumé impulsively. Instead, let it go cold then look at it again through the eyes of a stranger; ask yourself what you would think of the person described in the résumé. Would you understand whom they work for and what they do, and be impressed by their accomplishments if you had no prior knowledge about them? When you hold up the description of your target job together with your résumé, is the fit obvious? Is your résumé clear and straightforward? Does it include all of your relevant accomplishments?

Also, check that your previous jobs are described in the past tense. Confirm that each bullet conveys a unique, distinct accomplishment without covering overlapping info. Proofread for typos.

Once your résumé passes muster, show it to your trusted advisors and encourage them to be critical. Why? **Because the only way to *really* find out how your résumé comes across to other people is to ask other people how it comes across.**

Whatever problems your advisors find with your résumé will also be found by hiring managers, who are, after all, ordinary people, not organically different from anyone else. It is much smarter to face constructive criticism that can help you find and fix résumé flaws than to save your feelings now but let your résumé flaws eventually silently sink your prospects.

Perseverance Success Story!

I Got the Job!

By Andrew McDonald, Engineer

After working at the same federal agency for 7 years as a mechanical engineer, I decided that it was time to move on and find other challenges. I started looking for a new job. Now, I am working for another federal agency, learning new things and earning a significantly higher salary.

I landed my promotion strictly through my own efforts; I had no contacts helping me. I did it by:

1. **Searching USAJOBS** at least once a week: I was diligent about regularly searching USAJOBS, because each job listed on the site has its own rolling window of opportunity. If I had not regularly checked the site, I might have missed out on applying for some great jobs.

   If I am going to submit a package, I want it to reflect my best effort. So I spent about 1 week on each opening that really interested me. I never used the shotgun approach because I believe that it only produces more rejections. Who needs that?

2. **Using keywords:** I incorporated keywords from job descriptions in vacancy announcements into my résumé and KSAs. For example, because the responsibilities for the job description for my current job included "blueprint reading" as an important responsibility, I included it in my résumé and KSAs. Although I ordinarily wouldn't have mentioned such an obvious duty, I knew that doing so might improve my chances. Anything for a higher score! Also, I noticed that some vacancy announcements even list keywords that are desirable in applications. If you find such keywords listed in a vacancy announcement for a job that is similar to your target job, mention them throughout your application.

3. **Researching the agency:** I read through the website of each agency that I applied to. Based upon this research, I was able to specify in my cover letter how I would be able to contribute to the agency's goals.

4. **Telling success stories:** My KSAs included examples of my projects that showed that I was qualified for the target job. I found it useful to put these stories into the format suggested in this book; for each story, I described necessary background information, my actions, evidence of results, and objective validation of my success. (See worksheet for effective storytelling in Chapter 10.)

5. **Designing graphically pleasing layouts:** When I was on a selection panel for hiring another engineer, I learned what torture it is for hiring managers to trudge through the long, densely worded paragraphs. The experience made me appreciate easy-to-read, graphically pleasing layouts. So my goal was to design application documents that presented my credentials to hiring managers in an easy and efficient manner. I did this by:

   ➤ "Bulletizing" my résumés and KSAs as much as possible.

   ➤ Repeatedly examining the hard-copy versions of my documents. Because the layout on a computer screen is subtly different from that of a hard copy, you have a greater chance of missing typos and column misalignments on the computer.

   ➤ Checking that headings stood out, information was distributed on the page in a balanced way, font sizes were easy to read, and that I had used enough white space to break up the text without wasting space. I made sure that my layout was consistent (fonts, margins, etc.) throughout all of my documents.

   ➤ Using as few words as possible in order to make the best use of the precious seconds that the hiring manger spent on my application.

6. **Working on my résumé and KSAs only 15 minutes per day:** I found it much easier to attack these very difficult-to-write documents a little bit a time, and not to even try to finish them in a single session. This multisession approach enabled me to improve my application by repeatedly reviewing and editing my answers.

   When KSA ideas occurred to me when I was doing other things, I quickly jotted them down and then incorporated them during my next writing session. Because of such improvements, my answers were more thoughtful than they would have been if I whipped out my application in a single sitting.

7. **Recruiting a colleague to provide feedback:** I recruited a colleague to provide me with objective feedback on my résumé, KSAs, and cover letters. This person helped me simplify passages that were too technical for nonengineers, edit unnecessary information, and add background information where needed. Seeking and using my colleague's feedback took extra time. But this time was well spent because, from my experience serving on a selection panel, I know that the quality of applicants' KSAs determines who gets the job.

8. **Preparing for the interview for my current job:** I reviewed Internet sites that provided "how-to" advice on interviewing and listed standard interview questions. Sure enough, many of those standard interview questions did pop up in my interview. But because I was prepared to answer these questions, I handled them with more confidence and speed and with less fumbling than I otherwise would have.

For example, when my interviewer asked me to discuss an on-the-job mistake that I had made, I could—because of my preparation—quickly cite a nonserious scheduling snag that had developed on one of the construction projects I was managing. I was careful not to say that I had messed up the project irreversibly. Instead, I emphasized how I quickly resolved the scheduling problem, reworked the schedule to prevent delays in the completion of the project, and learned from the experience how to avoid similar snags in the future.

During the interview, I also mentioned some specific information about the hiring agency's recent construction projects that I had read about on its website. I thereby showed my interviewers that I gone to the trouble to research its activities.

Shortly after the interview for my current job, I was offered and accepted the job. My new agency operates under a pay scale called pay banding, which gives managers more flexibility in setting salaries than does the General Schedule system under which my previous job operated. Because of this difference and because my current boss was impressed with my qualifications, my new agency significantly beat my old salary. I didn't even have to negotiate for a promotion. Moreover, as I had hoped, I am now managing very different types of projects than I had managed at my previous job, and I am broadening my experience.

During my job search, which lasted over a year, I was rejected for a number of jobs. With some applications, I did not even get a response. But I didn't let the disappointments stop me. I expected this and persevered. **I also found it helpful to keep reminding myself that if you put in the extra effort to create a concise, eye-catching, and verbally pleasing application, I would eventually be rewarded because, as writer Silvana Clark said, "There is so little traffic on the extra mile."**

Résumé Padders Need Not Apply

If you lie on your application or in an interview for a federal job, you will likely end up having some 'splainin' to do, as Ricky Ricardo would say.

How the Mighty Have Fallen

Consider the cautionary tale of Laura Callahan.* In April 2003, she landed a coveted position as the Deputy Chief Information Officer in the Department of Homeland Security. But when Callahan—who often used the title Dr.—was screened for a top secret security clearance, investigators discovered in May 2003 that the BA, Master's degree, and PhD in computers listed on her résumé were from a diploma mill that was located in a refurbished motel. Ouch!

Callahan's troubles only snowballed when—in the wake of the brouhaha over the bogus degrees—many of her colleagues unleashed a torrent of allegations against her for other whopping ethical and managerial blunders made during her previous high-level stints at the White House and Department of Labor. After being suspended from her federal job, Callahan resigned in March 2004.

"Oops! The padding just fell out of your résumé."

Sour Toppings

Although Callahan was evidently not qualified for her job, many professionals who do have enviable qualifications top them off with false degrees or phony experience. Too bad. The principle ignored by such embellishers is that, even ethics aside, it is usually more effective to trumpet genuine achievements through the methods discussed in this book than to trump-up false achievements. In other words, spend your energy finessing descriptions of your finest qualifications rather than creating phony toppings that can end up biting you back.

*See Wikipedia's article on Laura Callahan and the article's references.

What This Means for You

Federal job applications that include false or inflated credentials are more likely than ever to be discovered. Why? Because after the Callahan scandal, many human resource staffers were trained how to spot fabrications. Applicants who are busted for lying may be barred from reapplying to the federal government. And applicants who do manage to get hired under false claims may be fired, fined, or even jailed.

Which does not mean that you must spotlight your weaknesses under klieg lights. But it does mean that you shouldn't invent degrees, titles, or experience that you simply don't have, or cover gaps in your résumé with whole cloth. Here's a litmus test: If you can't imagine a credential holding up under a background check, don't use it.

CHAPTER **10**

Writing Killer Application Essays (KSAs and ECQs)

"Good writing is clear thinking made visible."
—BILL WHEELER, WRITER

"It's plotted out. I just have to write it."

Most job seekers would rather eat ground glass than write application essays. So many of them procrastinate with their essay writing for days or weeks. Indeed, it is not uncommon for job applicants to live with their application essays hanging over their heads until they either come perilously close to nervous breakdowns or to missing application deadlines—whichever comes first.

When typical job applicants do finally work on their application essays, they are invariably overwhelmed by self-doubt . . . page fright. Most of them have no clear idea what to say in their essays, or how to say it. (Application essays are frequently called KSAs, short for knowledge, skills, and abilities or ECQs, short for executive core qualifications.)

The critical importance of essays and the vagueness of most essay questions compound the pressure. With every sentence that job applicants slowly, painstakingly squeeze out of their brains, they wonder, "Is this wrong? . . . or right? . . . Is there a better way to do this?"

Worse still, typical job applicants taunt themselves by imagining the competition effortlessly churning out perfect essays (whatever "perfect" is), landing jobs that should rightfully be theirs, and stealing their futures. Mired in uncertainty, these unfortunates typically discard draft after draft, only to start over again, each time more stumped and insecure than the previous time. One step forward . . . two steps backward.

Although essay writing does demand some time and thought, it does not have to be sooooo painful. In fact, most of the agony of essay writing is rooted in the uncertainty of the assignment. After all, federal agencies generally do not disclose what constitutes winning essays, distribute model essays, or warn of common essay blunders.

No wonder most essay writers feel like they do not know what they are doing—no one has given them a clue about what they should do.

But by providing you with guidance, examples, and templates, this chapter, along with this book's CD, will free you from the "flailing around in the dark" feeling, and help you bypass the bewilderment that typically bogs down KSA and ECQ writers. It gives you everything you need to quickly churn out eye-catching application essays that will make a fast, easy, and impressive read for hiring managers.

Why Essays Are Required

Why do hiring agencies put applicants through KSA or ECQ hell? Why don't they just base their hiring decisions on résumés and cover letters, like other employers do? Hiring agencies require KSAs or ECQs in addition to résumés because:

Time and time again, hiring managers have described my clients' application essays as the best they have ever seen. By using this chapter's essay writing techniques, you will similarly impress hiring managers.

> ➤ Résumés usually list credentials in chronological order. To evaluate them, hiring managers must tediously comb through them to tease out relevant credentials. By contrast, essays force applicants to consolidate their own relevant credentials themselves. Voila! No teasing out or combing required for hiring manages. Therefore, essays shift the burden of work from hiring managers to applicants.

> ➤ KSAs and ECQs contain more detail than résumés.

> ➤ KSAs and ECQs provide a screening device. Applicants who do not answer essay questions usually automatically weed themselves out of competitions.

What's in a Name?

Application essays go by many names: KSAs, ECQs, Technical Factors, and many others. Some online applications do not even give a name to essay questions; they merely list a series of essay questions with windows for answering them.

But no matter what an essay question is called, and no matter what level or type of applicant it addresses, the principles for crafting eye-catching, clear, and impressive essays are the same.

What to Say

Remember that the purpose of your essay is to prove that you are qualified for your target job. Therefore, your essays should serve up your best evidence that you're qualified for the job (i.e., your best academic and professional credentials and success stories that parallel the demands of the job).

Here's how to figure out which credentials to include in each essay included in your target job's application:

➤ Write down each essay question followed by about half a page of blank space.

➤ Review your résumé and other success documents, Chapter 7, and the "KSA-ECQ Prep" section of this book's CD.

➤ List under each essay your academic degrees, research projects, training courses, certifications, work projects, positive feedback, and other achievements that answer each question and parallel the demands of your target job. Don't omit credentials from your essays just because they are featured in your résumé. Taken together, your KSAs or ECQs should fully represent you without your résumé.

➤ Some tips for parceling out your credentials among your essays for maximum impact:

➤ **Hit hiring managers with your best shot up top:** Because readers remember best what they read first, position your best credentials in your first essay, if possible. And even though applications don't ask for a career overview, consider starting your first essay with a career overview that concisely ticks off your most relevant credentials. An example of this type of summary is provided in the document entitled "Sample Career Overview," included in the "KSA-ECQ Prep" section of this book's CD. Similarly, consider ending your final essay with a parting salvo that summarizes your top credentials and reaffirms your enthusiasm for the opening.

➤ **Don't leave a KSA or ECQ blank:** As explained in Chapter 6, essays are rated according to a point system. This point system assigns zero points to a blank essay, but assigns at least some points to a weak answer. Therefore, you will earn more points by providing a weak answer than by providing no answer to a KSA or ECQ. If you don't have any education, work experience, or volunteer experience that fulfills a KSA or an ECQ, do some reading or interview relevant professionals about the topic. Then describe these activities and what you learned from them in your essay.

➤ **Say it differently if you say it again:** Because essay questions are often redundant and overlapping, you may have to repeat some credentials in more than one essay. If you do, emphasize different angles of them each time you cover them, if possible.

HOT TIP
The Secrets to ECQ Success

The secrets to writing successful ECQs for senior executive service (SES) jobs are the same as those for writing successful KSAs. In addition to receiving ECQ guidance from this chapter and the cheat sheets featured on this book's CD, access ECQ advice and sample essays at http://www.opm.gov/ses.

- ➤ **Yesterday counts more than yesteryear:** Emphasize your recent achievements, if possible. Try not to focus on work experience older than 10 or 15 years.

- ➤ **Don't waste your education:** Mention your undergraduate and graduate degrees, certifications, and training courses. (Bear in mind that college and graduate degrees are almost always relevant to essay questions addressing communication skills. After all, it's pretty hard to earn a degree without being able to speak or write.)

- ➤ **SOS on your KSAs:** If you can't decide which credentials to include in your answer for a particular question, imagine being asked that same question in an interview. The same credentials you would recite orally should go in your essay.

- ➤ **Conquer writer's block:** You don't necessarily have to start writing your essays at the beginning. So if you have trouble with the first question, attack the last question or a middle question first, and then work back to the beginning. And if you have trouble crafting the beginning of a particular essay, write the middle first, and then work back to the beginning.

How to Say It

Once you decide which selling points to include your essays, its time to decide how to format and phrase them for maximum impact. Remember: your essays should be crafted to quickly catch and keep the attention of hiring managers who know nothing about you and will only spend a few minutes learning about you.

You can craft your essays to be eye-catching, easily skimmed, easy-to-understand, and error-free by, as explained below, citing specifics and examples, following a clear organization, using effective formatting, communicating clearly, using a human, energetic voice, and applying quality controls to your documents.

HOT TIP
Shortcut to Great Essays

You've heard of self-cleaning ovens, right? Well the cheat sheets and essay outlines provided in the KSA-ECQ Prep section of this book's CD and website are about the closest I can come to giving you self-writing essays.

Cite Specifics and Examples

If your essay relies on platitudes or generalities that could apply to every other professional with your job title, it will bore hiring managers and fade into the pack. But if, on the other hand, it provides concrete, specific examples of your successes, it will give hiring managers a vivid, distinct impression.

One way to provide a persuasive example is to cite a relevant success story—a narrative that describes how you accomplished a specific goal or solved a problem that relates to the opening. For advice on how to tell a compelling success story, see page 139.

Structure Each Essay with a Logical Organization

The facts in each essay should not be slapped haphazardly together in a disjointed manner; rather, they should be sequenced in a logical order or framework. There are almost an infinite number of ways to organize an essay. And you should, of course, base your strategy on the question and your relevant experience.

Here are some options for organizing your essays:

> ➤ Bulletize relevant work achievements under one heading and then bulletize relevant academic credentials under another heading.

> ➤ Cover a single success story in an essay, with components of the story covered under different headings as suggested in Figure 10-1 on page 171.

> ➤ Cover multiple success stories in an essay, with each story distinguished by its own heading.

> ➤ Itemize relevant achievements in a bulleted list—a simple but effective strategy.

> ➤ Use some combination of the techniques covered above.

To see these techniques in action, review the sample stories and essays at the end of this chapter. Notice that the headings in each document broadcast the logic of each document; so you don't even have to read each document from start to finish to understand its logic and essence—you can get their gist just be skimming them. Similarly, your essays should use headings to distinguish each section and support easy skimming. Also, use the sample outlines provided in the KSA/ECQ section of this CD's book.

Test that your essays are organized logically by asking yourself why you sequenced your paragraphs and sentences the way you did. If you can't explain their organization, rethink it. Also, check that your organization is reflected in your headings. In particular, be sure to set off descriptions of your "results" and "feedback" with headings. By doing so, you will emphasize your reputation as a producer and make your successes apparent even to hiring managers who only skim your essays.

Use Effective Formatting

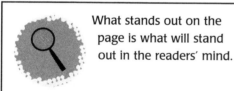

What stands out on the page is what will stand out in the readers' mind.

If you bury your credentials in miles of monotonous, featureless text, you will dig your own grave. But if, by contrast, you use formatting features, such as headings, bullets, and white space, you will grab the attention of hiring managers, send their eyes flying down the page, and quickly and persuasively convey your key selling points.

Don't believe me? Then compare the me-o-centric essay on page 137 with the stories and essays provided on pages 154 to 170. Aren't the well-formatted documents more inviting and easier to skim and read than the me-o-centric essay?

Instructions for formatting online applications is provided in Chapter 8 and a KSA using these online features is provided in the "Sample Online Essay" included in the "KSA and ECQ Prep" section of this book's CD. In addition, instructions for formatting hard-copy documents is provided are Appendix 4.

Communicate Clearly

Your application will probably be judged by nonspecialists who know nothing about your current organization and are strangers to your field. Moreover, even hiring managers who are familiar with your current organization and your field will be unfamiliar with the particular projects, programs, regulations, databases, IT systems, analytical tools, specialized terms, and acronyms that you cite. Unfortunately, hiring managers who don't understand an essay on the first pass are probably not going to take the time to study it until they "get it." Rather, once they hit a confounding "huh?" passage, they will probably skip ahead or onto another application without giving you the credit you deserve for your achievements.

The only way to guarantee that all of your hiring managers will understand all of your achievements is to explain them in straightforward, everyday terms rather than in bureaucratese, legalese, or scientificese.

Many applicants wrongly believe that their essays will sound unprofessional if they exclude jargon. But studies show that even specialized professionals, like lawyers and scientists, are more impressed by easy-to-understand texts than those written in traditional bureaucratese, legalese, and scientificese. Likewise, hiring managers will be more impressed by your essays if they are conveyed in easy-to-understand terms rather than specialized terms.

HOT TIP
Be Pro-Bullet

Whether or not you are pro-gun control, you should be pro-bullet. That is, your application documents should—wherever appropriate—break up paragraphs into bulleted or numbered lists (that are preceded by headings and/or a summary sentence).

Why? Because bulleted and numbered lists promote easy, fast reading and help break up text into manageable chunks—exactly what hiring managers want. As one hiring manager explains, "Many job seekers wrongly believe that bullets are too informal for job applications. But hiring managers prefer applications that fire off credentials with the rat-tat-tat of machine guns unloading their ammunition."

ON THE CD ...

This book's CD features tips, cheat sheets, examples, and sample essay outlines to help you quickly churn out first-rate application essays.

Many applicants also wrongly believe that their work is too technical to be explained in plain language. But publications like *The Wall Street Journal* and *Newsweek* regularly cover specialized topics in business, government, and science in reader-friendly language without sacrificing accuracy. They thereby prove that there is hardly any topic too technical to be explained in laymen's terms.

ALBERT EINSTEIN ON PLAIN LANGUAGE

Most of the fundamental ideas of science are essentially simple and may, as a rule, be expressed in a language comprehensible to everyone.

To help convince you of the power of plain language, Table 10-1 features three hard-to-read excerpts from real life KSAs and their plain language rewrites. Don't you think the plain language rewrites are clearer and more impressive?

T A B L E 10-1 Plain Language Rewrites	
Hard-to-Read Excerpt	**Plain Language Rewrite**
The drop date of the numismatic product was delayed.	The new coin was released late.
In my prior role, several efforts were utilized in finding solutions to track all issues associated with the Mail Order and Catalog System (MACS) maintained by the ERP. PVCS tracker was used to identify System Problem Reports (SPRs) and System Change Requests (SCRs).	As an IT specialist at Amazon.com from 2002 to 2004, I recalibrated systems used to identify errors in the company's marketing database, which is known as the Mail Order and Catalog System (MACS). I thereby significantly boosted the accuracy of MACS.
SG & A is down. I'm a believer in TPM.	As Plant Manager, I solicited employee suggestions for reducing wasted raw materials by 20 percent.

Translate your KSAs or ECQs into plain language by doing the following:

> ➤ **Write in short sentences and short paragraphs.**

> ➤ **Don't ask hiring managers to look for a needle in a haystack.** Instead give them just the needle without the haystack. Do so by eliminating unnecessary information; ask yourself if each credential you cite could realistically help you nail the job. If a credential probably couldn't do so, purge it.
>
> Also scrupulously examine each sentence for unneeded words. One way to eliminate excess words and to inject vigor into your writing is to rebuild sentences that contain a version of the passive verb "to be" around more energetic verbs. The telltale signature of the verb "to be" is the presence of the words: am, is, are, was, be, been, and were. In particular, almost any sentence that contains the phrase "there are" can be restructured around a more energetic verb. Compare the following "before" and "after" versions in Table 10-2.

TABLE 10-2	Energetic and Concise Rewrites
Before: Passive and Wordy	**After: Energetic and Concise**
There are many ways in which the program was successful. WORD COUNT: 9	The program succeeded in many ways. WORD COUNT: 6
I was responsible for editing the Director of the Customer Care Center's outgoing correspondence sent out under her signature. WORD COUNT: 19	I formatted, proofread, and fact-checked about 20 letters from the Director of the Customer Care Center per week. WORD COUNT: 18
Following termination of the contract, there was a marginal incrementation in workload, and, at this moment of time, it would appear that there has been a significant degree of improvement in profit capacity. WORD COUNT: 33	When the contract ended, our office's workload increased, but profits soared. WORD COUNT: 12

The "after" versions of the above examples are clearer and shorter than the "before" versions because they:

➢ Eliminate empty phrases, such as "at this moment in time."

➢ Replace wordy phrases with shorter ones.

➢ Use common words, like "ended," instead of pompous words, like "termination."

➤ **Orient readers:** Remember that hiring managers know nothing about you . . . until you tell them. They may read your KSAs before your résumé or forget your résumé by the time they read your KSAs, so assume no prior knowledge of your readers. As soon as hiring managers start reading your KSAs, they will want to know what your profession is and who your current and previous employers are. So just as you would introduce yourself to business associates when you first meet them in person, introduce yourself to hiring managers when you first meet them on paper by identifying your titles, employers, and dates for jobs described in your essays (Table 10-3).

TABLE 10-3	Orienting Rewrites
Confusing	**Orienting**
In my current position, I . . .	As a contract manager at the Immigration and Naturalization Service since 2006, I . . .
In my previous position, I . . .	In 2006, when I worked as a contract manager at the Bureau of Land Management, I . . .

➢ **Favor specific terms over vague, mealy words:** For example, the wimpy verbs *to help*, *to participate in*, *to join*, and the equally unimpressive *to be involved with* can usually be replaced by terms that precisely define what exactly you accomplished. By providing this specific information, you will portray yourself as a mover and shaker rather than as a hauler and carrier whose greatest contribution amounted to little more than just being there (Table 10-4).

TABLE 10-4	Specific Rewrites
Before: Vague	**After: Specific**
I help my supervisor keep track of ongoing cases.	On my own initiative, I created and now manage a case tracking system that automatically warns of approaching milestones.

To *improve* is another vague verb. Replace it with terms that define exactly what you improved (Table 10-5).

TABLE 10-5	Precise Rewrites
Before: Vague	**After: Specific**
Under my leadership, the Office of Sales and Marketing improved customer service.	Under my leadership, the Office of Sales and Marketing slashed average order delivery times from 8 to 4 days.

Table 10-6 has two more examples of credentials that sound more impressive when they are described in precise terms.

TABLE 10-6	Precise Rewrites
Before: Vague	**After: Specific**
I have briefed Congressional staffers.	During the last 2 years, I briefed the Director of Communications of the House Ways & Means Committee six times about the Security and Exchange Commission's budget requests.
I handled some major contracts.	I successfully directed cradle-to-grave contracts for four multi-year, multi-million dollar contracts for staffing ABC Inc.'s computer help desk.

Try to replace vague terms with precise terms that create verbal pictures that will lodge in the memories of hiring managers. Aren't the precise "after" versions of descriptions of achievements (Table 10-7) more memorable than their vague "before" versions?

T A B L E 10-7 Precise Rewrites	
Before: Vague	**After: Specific**
I produced a catalogue.	I designed the layout and all graphics for a 75-page, full-color catalogue that was packed with photographs of electronics products. The catalogue generated $5 million in revenues in 2 months.
My communication skills have been important to my career.	My ability to convey technical information to general audiences has helped me advance from a GS-5 position to a GS-14 position in 6 years.

Here are several examples of vague sentences from real-life KSAs that created more questions than they answered:

> *The agency is achieving its vision of its mission in the community.* (Huh? Watch out for sentences like this one that are composed of meaningless strings of buzzwords.)

> *My credentials speak for themselves.* (Nothing speaks for itself. If information is only implied or hinted, it is as good as unsaid.)

> *As Deputy of the Foreign Press Bureau in Croatia in the early 1990s, I recruited and supervised a corps of novice press officers under the most demanding circumstances imaginable.* (Oh! What juicy, impressive war stories this applicant would have told if only he had understood that most hiring managers weren't in Croatia during wartime, and so couldn't possibly imagine what conditions there were like.)

> **Eliminate stilted terms:** Don't include terms in your applications that you wouldn't use in ordinary conversation. For example, strike from your applications words like "herein," "in accordance with," and "the aforementioned."

> **Provide background for nonspecialists:** Explain specialized concepts. Also, define or replace technical terms with everyday words, when possible. This is important because if you're like most professionals, you're probably so fluent in your field's jargon that you're desensitized to it; it rolls off your tongue and keyboard naturally, without a thought. So consciously scrutinize your documents for concepts and terms that would stump the uninitiated.

➤ **Purge bureaucratic terms.** For example, don't name forms, regulations, programs, and laws solely by their identifying numbers. Instead, identify them by titles or words that define their functions. For example, see Table 10-8 here.

TABLE 10-8	Plain Language vs. Jargon
Jargon	**Plain Language**
A-76	The competitive sourcing program, a high-priority federal program that will privatize some federal jobs
SF-52s	Personnel documents
ISO 14001	International Standard 14001, which is composed of voluntary standards addressing the environmental performance of manufacturing organizations

➤ **Omit abbreviations and acronyms altogether, when possible.** When you must use them, define them.

➤ **Specify frequency:** For example, if you represent your office at meetings, state whether these meetings are held on a weekly, monthly, or bimonthly basis. Alternatively, if you write reports, state how frequently you produce them.

➤ **Cite numbers correctly:** Use the numerical form of 10 to 999,999. Write out numbers that are in the millions and higher. For example: $2 million. Double check the accuracy of all numbers that you cite. (Wrong numbers serve as quick credibility busters.)

➤ **Replace formulas with short verbal summaries.**

Use a Human, Energetic Voice

Many applicants wrongly believe that to sound professional, their essays must sound stilted and pompous. Rest assured: You will express your big ideas more persuasively and through small, everyday words that convey a human voice than through stuffy , specialized terms. After all, the great speeches of history, such as those by Abraham Lincoln, Franklin Roosevelt, and John Kennedy, were all built on simple words that convey a human voice.

By contrast, documents composed of bureaucratic, inflated language never make it into the history books because they are dull and forgettable. (I have yet to see a list of great books that includes the Code of Federal Regulations.) In other words, if you remove the humanity from your writing, your writing will be inhumanely boring and unmemorable. Although no one expects your KSAs or ECQs to have the resonance of a presidential speech, they will be more memorable if they—like other memorable texts—are built on plain language.

To convey an energetic, human voice:

1. **Open with a bang:** Most essays begin with a boring introductory sentence, such as "Throughout my career, I have written many important documents." Granted, such an opener is not technically wrong, and would not dash your chances of landing the job. But nor would such a bland, yawn-provoking lead sentence likely engage or stick in the craw of a hiring manager who reads dozens of KSAs that all begin with similar sentences.

   Rather than waste your openers on ho-hum sentences, try to open your essays (and stories) with lively leads that will reel in readers with a hard-hitting statistic that defines a problem that you have addressed, a vivid image, a quote, a reference to a high-profile news event that overlaps with your work, or another dramatic device. Here are several examples of stand-out essay openers:

   ➤ *As a customer care operator at the U.S. Postal Service, my switchboards light up like Christmas trees throughout the Christmas season. I keep up with my heavy workload during the busy holiday season by . . .*

   ➤ *As a contract manager at the Federal Reserve since 2002, I design contracts that get the biggest bang for the buck. For example . . .*

   ➤ *After my office's budget was cut by 10 percent, I developed innovative ways to do more with less. For example . . .*

   ➤ *Golda Meir said, "You cannot shake hands with a clenched fist." Prime Minister Meir's philosophy guides each Alternative Dispute Resolution negotiating session that I lead between employees and managers. During these sessions, I . . .*

   ➤ *Coin collectors often describe coins as "time capsules" that preserve history. More than ever, this concept came alive for me when, as a program analyst at the U.S. Mint, I helped organize a Presidential ceremony held on July 26, 2001 honoring the Navajo Code Talkers of World War II who used their native language as an unbreakable military code. My contributions to this event included . . .*

   ➤ *Nothing boosts organizational morale like an active incentives award program. As Human Resources Director of Data Consulting Inc., I innovated low cost ways to reward our most productive staffers. For example . . .*

BROTHERLY ADVICE FROM BILLIONAIRE WARREN BUFFET

Warren Buffet advises, "Write with a specific person in mind. When writing Berkshire Hathaway's annual report, I pretend that I'm talking to my sisters . . . though highly intelligent, they are not experts in accounting or finance. They will understand plain English, but jargon may puzzle them.

"No siblings to write to? Borrow mine: Just begin with 'Dear Doris and Berti.'"

> *If your staff suffers from meeting overload, I have the cure! As a conference planner and facilitator at Meeting Managers Inc. since 2006, I have been running effective, productive, and even fun meetings and conferences that make disorganized, pointless, and endless events a thing of the past. Here's how I do it . . .*

> *On January 1, 2003, as I arrived at my job as a senior attorney at the United Nations, my boss ran up to me and said, "I need you to deliver an opening statement at the war tribunals trial in the Hague by January 30. Can I count on you?" The challenges of this assignment included . . .*

2. **Infuse your essays with life!** Express what you like about your job, what drives you, and/or why it is important. For example:

   > *I earned a B.A. in International Relations because diplomatic strategies have prevented many wars. I hope that by pursuing a career at the State Department, I can help defuse heated international conflicts.*

   > *As a software engineer, I consider nothing more gratifying than digging into a vexing technical problem that has stymied everyone else, and solving it, no matter what it takes. Here are some examples of impossible-to-solve problems that I have cracked . . . .*

   > *Journalism suits me to a "T" because I am inveterately curious. I love asking questions.*

   > *My work is more than just a job for me. It is a passion. Every time I help the Consumer Product Safety Commission pull a defective toy from the market, I know that I may be saving a child's life.*

   > *I am eager to contribute to the mission of [name of your target agency goes here] as a [name of your target job goes here] because [your reason goes here]. I have previously demonstrated my dedication to this field by using my [type of relevant skills go here] skills to advance the following projects:*

3. **Be positive:** many applicants mistakenly believe that they will somehow impress hiring managers by putting themselves down in an essay. NOT! There is simply no way that you will curry favor with hiring managers by volunteering information about your shortcomings, botched projects, missed deadlines, or other failures on an essay.

HOT TIP
Show Your Passion
Passion is a primary element of effective communication. In fact, in an article in *O, The Oprah Magazine*, about how to communicate effectively, the late attorney Johnnie Cochran said, "Passion and preparation are unbeatable if you're to be an effective advocate."

By conveying passion and humanity in your essays, you will make your essays interesting and convince hiring managers that you are the kind of self-motivated, low-maintenance employee whom any supervisor would treasure.

Nevertheless, many job applicants include confessional information in their essays. I even read one KSA by a NASA employee who personally accepted some responsibility for the Challenger accident. As if any hiring manager would hire a walking disaster!

Never reveal unflattering information about yourself in an essay. Remember: In the United States, you have a Fifth Amendment right against self-incrimination; you don't even have to testify against yourself when you commit murder, let alone when you innocently apply for a job. Moreover, take some advice from my mother, Dr. Dorit Whiteman, who is a clinical psychologist:

"Don't ever put yourself down in public. There are enough people out there who are more than willing to belittle you. Don't ever make it easy for them."

So instead of giving potential employers ammunition against you when they are not even asking for it, spin your stories whichever way makes you look best, as long as the information that you provide is truthful. Table 10-9 is an example of effective spin in a KSA that removes self-incriminating information about a missed deadline.

TABLE 10-9 Avoid Self Incrimination	
Before: Self-Incriminating	**After: Innocent and Impressive**
I managed a major renovation of office space in the National Federal Center in Washington, DC. Unfortunately, we missed the 3-month deadline for the project.	I managed a $5 million renovation of 15,000 square feet of office space in the National Federal Center in Washington, DC. This project was complicated by the unexpected discovery of asbestos in the building's ceiling paint.
	To safely remove the ceiling paint, I quickly met the many administrative requirements for hiring asbestos-removal contractors. Because of my effective project management, my three-person team and I completed the entire project in only 97 days and within budget, despite the unanticipated expenses.

4. **Maximize your stature:** Include credentials that describe your highest level of responsibility; exclude credentials or words that diminish your stature. For example identify which activity—by its relatively low level of responsibility—reduces the applicant's standing in the following real-life KSA excerpt:

    As Director of Communications for the Vice President of the United States, I prepared position papers on issues such as partial-birth abortions, Middle East peace talks, and national environmental regulations, and I wrote Boy Scout congratulatory notes.

5. **Title-drop:** Cite the titles of your highest-level references in your KSAs, particularly if they include inside contacts at your hiring agency.

6. **Cite your positive feedback:** Validate your achievements by citing the types of feedback suggested in "The VALIDATION Generator" in Chapter 7. Notice how the sample stories and essays provided in this chapter and on this book's CD do so. In particular, cite your record of earning very positive performance reviews, and quote praise from your evaluations and awards and oral praise you have received from top managers.

   Suppose you're a current fed on a pass/fail rating system, and you have received passing ratings with positive written or oral feedback from your boss. Then, you may honestly state in your essays and résumé that you have received positive performance evaluations. After all, you have earned the highest possible grades provided by your agency's system.

Quality Controls

1. **Don't leave your essays to the last minute!** It is virtually impossible to dash off a quality application in a single sitting. You need at least several sittings to develop the perfect content and structure for them and to debug them of errors and typos.

2. **Take breaks from working on your essays:** Each time that you return to your document after a break, you will bring a fresh perspective to your work that will help you improve it. Why? Because your fresh perspective will show you what is *really* on the page rather than what you *think* is on the page.

3. **Keep checking:** Periodically review Chapter 7 for tips on how to convey your achievements persuasively. And every time you read your essays, make sure that they incorporate the principles described in that chapter. Also check for:

   ➤ Important credentials and success stories that should be added or replace those that were included

   ➤ Results you produced and positive feedback you received that should be added

   ➤ Logical leaps that should be bridged

   ➤ Unnecessary information or words that should be eliminated

   ➤ Vague generalities that should be described more specifically

   ➤ Negativities that should be eliminated

   ➤ Terms that should be defined

   ➤ Grammatical errors

   ➤ The accuracy of any numbers that you cite

4. **Use more editing tips:** See Chapter 8 for editing tips for online applications. See Chapter 9 for editing techniques for résumés; apply those techniques to your KSAs and ECQs as well.

> **THE MADDENING EDITING AND REVISING PROCESS**
>
> Many people wrongly believe that it's faster and easier to write a short, easy-to-understand document than a long, technical one. Quite the opposite. As Blaise Pascal, a 17th-century scientist said, "I have made this letter longer than usual because I lack the time to make it short."
>
> Even expert writers must repeatedly revise in order to convey information clearly and concisely. For example, it took Pulitzer Prize winner Ernest Hemingway nothing less than a slavish devotion to the editing process to achieve his trademark simple, direct style. He rewrote the ending of the classic *A Farewell to Arms* almost 70 times!

No, This Is Not a Joke: This Is an Excerpt From a Real-Life KSA

"Another Leadership role currently serving is President of the Bethesda Station Homeowners Association and representatives a community of more than 500 single-family dwellings. Leadership abilities involve frequent interaction with county managers, officials, and politicians in an effort to improve the quality of life, promote growth, and maintain harmonious relations amongst a very diversified which population is in excess of 5,500 people."

The many errors in this KSA excerpt are not this book's mistakes. These mistakes were in a real-life KSA. (Notice that according to the numbers provided in this excerpt, each home in the Bethesda Station Homeowners Association houses an average of more than 100 people: a tad crowded—wouldn't you say?)

But the real kicker is that the craven carelessness reflected in this KSA excerpt is NOT unusual. Agencies are literally flooded with applications that reflect as much sloppiness as this excerpt. It goes to show: if you repeatedly and meticulously proofread your KSA until it is error-free, your KSAs are virtually guaranteed to stand out from the pack for the right reasons.

The Importance of Storytelling

Most job applicants fill their KSAs and ECQs with job descriptions. (See the sample me-o-centric essay on page 137.) I call these documents "job description essays" or "me-o-centric essays." Their telltale signature is their repetition of the pronoun "I," the word "me," and clauses such as "my responsibilities include . . . " or "my duties include . . . "

What's wrong with job description essays? Dominated by lists of activities that are devoid of a theme or plot, job description KSAs are boring. Put another way: reading a job description KSA is about as interesting as reading someone else's mile-long "to do" list. And a boring KSA is unlikely to be read, much less remembered. What's more, because job description KSAs focus on what the applicant was supposed to do rather than what they actually accomplished or achieved, they are generally unimpressive. (Your job description may say that you will land a rocket on Mars . . . but did you actually do it?)

Success Stories

How can you craft KSAs and ECQs that are impressive and memorable? One important way is to tell a relevant success story—a description of how you accomplished a specific goal or solved a problem that relates to the opening. No matter what level you have reached in your career—whether you are applying for an entry level or executive position, your KSAs and ECQs should contain at least a few success stories. Here's why:

1. Success stories are memorable. Because success stories are conceptually united by a dramatic narrative, they are like verbal Velcro that wraps around and sticks to the reader's brain. Indeed, even a short essay that describes a single success story will likely be more memorable and impressive than a long job description essay that rattles off paragraph after paragraph of responsibilities that are only linked by the fact that they are performed by the same person.

   The memorable, persuasive punch provided by storytelling has compelled almost every successful politician—from Abraham Lincoln, to Ronald Reagan, to Bill Clinton—to use this device to woo votes. You can use this same technique to wow hiring managers.

2. Success stories are impressive. By telling success stories that transcend descriptions of ho-hum, day-to-day chores and that highlight your save-the-day moments and your Superman, home run, gold medal achievements, you will prove that you are a producer. You will thereby get hiring managers salivating at the prospect of hiring you to produce at their agencies.

   Your success stories will help you stand out from the pack: by telling success stories that capture the uniqueness of your problem-solving and goal-reaching experiences, and de-emphasizing responsibilities that are indistinguishable from those of hundreds of other government employees who have the same job title as you, you will distinguish yourself from the pack.

Don't pressure yourself to find a single blockbuster story that captures all of the credentials that you want to convey in a particular essay. You may answer an essay with more than one story and/or include additional credentials in your essays besides those that are embedded in stories.

Power Lawyer Gerry Spence Explains Why Stories Persuade

(From the audio version of *How to Argue and Win Every Time** by Gerry Spence.)

Gerry Spence is one of the nation's best known and most respected trial lawyers. In practice for more than 40 years, he has never lost a criminal case. His hundreds of victories include many high-profile cases, such as the Karen Silkwood, Imelda Marcos, and Randy Weaver cases. Here Spence explains why story-based arguments are so compelling. (Remember that each of your essays is essentially an argument for why you should be hired.)

Photo by D.J. Bassett.

Every argument in court or out, whether delivered over the supper table or at coffee break, can be reduced to a story. And the strongest structure for any argument is always story.

Storytelling has been the principle means by which we have taught one another from the beginning of time. We are indeed creatures of story. The stories of our childhood remain with us as primary experiences against which we judge and decide issues as adults. They are forever implanted on both our conscious and unconscious.

Movies, television, and theater are highly developed forms of storytelling. The most effective advertisements on television are always mini stories that take little more than half a minute. Jokes are small stories. Christ's parables are stories.

Before we can tell an effective story to the other, we must first visualize the picture ourselves. Begin to think in story form. Why? Because the story is the easiest form for almost any argument to take.

You don't have to remember the next thought or the next sentence. You don't have to memorize anything. You already know the whole story. You see it in your mind's eye. Whereas you may or may not be able to remember the structure and sequence of the formal argument.

The story argument is so powerful because it speaks in the language form of the species. Its structure is natural. It permits the storyteller to speak easily, openly from the heart zone. It provokes interest. It is an antidote to the worst poison that can be injected into any argument—the doldrums.

*Published in 1995 by Audio Renaissance Tapes. Reprinted with permission.

Don't Be a Me-O-Centric

Have you recently met a me-o-centric person—someone who is single-mindedly focused on himself or herself?

If so, chances are that you hardly remember the me-o-centric's words. How come? Because the me-o-centric's preoccupation with "me," without regard for the interests or activities of others, is monotonous and boring. Moreover, the me-o-centric's tendency to begin every sentence with the pronoun "I" offers all of the dynamism of a sleep-inducing white noise machine.

Shortly after starting a conversation with a me-o-centric, most people either physically move away or mentally drift away. Soon after the contact is over, any memory of the me-o-centric's words fades away. Just as forgettable as me-o-centric monologues are me-o-centric essays. Try to slog through, for example, the me-o-centric essay in the following section.

Now, without looking back at the essay, describe the writer's work. Chances are you don't remember much about it. How come? Because, like me-o-centric monologues, this me-o-centric essay is boringly self-absorbed—as reflected in its overuse of the "I" pronoun.

Moreover, any KSA or ECQ that is single-mindedly focused on "I" isn't explaining the benefits to people and programs yielded by the work done by "I." By ignoring their own results and how they benefited their employers, me-o-centrics sacrifice their best-selling points. (You might even say that me-o-centrics are victims of their own self-centeredness.)

Also missing from the me-o-centric essay is an overarching theme or framework that unites its content. Disjointed and incohesive, the essay's facts fail to lodge in the reader's mind. Instead, they slip through the reader's mind like sand through a sieve.

By contrast, success stories are held together by the glue of a plot. Therefore they are more memorable than me-o-centric essays. In addition, success stories are—by definition—focused on results that solved problems or achieved goals impacting organizations and people other than the writer. Therefore, they are more impressive than the dull, this-is-what-I-do-everyday descriptions of me-o-centric essays.

Sample of Me-O-Centric KSA

Describe your experience applying procedural knowledge and analyzing policies in performing your job:

I am responsible for developing OGE policy, staffing and recruitment, position classification and position management, pay and allowances, time and attendance, health and life insurance programs, employee relations, and discipline. My duty is to function as the agency's Training Officer and conduct career development. I counsel employees on retirement, benefits, and TSP. I administer the agency's performance management system. I administer the agency's injury compensation program. The Personnel Office at OGE functions as a Delegated Examining Unit. As the Personnel Officer, I manage all aspects of merit staffing procedures. This involves the ability to analyze jobs to identify the knowledge, skills, and abilities required for effective work performance. I analyze, interpret, and apply qualification standards to prospective applicants. I develop rating schedules and crediting plans. I write job descriptions and ensure that vacancy announcements are posted on USAJOBS. I have served on many selection panels. I am responsible for candidates under the terms of OGE's merit promotion plan. I have in-depth knowledge of Title 5 staffing and employment regulations. I have knowledge of personnel rules and regulations relating to staffing, recruitment, and benefits. My policies and programs have been used as templates by other offices. I accomplished staffing and recruitment in all targeted areas for the IRS: Examination, Collection, Agents, Criminal Investigators, and Taxpayer Service Representatives while serving as a staffing specialist for the IRS. I have knowledge of federal employment rules, regulations, practices, and merit principles. I am able to apply these policies to recruitment and selection, and other components of personnel. I consulted with management concerning both the immediate and long-range goals of the organization and developed approaches to improve operations in these areas. I am able to analyze and synthesize a variety of information from IRS functions and devise solutions to staffing and recruitment needs. I have the ability to analyze problems and exercise sound judgment in staffing and classification decisions. I have knowledge of special hiring programs such as Public Law 105-339: Veterans Employment Opportun-ities of 1998. I have knowledge of the legal authorities used for these types of appointments. I have prepared recruitment packages with materials for varied audiences and cover letters to various universities, law schools, and legal journals to recruit attorneys for the Office of Government Ethics. I have also recruited for the positions of Ethics Specialists and Administrative staff using the Internet, professional publications, and career fairs. While at IRS, I prepared recruitment packages aimed at recruiting accountants, attorneys, and taxpayer service representatives to the organization. I provide expert advice and on matters relating to overall HR programs and processes to employees, applicants, and the general public. I act as a coach to my Personnel Assistant and clerk. I have established collaborative work relationships with coworkers and personnel from other federal agencies. I am an excellent supervisors. My staff appreciates my guidance. I have worked on teams and on-going assignments as well as on project work groups for the IRS and VA. I am an effective communicator, often making presentations on policies, procedures, and programs to senior level management. I am adept at Powerpoint. I am also a good writer. I have written reports, policies, and programs.

Diagnosing a Me-O-Centric KSA

Notice how almost every sentence and important clause in this me-o-centric KSA begins with the pronoun "I" or the word "my"—the stylistic signature of the me-o-centric. Notice too how this unformatted essay, which features no paragraphs or headings, looks dense and overwhelming. And since nothing stands out off this KSA, nothing from this KSA will lodge in the memory of a busy, time-pressured hiring manager.

Picking Powerful Stories

Grist for Stories

Chapter 7 can help you mine your experience for powerful success stories. Remember to favor stories that closely parallel the demands of your target job, and capture your biggest successes, i.e., those that involved the largest numbers of people, largest amounts of money, the approvalsor participation of high level officials, or most favorable press coverage.

If you are not a new graduate, your stories should primarily come from your work experiences. However, you may also cite nonwork stories that are based in your academic experiences, activities in professional organizations, community work, volunteer jobs, hobbies, or reading.

Just be sure that your nonwork stories, like your work stories, reflect traits demanded by your desired job. For example, you could answer KSAs and ECQs addressing leadership or negotiating skills by discussing how you swayed a jury while serving on jury duty, started a neighborhood crime watch in your neighborhood, or negotiated an economical maintenance contract for your condo complex while serving on the condo board.

What Have You Done for Me Lately?

The more recent your power stories, the better. If possible, favor stories that describe your achievements form the last 5 or 10 years. Why? Because potential employers are way more interested in learning about who you are now and what you offer now than about who you were and what you did eons ago. And after all, our careers are supposed to reflect an upward momentum.

Danger Zones

Steer clear of stories that might offend hiring managers or suggest to them—however wrongly—that you might be a negative, high-maintenance employee. Such stories include those that so much as hint at your:

> ➤ Religious beliefs

> ➤ Personal problems or shortcomings

> ➤ Criticisms of former or current employers, employees, or colleagues

> ➤ Tendency to break rules on the job or elsewhere

Also keep your political views to yourself, unless you are applying to Capitol Hill jobs. In addition, if you cite your position as a staffer for a member of Congress as a credential, tone down the potentially partisan implications of your position. Do so by referring to your superiors by title rather than by name. For example, say, "I served as a legislative assistant for a senator from Colorado," rather than, "I served as a legislative assistant for Senator John Doe (R-CO)."

Features of a Powerful Story

Many storytellers omit critical information that seems self evident to them but that is not at all obvious to strangers to the situation. These storytellers thereby confuse and alienate their audiences. This is not a good thing to do when you are asking your audience for a job. You can avoid this pitfall by running your stories (as well as the rest of your application) by an objective editor(s) who can tell you whether your train of thought will be clear to hiring mangers who are unfamiliar with your projects.

The critical components of an effective story include (see Figure 10-1 on page 171):

1. **A concrete problem or goal:** Only provide as much information as necessary to provide context; set the stage for explanations of your achievement, and underscore the wisdom of your strategy.

    Eliminate any information that is not needed to understand your contributions. Why? Because most of your essay should be devoted to your problem-solving or goal-reaching strategy—rather than to an inventory of your agency's problems. In other words, emphasize your contributions and achievements.

    If possible, document the existence of the problem or the size of your goal with supporting statistics or other numbers. (Managers: See "Metrics for Managers" in the "Application and Interview Warm-Up Tip Sheets" folder in this book's CD.) Also explain why the problem or goal you attacked was important to your agency. Was, for example, an obstacle you removed wasting time for staffers, costing money, damaging productivity or morale, creating a safety hazard or legal liability, or tarnishing your organization's reputation?

Orient your readers by identifying the year, your title, and the name of the organization that employed you when you began addressing the problem or goal. Why? Because titles and dates give your story credibility. In addition, titles give you a more authoritative, commanding presence than vague references to "my previous job" or "my current job," which are meaningless to hiring managers who don't know you.

Examples of problems suitable for essays include:

➤ The need to do more with less

➤ A bad trend, such as an increasing accident or turnover rates

➤ The need for a better tracking system for supplies or project progress

➤ Poor results on an audit, survey, evaluation, or in the President's Management Agenda

➤ Poor sales, profits, or customer service

➤ High employee turnover, or poor employee morale

➤ An ineffective or inefficient system or process

➤ A back-log of work

➤ A disorganized office or gap in office capabilities

➤ An uninformative or outdated website

➤ Inappropriate use of an employer's credit cards by employees

➤ The need to cut costs

Examples of goals suitable for essays include the need to:

➤ Improve awareness of a problem, situation, or event

➤ Save money or time or improve efficiency

➤ Quickly procure goods, services, software, or hardware

➤ Win a legal decision

➤ Develop a new policy or regulation

➤ Organize a meeting, conference, or other event

➤ Produce a document

➤ Conduct an investigation, audit, or survey

➤ Launch a product

➤ Avoid controversy or confusion when a new regulation is released

➤ Avoid a potential catastrophe, such as a shortage of human capital

2. **Your problem-solving or goal-reaching actions**—for example:

   ➤ Automating a process

   ➤ Passing or enforcing a regulation

   ➤ Creating a team, task force, or organization

   ➤ Researching alternative solutions to a problem

   ➤ Designing and running a marketing or public awareness campaign

   ➤ Improving personnel policies

   ➤ Identifying inefficiencies in a system or processes and fixing them

   ➤ Consulting with experts

   ➤ Planning and arranging a meeting, conference or other event

   ➤ Reducing costs or boosting sales

   ➤ Creating/updating documents or websites

   ➤ Arranging or providing training

   ➤ Soliciting the cooperation of stakeholders

   ➤ Putting a contract or other project on a "fast track"

   ➤ Proving the cost-effectiveness of a purchase

   ➤ Keeping a project a high-priority with senior management

   ➤ Securing funding for projects

   ➤ Systematically prioritizing tasks and then completing them

   ➤ Getting "buy-in" for an approach from senior management or regional offices

3. **Challenges you conquered:** Don't pretend that your job is easy. You should, by all means, describe any factors that complicated your project. By doing so, you will help illuminate your tenacity and problem-solving skills.

But be sure to describe your challenges objectively and in impersonal terms, without reflecting bitterness or resentment or contempt for your employer, boss, or colleagues. No grumbling!

Emphasize what you did—not what was done to you or how you were overburdened or victimized. That is, focus on how you used your knowledge and creativity to deftly conquer your challenges rather than on how you were personally wronged when the project was assigned to you or as it progressed—no matter how wronged you were.

Examples of challenges suitable for essays include:

➤ The precedent-setting nature of your work and the unavailability of templates or models to follow (i.e. the need for you to blaze an entirely new trail)

➤ Risks that you faced

➤ Staffing, equipment, or geographic constraints

➤ Constraints created by a tough economy or a tight budget

➤ Tight deadlines

➤ Entrenched, change-resistant bureaucracy

➤ Hostile stakeholders or hostile press

➤ Varying perspectives of members of a workgroup that must reach consensus

➤ Lack of consistent commitment from senior management

➤ Last minute schedule or policy-changes that required accommodation

➤ Racial or gender glass ceilings

➤ The inaccessibility of important data

➤ A sensitive political situation

➤ A database or computer system that is crippled by bugs

➤ Office reorganizations or moves

➤ Changing leadership within an office

➤ Office closures due to bad weather or other causes

4. **Positive results:** Provide evidence that you solved the problem or achieved your goal that you identified in the beginning of your story. (See Chapter 7 for tips on how to quantify your activities and results and how to title-drop your high-level contacts when you describe your praise. Also see "Metrics for Managers" in the "Application and Interview Warm-Up Tip Sheets" folder in this book's CD.)

    Examples of positive results include:

    ➤ Improvements in an alarming trend

    ➤ Improved survey results

    ➤ Improved customer satisfaction

    ➤ Finalization of a regulation

    ➤ Launch of a website that receives many hits per day or the production and distribution of a document to the public, Congress, other government organizations or stakeholder groups (Cite circulation of publication, if its circulation is high.)

    ➤ Positive press coverage

    ➤ The receipt of awards to your agency because of your contributions

    ➤ A successful product launch or improved product sales

    ➤ Resolution of an important question

    ➤ Improvements in customer service

    ➤ Improvements in a system or process

    ➤ A successful meeting, conference, or other event

    ➤ The development of consensus on an important issue among experts

    ➤ Increased profits, savings in money or time, and improvements in efficiency

    ➤ Improved awareness of a problem, situation, or impending event

    ➤ The creation of a network of professionals promoting information exchange

    ➤ Acquisition of needed products or services

    ➤ Elimination of a back-log of letters, product orders, or contracts

    ➤ Improved office organization

    ➤ The seamless management transition

Be sure to mention, if possible, any evidence that you exceeded expectations or went beyond the call of duty by, for example:

➤ Beating a deadline

➤ Beating a quota or average production levels

➤ Completing a project under budget

➤ Attracting a particularly large crowd to a conference, training, or other event

➤ Working exceedingly long hours

➤ Maintaining a hectic travel schedule

➤ Having your documents (or other work products) approved by supervisors or senior officials without drawing any substantive suggested changes or requiring redundant efforts

5. **Feedback that you received:** If possible, provide objective evidence of your success. See the Validation Generator in Chapter 7.

"I wrote another five hundred words. Can I have another cookie?"

Five Story Makeovers

Provided here are five story makeovers, including a "before" and "after" version of each story. These stories are based on stories from real-life, winning KSAs and ECQs. (Names of offices and other details have been changed to disguise the identities of their writers.) Even if these example stories are not related to your field, they will give you ideas on how to convey your success stories persuasively and will help get your creative juices pumping.

Notice how the "after" version of each story is enhanced by the following formatting features:

➤ **Short sentences and short paragraphs.**

➤ **Headings:** Headings help underscore the logic of a document and encourage the reader's eye to whiz down the page. In addition, the "results" headings in the "after" versions of these essays help guarantee that their authors will be pegged as producers by hiring managers who only glance at these documents without reading them word for word.

➤ **Bulleted or numbered lists:** Bulleted lists of an applicant's activities, skills, or results are used to replace long-winded sentences that repeat the me-o-centric word "I" over and over again. Lists also encourage fast reading.

Side-by-Side #1: The Me-O-Centric

**Describe your experience in working with methods, procedures, and regulations as re-
lated to civil rights laws.**

*As a result of my extensive training and daily responsibilities, I have obtained a thorough knowl-
edge of EEO principles, laws, policies, and regulations. As EEO counselor, this knowledge allows
me to advise employees and applicants seeking guidance on EEO policies and practices and com-
plaint procedures. I have the knowledge required to apply EEO rules and regulations appropriately, allowing the entire process to progress smoothly. I can research various laws and policies relating to the Civil Rights Act of 1963 with complete understanding of its relationship to the issues
involved. I understand various authorities relating to persons with disabilities and minorities and
women. I have also conducted training explaining employee rights and responsibilities. I act as a
coach to my personnel assistant and clerk.*

Typical of me-o-centrics, this me-o-centric presumes that her list of responsibilities and areas
of knowledge will attract employers. But she has inadvertently overlooked what most attracts
employers: evidence that she fulfills her responsibilities and applies her knowledge to solve
specific problems and achieve concrete goals. A few sentences, for example, about how the
author skillfully recruited a sought-after lawyer who won important cases for his agency, or
about how the author's coaching helped propel her personnel assistant through the ranks
would have been more memorable and more impressive than this collection of vague "I"-
isms.

Side-by-Side #1: The Reformed Me-O-Centric

**Describe your experience in working with methods, procedures, and regulations as re-
lated to civil rights laws.**

*As an Equal Employment Opportunity (EEO) counselor at the Equal Opportunities Administration,
I am helping to shatter glass ceilings all over Iowa. Most recently, in 2006, I helped the Iowa City
Fire Department, which was entirely male, adhere to EEO regulations. I did this by designing and
delivering five day-long workshops on EEO regulations for senior managers, who were almost
unanimously opposed to hiring female firefighters. These workshops covered:*

- *All applicable EEO regulations on discrimination.*
- *Examples of how state agencies were heavily penalized for breaking EEO regulations.*
- *Testimonials from male firefighters whose lives had been saved by female firefighters.*

RESULTS: *Within 2 months of participating in my workshops, the Iowa City Fire Department hired
10 female firefighters.*

Notice how, in less than 10 sentences, this applicant tells a story that clearly defines a
problem, her solution, and impressive results. In addition, by including a bolded "Results"
section, the author shrewdly gives her results extra oomph and broadcasts them to skim-
mers.

After reading this essay, turn away from it and try to describe the author's achievements.
Chances are you will recall more of this applicant's achievements than of the me-o-centric's achievements. Likewise, so would hiring managers.

Side-by-Side #2: The Fixer in Search of a Problem

Describe your experience analyzing procedures.

When I assumed responsibility as the deputy director for IRD in January 2006, I inherited a problem from my predecessor. I discovered that our command had accrued monthly fees of $800 and had accrued a total of $11,000 in outstanding fees to date for storage of used equipment and furniture. Through extensive research, I found that our organization had made a verbal agreement with the contractor to pay monthly for storage of the items, but had later decided to back out of the agreement. So, for several months, we were receiving bills, but leaving them unpaid. To resolve this issue, I sent a two-person team to inventory the items in storage and find an interim temporary storage facility on the base to house the items. I paid the contractor the amount we had incurred to date and arranged for immediate shipment of the items, which closed out our obligation to the contractor. As a result, I implemented two polices—(1) the command would utilize all items in storage first, prior to ordering new; and (2) made it clear to all members of our command that they would work through the IRD and our resident military contracting officer before going to any outside commercial contractor for this saves time, money, and any potential legal action that could have an adverse effect on performing our mission.

This applicant knows that he confronted some important problems and he is confident that he developed some mighty impressive solutions for them. But he's apparently unsure of which solution addressed which problem. His confusion is exposed by his failure to clearly articulate a problem.

At first blush, the essay's first few sentences seem to be building toward a discussion of the office's inability to pay the $11,000 storage fees or of the bogusness of the fees. But no, as it turns out, those weren't problems at all. The problem—only discernible by reading the essay several times and by reading between the lines—is that the IRD (whatever that organization is?) has been wasting money on unnecessary contracts for storage services, and, as the essay's last line implies, for other services as well.

In addition to failing to define this central problem, the author ignores an important problem that he inadvertently introduced: the failure of the IRD to pay its bills on time—not exactly an image-building maneuver. By failing to disclose how he addressed this problem—if at all—the applicant spotlights his own inadequacies. (Someone should tell this guy about his Fifth Amendment right against self-incrimination.)

Side-by-Side #2: The Efficient Fixer

Describe your experience analyzing procedures.

Since becoming deputy director of the Intelligence Resources Division (IRD) in January 2006, I have saved my office almost $20,000 by eliminating unnecessary contracts.

Problem: *I was initially alerted to IRD's over-eagerness for outsourcing by a bill for $11,000 that IRD received from a commercial storage company for storing some of IRD's furniture and equipment. The bill had been accruing for over a year without IRD making a single payment on it. Moreover, because our furniture and equipment was still languishing in the storage facility at $800 per month, the meter was still ticking. So I gave this contract my full and immediate attention.*

Action: *After swiftly verifying that the charges were legitimate, I found space in IRD's own storage facilities for holding the furniture and equipment. Then I worked quickly to:*

- *Restore IRD's good standing in the community by sending the storage facility a letter of apology for IRD's delinquency and paying our bill in full.*

- *Stop further unnecessary storage fees from accruing by arranging for the transfer of the stored furniture and equipment to IRD's storage facility.*

- *Ensure that the stored furniture and equipment be distributed to IRD staffers before we purchased any additional pieces.*

- *Establish regulations that channel all of the base's contracting requests through my office for stringent screening. Since these regulations took effect, my office has identified and cancelled many other unnecessary contracts for storing equipment, renting vehicles, and obtaining plumbing services.*

Recognition: *Please note these comments from the Assistant Secretary for Intelligence on my 2007 performance appraisal: "With his ability to sniff out unnecessary contracts, Bill has helped transform this office from a chaotic free-for-all into a well-oiled-machine."*

This applicant wisely hits readers with his best shot up front: his $20,000 savings. (Notice how he quantified and tallied his savings to yield an impressive total figure.) Then the applicant methodically defines the problem and his solution to it. And by quoting praise from his performance evaluation, he provides vivid proof of his supervisor's satisfaction with his results. (Note that this applicant name-dropped his supervisor's impressive title.)

Side-by-Side #3: The Abused Employee

Describe your experience managing financial data.

In 2004, the U.S. Postal Service awarded the Breast Cancer Stamp to a new advertising agency. This is a high profile contract with a very large dollar value, $15 million per year.

I inherited a major problem because the advertising agency had never before handled a government contract. It had no idea how to do invoices. The accounting department refused to review them and higher-grade Brand Managers were too busy, so this process was pushed on me. By the beginning of 2003, the situation was so bad that the contract was at the center of a major lawsuit. For each month, there were 508 binders, which I had to review at least 3 times and create a discrepancy list to wipe out basic errors. The work is so enormous that we are still processing last year's invoices.

The vendor does not have knowledge of cost accounting standards. The vendor submits disorderly invoices that have no regular format (no spreadsheet, no accounting codes). Annually submit 60 to 70 task orders and this is not computer entered and I must keep this in my mind and delve into a pile of binders and read each page and detect hidden errors with my eagle eye. Materials are often entered without unit price or quantity. And only through individual research I prevented the U.S. Postal Service from overspending. Provided discrepancy lists that assisted in the contract being rescued at that time, meanwhile saved money to a large extent, which influenced savings of $17K after second review.

This type of review I single-handedly created and implemented in order to deal with the crisis. During my vacation in 2004, management could not find a single person to process the last quarters' invoices, as a result they had to get four people from across the divisions to receive the invoices in PeopleSoft for me and when I returned, unfortunately for me everything was entered wrong.

Whoa! This applicant sounds like he is primed for workplace violence!

No matter how justified this applicant's anger may be, the appropriate venue for venting is not an application essay. His resentment will only backfire by arousing suspicions that he is the problem—not everyone around him, as he claims. It's been said that the sweetest revenge is success. This applicant would better serve his cause by channeling his energy into writing a positive, dispassionate account of what he achieved under difficult circumstances, rather than into writing a treatise of the injustices foisted upon him.

Side-by-Side #3: The Recovered Abused Employee

Describe your experience managing financial data.

Problem: As an accountant, I manage financial records for the U.S. Postal Service's high-profile $15 million-a-year Breast Cancer Stamp Program. About 50 million breast cancer stamps are currently sold annually. Records management for this high-dollar project—already labor intensive—has been particularly challenging since 2004, when advertising for the program was contracted out to an agency that had never before handled a government contract.

Solution: Because the contracting advertising agency's invoices and task orders almost always deviate from standard accounting protocol and are prone to costly errors, I single-handedly process them according to a unique and painstaking accounting protocol. My protocol involves:

- *Reviewing hundreds of invoices that are submitted each month at least twice, scrutinizing them for errors, and cross-checking them against previous invoices to ensure that we are not being charged more than once for the same service.*

- *Conducting daily reviews of 60 to 70 hard-copy task orders and cross-checking them against previous orders.*

- *Researching accounting codes, unit prices, and quantities of purchased products, which are almost always omitted from task orders and invoices.*

- *Accurately entering all invoices and task orders into accounting records stored in PeopleSoft.*

Results: By regularly identifying and doggedly pursing financial discrepancies and overcharges, I helped save the U.S. Postal Service $17,000 in unwarranted changes since 2004. Through my contributions to this project, I have earned a reputation as an exceedingly conscientious and eagle-eyed financial manager.

Notice how "the recovered abused employee"—unlike "the abused employee" explicitly mentions his involvement in the important Breast Cancer Stamp Program in the very first paragraph of the essay.

Moreover, the applicant factually states what he did . . . not what was done to him. Untarnished by his resentful comments, his accomplishments shine brightly.

Side-by-Side #4: The Wallflower

Describe your experience leading change.

I served as the Internal Revenue Service's representative to the Congressional Task Force for Improving Government, an interagency task force. I facilitated partnerships among high-level federal officials from a number of executive agencies and representatives of a network of community-based organizations that are dedicated to encouraging lifelong learning for adults. This involved organizing meetings and developing and revitalizing several websites, including workers.gov, plainlanguage.gov, and FirstGov.gov.

This wallflower is too afraid of the spotlight to even provide his title or to define the problem that he addressed. In addition, he only glosses over his activities without explaining their importance. These flaws minimize his stature and achievements.

Side-by-Side #4: The Reformed Wallflower

Describe your experience leading change.

Problem: *In the year 2020, 60 percent of all jobs in the United States will require technical skills that are possessed by only 22 percent of today's workers, according to the U.S. Department of Commerce.*

Action: *As Assistant Director of the Congressional Task Force for Improving Government's 21st Century Workforce Team from May 2004 to January 2007, I worked to narrow the nation's skills gap by:*

- *Forging and fostering partnerships between 20 community-based organizations (Workforce Network Partners) that encourage lifelong learning and Assistant Secretaries from appropriate federal agencies, including the Departments of Labor, Education, and Commerce.*

- *Advising Workforce Network Partners how to secure federal grants to expand their adult education and lifelong learning programs.*

- *Developing and revitalizing interactive websites that provide information on best practices for improving adult education and lifelong learning programs. (These sites include workers.gov, plainlanguage.gov, and FirstGov.gov.)*

- *Managing a high-traffic list-serve that helped Workforce Network Partners exchange best practices information—despite the geographical distance between them and our program's tight budget.*

Workforce Results: *Under my leadership, the 21st Century Workforce Team and our partners built an electronic and organizational infrastructure that will help community-based organizations encourage lifelong learning and adult education for years to come. (The Workforce Team's websites, for example, currently receive tens of thousands of hits every day.) By propelling American workers into high- skill, high-wage jobs, this infrastructure will contribute to U.S. competitiveness.*

Oh! What a shot of courage can do! By starting the story with a hard-hitting statistic, this applicant establishes the national importance of his project. By stating his title, the full name of his organization, and the dates he worked there, this applicant gives himself authority and credibility. In addition, by explaining that he collaborated with Assistant Secretaries, this applicant proves that he has worked at a very senior level. All of the bullets in this essay reflect an energetic, multitalented individual. And this essay's "Results" section describes how he left a lasting and important legacy that will that will continue to address the problem introduced in his story's first sentence.

Side-by-Side #5: The Rambler

Describe your experience leading change.

For more than 30 years, most small construction sites in the United States employing fewer than 20 workers have been essentially exempt from requirements to provide safety training to their employees. These requirements are implemented by the Occupational Safety and Health Administration (OSHA). This exemption was implemented as a result of a deal brokered by several construction operators and lobbyists. It has remained in effect due to various examples of fancy political legwork.

During the late-1990s, fatalities at small construction sites climbed. Congress held several sets of hearings on the topic. Many editorials on the topic were published in newspapers. CNN did a special on construction safety. Safety at small constructions sites had clearly become an important problem. Something needed to be done about it. Finally, the OSHA leadership attempted to get rid of the exemption. As part of this effort, Congress authorized the expenditure of funds to provide safety training to construction workers at small construction sites.

We held 11 hearings before we inaugurated the Small Construction Site Training Program. These hearings were designed to collect comments from interested parties. They were held in many cities including New York, Boston, Washington, DC, Denver, Mexico City, and Los Angeles. Transcripts were made of public meetings and published on OSHA's website to allow those who had been unable to attend hearings to participate in the process.

The safety training program was delivered by the congressionally mandated deadline and was well received. It took effect a year later. Since 2004, fatalities at small construction sites have fallen significantly from their all-time high level. Achieving "buy-in" has proven to be critical to increased performance and has been the basis for rewarding employees for their work and innovation. This project was regarded as a great success, and OSHA received suggestions that the Part 56 experience be used as a model in other regulatory projects.

Get out the gong bell! This applicant was apparently too involved with his project to distinguish important from unimportant information. The politics described in the first few paragraphs are boring. They are also irrelevant because we don't need this information to understand the applicant's actions or achievements. Also notice that the final two paragraphs are mired in repetitive and technical information (what is Part 56?) that obscure—rather than enhance—the applicant's achievements. Moreover, the essay's final paragraph fails to identify who regarded the project as a great success. (For all we know, this applicant's fan is none other than his own mother!)

Side-by-Side #5: The Reformed Rambler

Describe your experience leading change.

Problem: Every year, hundreds of construction workers are killed by electrocutions, collapsing structures, and collisions between gigantic trucks. Nevertheless, construction operations that employ fewer than 20 construction workers have traditionally not been required to provide safety training to their employees.

Because of the long hours and lack of safety training at small construction sites, accidents soared at these facilities during the construction boom that started in the late 1990s. In 2003, fatalities reached a record high of 200 deaths per year—many of which could have been prevented by basic safety training. In response, in 2004, Congress ordered the Occupational Safety and Health Administration (OSHA) to develop a safety training program for small construction sites by 2005.

Solution: As Chief of OSHA's new Small Construction Site Training Program since its creation in 2004, I currently manage the Small Construction Site Safety Program. So far, this program has:

- *Produced an attention-grabbing video reviewing construction safety methods. This video, which was distributed to 50,000 construction sites, won the Occupational Safety Video of the Year Award in 2003.*

- *Created a new website on construction safety for small construction operators. This site, which is updated daily, receives more than 500 hits per day. Its offerings include free, downloadable scripts for construction safety trainings on varied topics from vehicle safety to electrical safety.*

- *Finalized requirements that every worker at a small construction site receive safety training by a certified construction safety trainer at least once every 6 months.*

To battle the popular misconception among many labor organizations that the training program would reflect undue industry influence, I invited all interested parties to comment on my office's efforts at 10 public, nationwide meetings held in 2004. At these meetings, a total of 98 construction workers, union representatives, safety trainers, members of academia, and construction operators provided suggestions—many of which were incorporated by the safety program.

In addition, I single-handedly put the training regulation on a fast track by keeping it a top priority for OSHA's senior management; answering the Office of Management and Budget's information exhaustive information requests as quickly as possible; and setting deadlines for each step of the regulatory process and working doggedly to meet them.

Results: Under my leadership, OSHA initiated the Small Construction Site Training Program in record time and met Congress's tight 1-year deadline. As a result, more than 100,000 construction workers now receive effective workplace safety training. Moreover, the Small Construction Site Training Program helped reduce deaths among construction workers at small operations by almost 50 percent, from 200 fatalities in 2004 to about 105 fatalities in 2006.

Positive Feedback: For my leadership role in Small Construction Site Training Program, I received the Secretary of Labor's Bravo Award. In addition, the program was praised by organized labor, federal officials, and union representatives at a ceremony hosted by Secretary of Labor Elaine Chao. Also, the union publication, Construction Safety Today, hailed the training program as "a giant step forward." Furthermore, construction operators have regularly suggested that the cooperative process used in developing the program serve as a model for the development of other training programs.

This story's opening is attention-grabbing and briskly establishes the problem's life-or-death importance. Moreover, the "Results" section quantifies the applicant's achievement and portrays the applicant's accomplishments in a precedent-setting light. Nice name-dropping too. Bullets and headings promote fast-reading. Note that the real-life version of this essay helped its writer land numerous interviews for GS-15 and SES positions.

Ten Example Essays

Although a KSA or ECQ may consist entirely of one or more stories, you may include additional information besides or instead of stories in your essays. The 10 essays on the following pages provide examples of how to do so.

These essays are based on real-life, winning KSAs and ECQs (the names of employers and other details have been changed to disguise the identities of their writers).

Even if the example essays on the following pages do not cover your field, they will give you ideas on how to describe your achievements and organize your essays; the organization of each essay is reflected in its headings; just by scanning them, you can get their gist.

Notice too that each essay identifies the applicant's title and employer—this information is critical to hiring managers. Moreover, these essays demonstrate various methods for quantifying activities, achievements and results, title-dopping, and providing objective validation to an applicant's success as discussed in Chapter 7; they also incorporate effective storytelling methods.

HOT TIP
For Non-Feds Applying for Federal Jobs . . .

Explain in your cover letter or the first essay in your application why you are eager to switch to the federal sector and that you are ready, willing, and able to quickly adopt whatever new approaches and technical techniques would be required by your sector switch. Also, provide an example(s) of how you have previously quickly integrated into a new environment and learned a new job.

Example Essay #1

Essay for Customer Care Manager position: Describe your communication skills.

My Current Job

The United States Mint gives the best customer service in the federal government, according to the American Customer Survey Index (ACSI). As an award-winning Customer Care Representative at the Mint, I contribute to the Mint's number one position by providing fast, efficient, and courteous service to Mint customers. I use my communication skills daily to:

> ➤ Process telephone orders for about $1,000 worth of coins, medals, jewelry, and other collectibles per day.

> ➤ Resolve complaints about lost or broken merchandise. I am adept at calming angry customers by providing them with accurate information and extending extra services—such as free overnight delivery—as warranted.

> ➤ Research customers' questions about the history of U.S. coins and medals.

> ➤ Explain the Mint's products, billing procedures, and shipping procedures to clients as I manage 50 ongoing corporate/ bulk order accounts.

Recognition

Since 2004, I earned three "Superior" evaluations on my annual performance reviews. I excel as a Customer Service Representative because I enjoy talking to people from all walks of life and all ages. This same trait would serve me well as a Customer Care Manager.

Example Achievement

The anthrax mail contaminations of 2002 were more than just headlines for me. Why? Because they triggered a month-long suspension of mail deliveries to the U.S. Mint's Customer Care Center. On the day that our mail deliveries résuméd, the mailman delivered a mountain of mail that completely filled a 10-foot-by-10-foot cubicle! I helped attack this mountain of mail by:

> ➤ Setting up a tracking system that flagged and gave priority to mail that was more than 2 weeks old.

> ➤ Drafting form letters to send out in response to low-priority, routine inquiries.

➤ Arranging for the hire of a temporary worker who helped process the backlog of mail.

➤ Working 3 hours of overtime every day for 21 business days.

Results

Within 1 month of the resumption of mail deliveries, the Customer Care Center's huge backlog of mail was completely dissolved. Because of my pivotal role in this project, I received an On-the-Spot Award.

Early Experience

From 2001 to 2004, I worked as an administrative assistant at the Department of Transportation. In this position, I answered about 20 controlled letters per week. My drafts for these letters were routinely approved by the Director of the Customer Care Center, without requiring any substantive changes.

Education and Training

➤ Concurrent with full-time job: 24 hours of coursework from Fairfax Community College; Fairfax, Virginia (2006–Present)

➤ Five 1-day courses in providing excellent customer service since 2006.

The structure of this essay would be adaptable to almost every job applicant's background. This essay structure would be particularly effective for an application's first essay, which should—for the sake of making the best possible "first" impression—include the applicant's most impressive achievements. In addition, this essay gets kudos for including a dramatic topic sentence; this applicant cleverly claims credit for the successes of her employer to which she contributed. This essay's other strengths include its success story that is particularly compelling because it was ripped from the headlines. In addition, the vivid imagery provided in the story adds to its punch. Also, this essay's "Recognition" paragraph tells why the applicant likes her job and thereby conveys her enthusiastic, go-getter personality.

Example Essay #2

Essay for Executive Assistant position: Describe your ability to organize an office.

Career Overview

As an administrative assistant with 10 years of experience working for Chief Executive Officers, Chief Financial Officers, Senior Attorneys, and Department Chiefs at General Electric (GE), Oracle, and other large corporations, I have reveled in every opportunity to replace chaos with order.

I am an expert in developing and maintaining logical filing systems that enable the entire staff—from entry level professionals to executives—to quickly and easily access varied types of hard-copy and electronic documents, such as contracts, reports, personnel records, letters and memos, policy documents, forms, and newsletters. My records management skills have frequently saved my employers large amounts of time and money.

Example Achievement

Background: As an Executive Assistant to General Electric's Chief Executive Officer (CEO) from 2003 to 2007, I frequently supported my supervisor as she negotiated multimillion dollar contracts.

Problem: During the CEO's high-pressure negotiations with ABC Corporation in 2006 on the renewal of a $10 million dollar contract to supply GE with large quantities of plastic, a disagreement developed between GE and ABC Corporation over the existence of an addendum to our current contract, which had been signed 3 years before. This addendum verified the existence of current contract terms that were significantly more favorable to GE than were those proposed by ABC Corporation for the renewed contract. Unfortunately, however, ABC Corporation had no record of the addendum and doubted its existence. Therefore, ABC Corporation would not agree to extend those favorable conditions to the renewed contract.

My Solution: Because I had maintained the original contract addendum in my files since it had been signed 3 years previously, I was able to immediately retrieve this document as soon as it was needed during the negotiations. The introduction of this document into the negotiations compelled ABC Corporation to sign a renewed contract that cost GE $50,000 less than the contract proposed by ABC Corporation would have cost.

Positive Feedback: While thanking me for swiftly producing the addendum, GE's CEO stated unequivocally that my solid record-keeping skills were solely responsible for the $50,000 in savings.

This applicant gets high points for name-dropping the titles of her high-powered supervisors and the names of the corporate giants that employed her in the very first sentence of her essay. In addition, this applicant tells a compelling, well-organized story that offers money-saving punch.

Example Essay #3

Essay for Administrative Assistant position: Describe your ability to arrange travel.

Federal travel management is currently being revolutionized by the federal e-travel initiative. As an expert in all aspects of the fast-changing federal travel arena, I would be able to smoothly steer your agency through this revolution.

Experience in Travel Management

Under the title of Travel Manager, I serve as the "Travel and Shipping Go-To Person" for 200 employees at the Department of Interior. My typical travel projects involve the following tasks:

➢ Purchasing airline and train tickets, reserving hotel rooms, and arranging car rentals.

➢ Preparing travel authorizations and issuing vouchers and itineraries under tight deadlines. I also ensure that all travel paperwork adheres to federal regulations, and is approved by the appropriate officials.

➢ Trouble-shooting through snags, such as lost tickets and cancelled flights, and accommodating last-minute schedule changes, stop-overs, side trips, and medical emergencies.

➢ Processing reimbursements of expenses quickly so that employees will not be delinquent on their credit cards.

Regulatory and E-Expertise

Every year since 2000, I have attended the annual Federal Travel Conference, where I have participated in workshops on the new federal e-travel initiative, the federal SmartPay System, and the Travel and Transportation and Reform Act, among many other topics.

I am an expert in using the Internet and Gelco's Travel Manager software to electronically process all aspects of travel—from planning to processing reimbursements. In addition, I am thoroughly familiar with all federal websites that address credit card use, travel regulations, per diem rates, international travel and shipping, as well as airline, hotel, and car rental websites.

Results

➤ My paperwork and travel arrangements are—almost without exception—flawless, requiring no redundant efforts. Moreover, because of my efficiency and courteous manner with internal and external customers, I am known as an exceptionally efficient and congenial professional.

➤ I wrote my office's 20-page Travel Manual, which my office's 200 employees treat as a travel Bible.

➤ By using electronic travel procedures and by training other professionals in their use, I have helped streamline my office's travel processes and helped transform my office into a user-friendly, paperless environment.

By citing the factors that are changing her field and proving that she has the training and knowledge to adapt to them, this applicant creates the impression of a prepared and forward-thinking professional. If you want to use a similar approach in your essays but have trouble identifying some of the factors that are impacting your field, conduct some online literature searches in publications such as *Government Executive* (www.govexec.com) or conduct keyword searches in Internet search engines using keywords from your field.

Example Essay #4

Essay for Engineering position: Describe your ability to work with diverse groups of people.

As Director of the National Financial Center's (NFC) Energy Conservation Program, I interact every day with professionals of all levels—from blue-collar laborers to pin-striped engineers and executives.

Internal Customers

The success of the NFC's Energy Conservation Program hinges on contributions of plant managers, building engineers, and the energy coordinators of each of NFC's five facilities. Even though I do not personally supervise these professionals, I have gained and maintained their cooperation by:

➤ Convincing them of the importance of energy conservation efforts.

➤ Quickly addressing their concerns and questions. Because I am fluent in Spanish, I can communicate directly with NFC's many Spanish-speaking laborers whose activities affect energy efficiency.

➤ Keeping all energy coordinators updated of changes in policy or regulations by providing them with easy-to-understand fact sheets and checklists.

➤ Advising each facility's energy coordinator on the development of its individual energy plan. I provide site-specific guidance that addresses the unique climatic demands of each facility's location and the unique constraints of each facility's buildings.

➤ Keeping each facility's energy coordinator informed of approaching deadlines.

➤ Meeting personally at least once every 6 months with the plant manager, building engineer, and energy coordinator of each facility. (Nothing beats personal contact!)

In addition, my annual plan for NFC's Energy Conservation Program has been enthusiastically approved each year by NFC's Director.

Results: Under my leadership, during the last 2 years, NFC's Energy Conservation Program has:

➤ Saved well over a $1 million dollars in energy costs.

➤ Reduced energy consumption by more than 2 million BTU per year.

➤ Won two annual Department of Energy Water Management Awards. No other federal agency has ever won this award 2 years in a row.

External Customers

Managing the NFC's Energy Conservation Program requires interacting with:

➤ Energy conservation experts at the Department of Energy. I participate in several DOE sponsored working groups, such as the Utility Partnership Working Group.

➤ Energy experts at monthly meetings of the Interagency Task Force on Energy Conservation.

➤ Representatives of utility companies with whom I negotiate utility contracts.

Results: Evidence of my ability to effectively represent NFC includes my record in saving NFC more than $50,000 per year in negotiated utility contracts and managing the completion of five contract energy conservation projects on time and within budget during 2006.

Notice how this essay's first "Results" section quantifies and takes credit for accolades received by the employer, and the second "Results" section cites the applicant's record in completing projects on time and on budget—both excellent strategies.

Example Essay #5

Essay for Chief Financial Officer position: Describe your problem-solving skills.

In January 2006, immediately after I became Chief Financial Officer of Global Electronics Corp.—an electronics distributor with annual earnings of more than $50 million—the company's CEO laid down the gauntlet by instructing me to "produce faster, more comprehensive, and cleaner financial analyses than Global Electronics has ever produced before."

Achievement #1: Fast Financial Analyses

Global Electronics has historically updated its financial statements and closed its books about 19 days after the end of each financial reporting period. (Each fiscal year has 14 reporting periods.) Under my leadership, the Office of the Chief Financial Officer (OCFO)—which includes 10 Accountants and 10 Financial Planners—sped the processing of the company's financial statements by:

➤ Consolidating over 150 expense accounts into 50 accounts, and thereby reducing opportunities for reporting errors from these accounts

➤ Providing training in automating accounting data to all 30 of Global Electronics Accountants

➤ Grading each of Global Electronics' 15 offices on the accuracy of its accounting data, and providing intensive guidance to offices that earned low grades

As a result of these activities, Global Electronics closed its books within 3 days of the close of the financial reporting period in January 2007. This was the company's the first 3-day close in the company's 20-year history. Global Electronics has closed out every subsequent reporting period with similar timeliness.

Achievement #2: Comprehensive Financial Analyses

Under my direction, OCFO initiated the production of new comprehensive reports of the company's financial/operational performance at the end of each financial reporting period. These reports include features such as comparisons of actual financial activity vs. planned activity for individual offices as well as for the entire company.

By posting these reports on the company's Intranet, OCFO allows all company managers—from the highest level executives to front-line managers—to easily access the same financial information at the same time. My office thereby promotes consistent and informed decision-making throughout the company as well as more proactive, agile decision-making than had been possible before. For example, during FY 2007, OCFO's financial reports supported precedent-setting midquarter adjustments to spending that accommodated fast-changing economic conditions.

Achievement #3: Clean Financial Analyses

During each of the 2 years in which I have served as CFO, Global Electronics' financial statements have been approved by its independent auditors. By contrast, the company had never before received unqualified opinions from its auditors for 2 consecutive years.

Education

I earned a B.A. in Accounting from the University of Colorado, and a Master's in Business Administration from the University of Chicago.

This essay opens with an attention-getting lead and then cites several impressive "firsts," which just goes to show that even those of us who lead tamer lives than Edmund Hillary and Tenzing Norgay—the first climbers up Mt. Everest—can take credit for pioneering some admirable "firsts" (without getting altitude sickness).

Example Essay #6

Essay for Program Manager position: Describe your ability to work in teams.

What Makes an Effective Team?

An effective team is more than just a group. It is group of professionals who each take the initiative, transcend rigid divisions-of-labor to advise and help one another conquer glitches, work doggedly and jointly to pursue a common goal, and then share the credit for their joint achievement. Of course, a natural simpatico and shared sense of humor among team members can also help grease the wheels within any working work.

Example Team Project

As the Special Assistant to the Assistant Secretary of Labor, I served as one of three organizers of the Mine Safety and Health Administration's celebration in 2006 commemorating the 30th anniversary of passage of the Mine Safety and Health Act. (This law was among the most important worker safety laws ever passed.) We were given a mere 2 months to organize this historic event, which was attended by more than 500 miners, widows of miners, mine operators, union representatives, state and federal regulators, and reporters.

Our planning of this event involved:

➤ Selecting and inviting speakers, and advising speakers on what topics to cover in their talks. We infused the event with a human touch of by including on the speakers list several miners' widows.

➤ Generating an invitation list of more than 500 of the major players in the mine safety field.

➤ Designing the event's program brochure, which reviewed the history of mine safety and featured eye-catching photos of miners. We also managed the $20,000 printing contract for production of the brochure.

> ➤ Constructing event displays, which included photographs, narrative texts, and historical objects.

> ➤ Addressing a myriad of logistical challenges, including managing the event's limited budget, finding and reserving a suitable meeting hall, and negotiating catering.

The two other event co-organizers and I met our tight deadline by demonstrating the principles of effective teamwork: We collaborated on each aspect of the project, kept one other informed of the progress of all tasks, and helped one another work through a myriad of logistical snags, such as computer programs that crashed at inconvenient times and speakers whose travel arrangements became problematic. In addition, each member of the event planning team carried more than his/her fair share of the load by working until at least 10:00 P.M. every workday and every weekend during the month before the event. Nevertheless, because all team members maintained good cheer throughout the high-pressure planning process, we maintained a productive esprit de corps.

Results: Evidence of my team's success included:

> ➤ Positive coverage of the event in trade publications. For example, the event was described in Mining Today as an "evocative, moving tribute," and in Worker Safety as "a lively history lesson."

> ➤ The heart-felt standing ovations given to many of the speakers that were selected by the event organizing tine.

> ➤ A $1,000 Team Award that was given to each team member.

If you are asked about your teamwork in essay or interview question, include in your response—as this applicant did—any team awards that you have won.

Example Essay #7

Essay for Office Manager position: Describe how you have demonstrated creativity.

Background

I became the Director of the Office of Information Technology (OIT) of the National Regulatory Institute (NRI) on October 1, 1999—only 3 months before the Y2K showdown of January 1, 2000. Talk about having to hit the ground running!

Without a moment to lose as the day of reckoning approached, I dove head-first into Y2K preparations on my first day on the job. And there was much to do. Like many other government organizations, NRI had received harsh criticism from the Government Accountability Office (GAO) because of its inadequate Y2K preparations. Moreover, most of OIT's 20-person staff lacked any recognition of the importance of systematically planning for Y2K.

Actions

I put NRI's Y2K preparations on a fast track by:

➤ Arranging for all of OIT staffers to receive immediate 2-day training on the importance of Y2K planning, which reviewed preparation strategies adopted by Fortune 500 companies.

➤ Directing the cataloguing of more than 5,000 hardware items and 300 software applications used at NRI. This action was necessary because NRI's documentation of its systems was outdated.

➤ Working with NRI's Office of Procurement to hire a contractor to test, modify, and then certify NRI's systems as Y2K compliant, and then working with this contractor as it completed these tasks.

➤ Managing the development of IRD's first Business Continuity Contingency Plan, which provided comprehensive analyses of the potential impacts of various types of system failures on all of NRI's operations, and developing IRD's first Disaster Recovery Plan for restarting operations after experiencing system failures.

➤ Preparing OIT's staff to implement our Disaster Recovery Plan.

➤ Creating a temporary command center at which the OIT staff monitored critical systems and coordinated activities with NRI's five field sites, as the clock rounded midnight on December 31, 1999.

Results

Most importantly, under my leadership, OIT's Y2K preparations ensured that NRI's Information Technology systems experienced zero system failures on January 1, 2000. Moreover, the Business Contingency Plan and Disaster Recovery Plan that my staff developed in less than 3 months has been incorporated into NRI's contingency planning for terrorist attacks.

The writer of this essay promises to fulfill every employer's desire to hire an employee who can take charge from their first day on the job without needing coddling or hand-holding. This story's appeal is enhanced by its description of a high-impact problem (Y2K) that everyone can remember. The real-life version of this essay helped its writer land a job in the senior executive service.

Example Essay #8

Essay for Program Manager position: Describe how you have demonstrated creativity.

Background

Recent budget cuts have forced me—like many managers—to find ways to do more with less. As the Director of the National Center for Strategic Development (NCSD), I enhanced the productivity of my 50-person office despite a 10 percent budget cut since 2005.

My Actions

Here is a sample of the innovative programs that I adopted during FY 2006:

➤ Initiated a formal program for soliciting anonymous employee suggestions. Employee suggestions submitted through this program inspired NCSD to develop a new monthly employee newsletter and to offer flexible work schedules to employees.

➤ Purchased and implemented an automated e-learning system that enables every employee to receive training in diverse topics such as communicating, negotiating, accounting, database management, and web development on their computers. This system has enabled NCSD to provide more training to more employees while slashing its training budget by 20 percent per year. This program has also enhanced NCSD's ability to provide cross-training to employees so that they can be transferred to the areas in which they are most needed.

➤ Issued an agency-wide directive to increase the use of incentives-based service contracts. This type of contract benefits NCSD because they are designed to encourage contractors to exceed minimum requirements on timeliness and quality. Because of my directive, during FY 2003, 70 percent of our performance based contracts were incentives based, compared to 10 percent in FY 2002.

➤ Developed a program for rewarding high-performing employees by giving them extra days off.

➤ Developed a telecommuting program for high-performers. This program serves as a low-cost incentives program and has allowed NCSD to reduce office space by 10 percent, and thereby save $2 million per year.

Results

These innovative programs:

➤ Are currently producing a gross savings for NCSD of $5 million per year.

➤ Helped increase scores on our yearly employee satisfaction surveys by an average of 20 percent.

➤ Enabled NCSD to avoid a lay-off during FY 2003 that would have otherwise been necessary.

These results prove that, contrary to popular belief, smart innovations don't need to break the bank. In fact, they can benefit the bank.

Many applicants are intimidated by essay or interview questions about "creativity" because they wrongly believe that they are expected to reel off accomplishments that would be worthy of Leonardo da Vinci. Not so. The "creativity" question usually means exactly the same thing as the question, "Explain how you have demonstrated that you think outside of the box." The essay answer provided here conveys a trait that every hiring manager wants: the ability to, like an alchemist, spin gold out of metal . . . or, at least, stretch the metal.

Example Essay #9

Essay for Writer/Editor position: Describe your communication skills.

I am a jack-of-all-trades communications expert who can produce varied documents for varied audiences. For example, I have prepared:

➤ **TECHNICAL MANUALS:** As a technical writer at Environmental Systems Research Institute from 1995 to 2000, I wrote four user manuals for computer mapping systems. Production of each manual required acquiring mastery of the associated software program, explaining its use in easy-to-understand instructions, and then meticulously testing these instructions for accuracy and usability. Each manual was distributed to more than 10,000 system users.

➤ **PRESS RELEASES:** As a communications officer at the Securities and Exchange Commission since 2000, I have written approximately 50 easy-to-understand press releases on complex issues involving corporate fraud, insider trading, and tax policy. Please note these comments from my supervisor on my latest performance evaluation:

"What did we do before Nancy worked at this office? This oft-used phrase aptly describes how valuable Nancy is to this office. Multiskilled, she brings unwavering energy and professionalism to an office that requires both in spades."

➤ **ARTICLES FOR THE POPULAR PRESS:** I have published more than 20 articles in national magazines and flight magazines on varied topics including energy and environmental issues, corporate finance, and personal investing. Because of the high quality of my articles and my ability to meet tight deadlines, my editors often asked me to submit additional articles. (See the attached list of my publications.)

➤ ORAL PRESENTATIONS:

➤ I have delivered presentations at the National Institutes of Health's (NIH) annual meeting in Bethesda, Maryland, on science communication every year since 1995. (NIH keeps asking me back because of the positive evaluations that my presentations have generated from meeting participants.) My NIH presentations—spiced with lively, humorous anecdotes—provide practical instruction in how to convey technical and scientific information in plain English. Each of my presentations has drawn about 200 professional communicators and government scientists.

➤ As a Program Analyst at the Environmental Protection Agency from 1998 to 2000, I delivered presentations on Clean Air Act requirements to members of the regulated community, which included some hostile audiences. These assignments tested my persuasive powers as well as my ability for quick thinking, maintaining grace under pressure, and anticipating audience questions.

➤ I have been a volunteer at the National Zoo since 1998. In this position, I spend one weekend afternoon per month presenting lectures that mix entertaining and factual information about wildlife to large crowds of visitors.

➤ I am an expert in using PowerPoint.

Education

I earned a B.A. in English Literature and an M.A. in Journalism with Distinction from Columbia University.

If you have provided stories in several of your essays, it is fine to provide one or two essays that do not tell stories. This is a good example of a nonstory essay that is nevertheless impressive and interesting because it is well organized with headings, cites specific examples, incorporates an attention-getting quote, quantifies achievements, and reflects a body of accomplishments.

Example Essay #10

Essay for Policy Analyst position: Describe your communication skills.

Eric Schrodinger, a Nobel Prize winner in physics, said: "If you cannot—in the long run—tell everyone what you have been doing, your doing has been worthless." As a scientist I share Schordinger's respect for the importance of communication skills. So while I earned a B.A. in biology from the University of Massachusetts, I participated in various academic and nonacademic activities that improved my writing and speaking skills.

Writing Skills

I demonstrated my effective writing skills by:

➤ Completing a three-credit independent project on the effects of growing deer populations and urbanization on Lyme disease in Massachusetts. This project involved summarizing the current literature; interviewing 15 wildlife biologists, epidemiologists, and urban planners; documenting an increase in Lyme disease in 3 counties over the last 20 years from state records; and synthesizing this information into a 30-page report. I earned an A- on this project. In addition, my advisor repeatedly complemented my ability to strategically balance the need to work with minimal supervision against the need to solicit guidance as appropriate.

➤ Earning a B+ in English Composition and Advanced English Literature during my junior year.

➤ Writing a five-page report on the ecology of the Hudson River as an Intern at the Office of Technology Assessment (OTA) during the summer of 2006. Because of the logic, conciseness, and accuracy of my writing, my supervisor, the Director of Natural Resources Programs, approved my report with few substantial edits and offered me a position for the summer of 2007.

Speaking Skills

I demonstrated my effective speaking skills by:

➤ Giving a 90-minute presentation on Elephant Ecology to my Wildlife Biology class. Completing this project required determining the structure of my presentation; becoming an expert in elephant ecology by scouring the literature; delivering a lively and informative presentation; designing reader-friendly PowerPoint slides; and answering 20 minutes of questions from students. My professor described my presentation as "a tour-de-force."

➤ Providing 2 hours of one-on-one tutoring per week to freshmen taking Introductory Biology during my senior year.

➤ Serving as co-captain of the varsity basketball team during my junior and senior years. In this leadership role, I often contributed to decisions on team management, coached team members, and counseled them on their personal problems.

This essay by a recent college grad builds a compelling case by citing coursework, grades, summer jobs, and extracurriculars.

MY GOAL AND WHY IT WAS IMPORTANT TO MY ORGANIZATION:

_____
_____
_____
_____
_____

MY ACTIONS TO ACHIEVE MY GOAL:

_____
_____
_____
_____
_____

SPECIAL OBSTACLES I CONQUERED, IF ANY:

_____
_____
_____
_____
_____

MY RESULTS:

_____
_____
_____
_____
_____

POSITIVE FEEDBACK, IF ANY:

_____
_____
_____
_____
_____

Figure 10-1. Worksheet for telling success stories. A worksheet similar to this one is included for your use in the CD and website accompanying this book.

CHAPTER **11**

Cover Letters That Open Doors

"You will automatically beat out 95 percent of your competition if you submit an error-free cover letter that concisely describes how you meet the requirements of the opening."

—A FEDERAL HIRING MANAGER

... AND THE LAST SHALL BE FIRST

Even though an effective cover letter is key to making a good first impression with potential employers, most job seekers thoughtlessly dash off their cover letter in the last minute. Whether your cover letter is the first or last step of your application preparation, devote enough time to it to create a first-rate document.

Your cover letter will probably be the first part of your application that hiring managers will read. What's more, your cover letter may be the only part of your application that hiring managers will *really* read.

Why? Because while many hiring managers only skim page after page of federal résumés and application essays, virtually all of them read one-page cover letters from top to bottom.

A skillfully crafted cover letter will get your potential employers panting with anticipation for the next page of your application and thereby kick open opportunities. Conversely, a flawed cover letter can get your application kicked out of the competition before it really has even begun.

And even though federal job applications never require cover letters, naked applications lacking cover letters stand out for all of the wrong reasons; they might as well have the words, "I don't care enough about getting this damned job to write a cover letter," written across the top of them.

In addition to introducing your applications, your cover letters will also play an important role in your networking campaign; as you meet key contacts and potential employers, they will invariably ask you to send them your résumé, which of course, should be introduced with a cover letter or cover e-mail.

But despite the potential make-or-break importance of effective cover letters, many job seekers completely omit them from their applications. Others submit typo-tarnished, long-winded cover letters that are the written equivalents of A&E Biographies, or terse cover letters that reveal only about as much information as a captured soldier may disclose to the enemy: name, rank, and serial number; neither of these strategies makes a compelling sales pitch.

In this chapter, you will learn about the multifaceted powers of cover letters, review sample effective cover letters, and learn how to write first-rate cover letters that will help you make a great first impression.

Cover Me: I'm Going In

Use your cover letter to:

➤ Introduce yourself: identify your current title and target job.

➤ Concisely summarize your most relevant educational and professional credentials: use bullets to encourage a fast read.

➤ Showcase knowledge of your target organization: explain why your target agency provides particular appeal and complement your target agent's recent achievements, if possible.

➤ Serve as an impressive writing sample: a skillfully formatted, well-written cover letter will provide tangible evidence of your communication skills.

> ➤ Convey enthusiasm and zest.

> ➤ Name a contact in your target organization who can vouch for you, if possible. Such name-dropping will help confirm your credentials as the zero-risk applicant.

> ➤ One more thing: state that you're applying for a noncompetitive appointment, if you're doing so.

Scoping Out Your Target Agency

Your target agency probably fills its openings with applicants who are passionate about the agency and the issues it addresses. Why? Because, hiring managers believe that employees work hardest and put their hearts and souls into what they are passionate about. In other words, they believe that applicants who show fire in the belly for their organization will turn out to be loyal, self-motivated, go-getters.

How can you prove that you are passionate about your target agency and its mission? By demonstrating your knowledge of your target agency in your application and interviews.

Remember that government organizations are as different from one another as are private companies. So in order to convey knowledge of your target organization's programs, goals, hot-button issues, achievements, and culture, you must research your target organization. Start your research by debriefing any of your target agency's employees who may lurk within your network. Also use the following free online resources to become an expert on your target agency:

> ➤ Your target organization's website. This is absolutely **required reading** for applying and interviewing for any job in a federal agency or Congress. Pay particular attention to your target organization's press releases, annual reports, and strategic plan.

> ➤ The websites of national newspapers, particularly *The Washington Post*. Also do keyword searches of your target organization on the websites of *Federal Times*, *Government Executive*, *The Hill*, *Roll Call*, *Federal Computer Week*, *Government Computer News*, and *FedSmith.com*. Such media research is important because, unlike private sector organizations, most federal agencies are frequently covered in the news.

> ➤ Scorecards of agency performance at http://www.whitehouse.gov/results/.

> ➤ The annual survey and agency profiles at http://bestplacestowork.org/BPTW/about/.

> ➤ The literature search function of your public library's website, which allows you to retrieve articles from magazines and newspapers from any computer for free. To conduct such searches, you need only provide a valid library card number.

> ➤ *Washingtonian* magazine's "Best Places to Work" issues, which appear every other year in the fall.

Cover Letter Tone

Your cover letter should convey a friendly, energetic, and efficient tone. And like all of your other application documents, it should prove that you care about your target organization by addressing its needs. Remember: hiring managers are only concerned about what you offer them and how you would solve their problems—not about what you want from them or their target opening.

Show that you care about your target agency by citing your knowledge of its recent accomplishments and by using terms like "offer" and "contribute" rather than phrases like "this would be a fantastic opportunity for me."

Outline of Effective Cover Letter

Your Address
City, State ZIP
Date

Name of Contact Person
Contact Person's Title
Name of Agency
Address
City, State ZIP   RE: Name and number of job opening

Dear Name of Contact Person:

OPENER: *An energetic, concise introduction of who you are, and how you would advance your target organization's mission. Cite one of your target organization's recent achievements, if possible.*

MIDDLE: *Several concise bullets of employer-centered information on your achievements/skills.*

CONCLUSION: *Thanks and look forward to hearing from you.*

Sincerely,

Your Name

Enclosures: Résumé and KSAs (if applicable).

> Notice how concise and to the point this format is. Also notice how space is saved by the "RE" and "Enclosures" lines that eliminate the need to provide this information in full sentences.

Cover Letter Dissection

The Salutation

Address your cover letter to the contact name on the vacancy announcement for the opening. Be sure to spell names correctly. If the contact person's first name is gender neutral (such as Terry or Sandy), call the contact to determine whether to address him/her as Mr. or Ms. If a contact person is not listed on the vacancy announcement, call the Human Resources office of the hiring agency to identify the proper recipient of your application. Alternatively, open your cover letter with "Dear Hiring Manager" or "Good Morning" rather than the impersonal "To Whom It May Concern" or the sexist "Dear Sirs."

The Opener

Purge clichéd phrases from your application, such as:

➤ Enclosed please find my application. (*snooze . . .*)

➤ Please accept the enclosed application. (*yawn . . .*)

➤ I am contacting you in order to . . . (*snore . . .*)

➤ I am interested in . . . (*someone get some defibrillator paddles to resuscitate this application!*)

➤ I am forwarding the enclosed résumé for your consideration . . . (*wake me up when you say something different from your dozens of competitors!*)

Instead of using a clichéd opener, use an energetic opener that demonstrates your knowledge of the agency and explains how you would contribute to your target organization's success. Also, be sure to identify your title right off the bat. For example:

➤ Congratulations to the General Services Administration (GSA) for excelling in the "teamwork" category on GSA's annual employee satisfaction survey. As a logistics expert and a veteran of several award-winning workgroups, I share GSA's team-friendly work ethic. Please consider me for the logistics specialist opening.

➤ As a contract manager with an MBA and 5 years of experience in innovative contract management, I am qualified to contribute to EPA's efforts to streamline procurement procedures, which were recently covered in *Fast Company*.

➤ I couldn't be more excited about the recent announcement that NASA will return to the Moon. I would welcome the opportunity to support NASA's many dynamic programs with my top-notch skills as an Administrative Assistant.

Alternatively, if you cannot cite any relevant information about the hiring agency, simply state your credentials:

➤ My qualifications match the qualifications that you seek for senior attorney. I am currently a senior attorney with Smith & Westlock, the largest firm in South Dakota.

➤ As an information technology analyst, I specialize in improving the efficiency of large networks used by federal agencies like yours.

➤ Does XYZ agency want to get more for less on its contracts? If so, I can help because I saved ABC agency $500,000 on its supply contracts last year as a procurement specialist at ABC. My credentials also include . . .

One *avant-garde* method of revving-up a cover letter is to begin with a memorable quote either about success, problem-solving, efficiency, or another topic relevant to the opening. You can obtain relevant quotes from "Googling" keywords like *quotations*, together with words like *goals*, *business*, and *success*.

Middle Paragraphs

➤ Emphasize your most relevant qualifications; do not repeat your entire résumé.

➤ Address each knowledge, skills, and abilities (KSA) question with a one-sentence bullet, if possible. Why? Because these questions identify the credentials sought by the hiring agency. By proving that you have those credentials right when you introduce yourself, you will immediately impress the agency's hiring managers.

Purge your cover letter of presumptuous statements, such as, "I know you will find that I am a perfect match for the position." Instead, describe how your credentials match the requirements of the opening, and let hiring managers decide for themselves that you're a perfect match for the position.

➤ Use the techniques discussed in Chapter 7 to describe your achievements. Do not provide job descriptions that describe duties and responsibilities.

➤ State whether you have veterans' preference or whether you want to be considered for a noncompetitive appointment.

➤ Explain any special situations presented by your application, such as your willingness to relocate or the 5-year gap in your work experience, which you spent caring for a sick relative. (Federal applications don't require coverage of credentials that are older than 10 years, so ignore gaps that are older than that.)

➤ Use active and conversational words rather than stilted, pompous, and bureaucratic words.

HOT TIP

If You Have Your Own Website . . .

If you have your own website that showcases skills relevant to your target opening, consider directing hiring mangers to it in your cover letter.

Last Paragraph: Au Revoir

➤ Identify the best way for you to be contacted. If your phone numbers and e-mail address are not on your letterhead, provide them in your closing.

➤ Express thanks for being considered.

Formatting and Length

➤ A cover letter should never exceed one page.

➤ Create a layout that is visually appealing and open. Margins should be 1.25 inches wide.

➤ Draw attention to your skills by using bold, bullets, indented margins, and columns.

Save Time and Space

➢ Identify your target opening in a "RE:" line of a paper application or in the subject line of an e-mailed application.

➢ Identify enclosures in an "Enclosures" line of a paper application.

➢ Add a P.S. to emphasize an important fact, observation, or credential. Why? Because studies show that a P.S. is the most read part of a letter. That's why so many fundraising letters include part of their pitches in a P.S.

Proofreading

Proofread your cover letter fastidiously. Indeed, most hiring managers say that typos in an application can kill an applicant's chances. And a typo that appears in a cover letter will invariably look as big as a barn! Proofread your cover letter by:

➢ Spell checking it. But don't rely solely on spell checkers, which cannot recognize all mistakes. For example, spell checkers won't flag words that should be capitalized or tell you if you used the word "their" instead of "there."

➢ Printing out your letter. You will find awkward passages and errors in paper copies of documents that you would miss on the screen. It is particularly important to print out e-mails. Never send an e-mail to a potential employer without first proofreading a paper copy of it.

➢ Reading your letter out loud.

➢ Asking yourself why your sentences are sequenced in their current order. If you don't have a good reason, your document is probably not logically organized, so rethink it.

➢ Getting distance from your letter, and then reading it again. If you are tight on time, let your letter go cold by doing something else—such as watering your plants—for a few minutes and then returning to your letter. Even a few minutes away from your letter will increase your objectivity and help you find mistakes in it.

➢ Soliciting objective, honest feedback on your letter from trusted advisors.

Figures 11-1 to 11-5 are examples of cover letters.

CAUTION
Don't Use Your Current Employer's Stationary

If you're a current fed, don't use the stationary or envelopes of your current employer to communicate with target employers. Doing so is a flagrant violation of federal regulations and will almost certainly trigger a rejection. Also, conduct your job search from your home e-mail account rather than from your employer's account.

CAUTION
Know Thy Reader

An application that was churned out on an assembly line without being tailored to the hiring agency usually gives itself away sooner rather than later. For example, I have seen many cover letters submitted to federal agencies that—believe it or not—profess the applicant's desire to "work for a company like yours," or work for a nonprofit company.

As one hiring manager explained, "If an applicant is that careless on a job application—something that he or she really cares about, that is in his or her direct interest, when they are supposed to be putting their best foot forward—I wouldn't trust them to work on projects that are not directly tied to their self-interest."

1234 Yellow Brick Road
City, State, Zip Code
January 31, 2008

Mr. Frank Howard
Personnel Analyst
US Mint
801 9th Street NW
Washington DC 20220

Dear Mr. Howard:

Subject: Marketing Manager Position (#08-65-59)

As a Marketing Manager at Wal-mart since 2002, I have been tracking the Mint's record-breaking sales successes. I would like to work to help the Mint increase its sales even further.

A synopsis of my credentials:

YOUR NEEDS	MY CREDENTIALS
Knowledge of business principles	Five years of experience as Marketing Manager at Wal-mart, and a B.A. in Business Administration from University of Maryland.
Computer proficiency	Expert in using PC Lotus, Ledger, Excel, PeopleSoft, PowerPoint, Word, and various web creation programs.
Negotiating skills	Saved Walmart $500,000 since 2000 by negotiating pricing of advertising. Completed training courses in negotiating.
Communication skills	Experienced in creating PowerPoint presentations summarizing monthly marketing trends for senior managers.

I am eager to speak with you about the Marketing Manager position. My telephone numbers are (123) 123-4567(w) and (012) 123-4567(h), and my e-mail address is Jones@e-mail.com. I sincerely appreciate your time and consideration.

Sincerely,

Trudy Jones

Enclosure: Resume and KSAs

Figure 11-1. What's not to love about this letter? The opener demonstrates knowledge of the organization. But even more importantly, the letter's table broadcasts the applicant's suitability for the opening—even to hiring managers who may only skim the letter. This memorable formatting is guaranteed to stand out from the pack. Directions for creating tables are included in Appendix 3: Formatting Tips. If you use this format, craft the "Your Needs" column to capture the requirements of the opening. If you don't fulfill some of the requirements of the opening, omit them.

1234 Yellow Brick Road
City, State ZIP Code
August 1, 2008

Ms. Jackie Harper
Personnel Officer
Office of Human Resources
Office of Management and Budget
4201 Wilson Boulevard
Arlington, Virginia 22230

RE: Project Management Position (111-PM-45)

Dear Ms. Jackie Harper:

Congratulations to the Office of Management and Budget (OMB) for winning the 2008 Presidential Award for Management Excellence! As a recent college graduate who is knowledgeable about the latest performance-based management techniques, I would like to join OMB's staff as a project manager.

My qualifications include:

- **A BA In Business Administration from Northwestern University.**

- **Polished communication skills:** All of my classes in my major required papers or oral presentations. My GPA in my major was 3.50, and I graduated with Departmental Honors in my major.

- **A proven record as a self-starter and team-player:** As an undergraduate, I juggled a heavy academic course-load along with a 15 hour-per-week campus job and my responsibilities as co-captain of the lacrosse team.

I would be happy to provide any additional information about my background that might be helpful. I will be moving to the Washington DC area within the next two months. I can be reached on my cell phone at (012) 123-4567 before or after I move to Washington DC. My e-mail address is Linda.Watson@e-mail.com. Many thanks for your consideration, and I hope to hear from you soon.

Sincerely,

Linda Watson

Enclosures: Resume and KSAs

Figure 11-2. An exemplary letter from a recent graduate. Notice how the applicant demonstrates knowledge of the National Science Foundation by referring to its recent management award, which was posted on results.gov. The applicant also cites her own grades as objective validation of her skills and mentions her extracurricular activities as evidence of her work ethic and team-friendly credentials.

LINDA WATSON
1234 Yellow Brick Road
City, State ZIP Code
Phone: (123) 123-4567 (w); (012) 123-4567 (h)
E-Mail: Linda.Watson@e-mail.com

January 31, 2008

Ms. Jackie Harper
Personnel Officer
Office of Human Resources
U.S. Fish and Wildlife Service
3345 Wilson Blvd.
Arlington, VA
20456

Dear Ms. Harper:

My qualifications match those of the "multitalented Webmaster" that you seek (Position 123-WM-789). My credentials include:

- Seven years of experience as a Webmaster at EPA designing and updating high-traffic websites that broadcast scientific information in engaging screen formats.

- A solid record of earning superior performance evaluations throughout my career.

- An M.S. in Systems Administration from the University of Colorado.

- A B.A. in Graphic Arts from the University of Colorado.

I would also bring to the position my lifelong passion for conservation, which is reflected in all of my work experience, and my hobbies, which include bird watching and reading publications such as *Wildlife Conservation* and *National Geographic*.

Attached is my resume and KSAs. I would appreciate the opportunity to discuss the position with you further and show you my portfolio of web pages. Thank you for your time and consideration.

Sincerely,

Linda Watson

P.S.   Congratulations on the favorable write-up of the Fish and Wildlife Service in last month's issue of *Government Executive*!

Figure 11-3. This letter is enlivened by the applicant's mention of her lifelong passions which relate to the writer's target job and the clever use of an attention-grabbing P.S.

SALLY BAKER

1234 Yellow Brick Road   •   City, State ZIP Code   •   123-123-4567

Mr. John McCarthy   December 15, 2008
Personnel Analyst
Small Business Administration
Two Gateway Center
Newark, NJ 07102
                                    RE: Administrative Assistant (XX-AA-123)

Dear Mr. McCarthy:

PROBLEMS CANNOT BE SOLVED AT THE SAME LEVEL OF AWARENESS THAT CREATED THEM.
                — ALBERT EINSTEIN

As an Administrative Assistant at Verizon, I continually strive — in the spirit of Albert Einstein's philosophy — to master new software and people skills that improve office organization. At Verizon, I am known as "the office fixer" and "the event fixer." I could similarly smooth the operations of your office.

I am an expert in:

- Organizing large events attended by dozens of high-level officials, including CEOs of telecommunications companies.

- Managing the busy schedules of executives using the latest e-mail, electronic calendar, and palm pilot software.

- Arranging conference calls and virtual meetings.

- Shepherding high-profile documents through the approval process.

- Establishing and maintaining electronic filing systems for easy retrieval. For example, during a pivotal point in my supervisor's recent contract negotiations with a contractor, I quickly retrieved an urgently needed legal document that compelled the contractor to agree to contract terms that saved Verizon $50,000.

I am methodical enough to comprehensively plan events and projects, and flexible enough to calmly confront the unexpected.

I would be happy to meet with you to discuss your needs and my skills further. Please call me at the phone number on my letterhead, or e-mail me at Sally.Baker@e-mail.com. I do appreciate your consideration.

Sincerely,

Sally Baker

Enclosures: Resume and KSAs

Figure 11-4. Effective use of the quote method. Notice how this applicant has skillfully tied the quote into her own on-the-job approach. Also notice how this applicant's credentials are crafted to sound impressive even without mention of awards or performance evaluations.

1234 Yellowbrick Road
Anywhere, USA
E-Mail: SSuccess@e-mail.com
December 1, 2007

Mr. Jayson MucketyMuck
Director of the Office of Executives
US Department of Energy
1000 BigWig Avenue
Washington DC 20008

Hello Mr. Jayson:

Thank you for requesting more information about my background. As we recently discussed, I am eager to contribute my communication skills and environmental background to Federal Energy Regulatory Commission's important work securing the US's energy security.

As a federal communications expert and freelance writer, I offer special expertise in conveying technical information in easy-to-understand language, pitching stories to the press, advising political appointees on sensitive issues, producing high-impact documents, and leading trainings on communication skills.

My credentials include:

☐ **A life-long passion for environmental and public health issues.** I have a Master of Public Health and a Master of Environmental Management from Yale University. Also, dozens of my articles have appeared in popular publications, such as *Audubon*, *National Parks,* and three environmental law reviews.

☐ **Fifteen years of experience promoting the achievements of high-profile agencies, including the Labor Department and EPA.** I offer a solid track record of earning positive press coverage for my employers in national media outlets; defending agency positions; and writing Congressional testimony, annual reports, speeches, talking points, and easy-to-read fact sheets and web documents.

☐ **Skill in working with editors in high-pressure, deadline-driven environments.** I have contributed to *The Washington Post*, WashingtonPost.com, flight magazines and law reviews.

☐ **Experience as a communications trainer/mentor.** I have delivered seminars on communication skills to The Council of Editors, The National Institutes of Health, and other organizations.

I would, of course, be happy to follow-up in any way that you might suggest. I will call you soon to discuss any leads you might have.

Thanks very much for your time and consideration.

Sincerely,

Susan Success

Attachments: Resume and list of publications.

Figure 11-5. This cover letter was successfully used to pursue a networking contact—not to apply for a specific opening. It quickly hits the applicant's high notes, effectively uses bullets, and warns the recipient of the sender's impending follow-up. When your networking contacts ask you to send your résumé and/or a concise summary of your credentials, do so immediately. Your speed and efficiency will testify to your efficiency and encourage your networking contact to similarly act quickly on your behalf. Also, if appropriate, accompany your networking letters with several relevant work products that showcase your skills, as covered in "Prepare to Give the Portfolio Treatment" in Chapter 13.

CHAPTER **12**

Waiting for a Response
to Your Application

"Between the wish and the thing lies waiting."

—UNKNOWN

How Long Will the Wait Last?

Granted, the federal hiring system is generally not known for its need for speed. Nevertheless, it has—in recent years—greatly accelerated its selection processes. I know from my own experiences and those of my clients that more and more agencies are meeting or beating new guidelines to complete each selection within 45 days of its closing date, which is comparable to the private sector.

An example of federal efficiency: I recently received an e-mail confirming that I ranked among the "best-qualified applicants" for a Labor Department opening the very same day that it closed, and then was invited to interview for the job 2 weeks after that. Nevertheless, some agencies still frequently miss the 45-day deadline, and so selection times vary from agency to agency.

Getting Status Updates

Once you have thrown your hat into the ring and submitted your application for a federal job, how can you track your application through the selection process?

Many agencies provide applicants with updates (either by e-mail or on password protected websites) confirming submission of their applications, informing them whether they qualified as a best-qualified applicant, and then telling them after a final selection has been made—whether or not they were selected. Check such confirmations carefully and immediately contact your target job's contact person if you identify a problem.

Communicating with the Silent Type

Unfortunately, some agencies do not communicate with applicants at all during the selection process. Believe it or not, some agencies don't even send out rejection e-mails. If your target agency is the silent type or if you have questions about your application, here's what you should do:

If more than 3 weeks have passed since your target job's closing date, call the agency contact person identified on your target job's announcement, and ask him/her if your application rated among the best-qualified applicants or, in government lingo, "made the cert." If not, ask how high you scored. The resulting feedback you receive may help you determine whether your application strategy is on the right track or warrants an overhaul.

Don't be shy about calling agency contacts: I have personally contacted many of them and I assure you that these staffers are generally very obliging and helpful. Keep in mind that it is their job to answer applicants' questions. You're well within your rights to consult them and you won't alienate the hiring agency or damage your application in any way by inquiring about its status.

If more than 10 days to 2 weeks have elapsed since your interview, or the date your interviewer promised to make a decision has passed, call your interviewer, reaffirm your interest in the job, and politely ask when s/he expects to make a decision.

Even if such contact yields no helpful information, you may further your case by staying in touch with your interviewer. I know, for example, of one busy hiring manager who had totally forgotten about an opening he was filling until he received a polite request for an update from an applicant whom he had interviewed some weeks before. The result: he hired the applicant.

If the selection process drags out, occasionally call or e-mail your interviewer, but not too often. As one hiring manager observes, "There is a fine line between getting credit for being persistent and for getting a reputation for being a persistent pest."

Solicit Feedback

If you're notified that you've been rejected for your target job, call your interviewer and express thanks for having been considered, mention your interest in future openings, and ask for some honest feedback on your interviewing skills. After all, you've got nothing to lose by doing so. And for your bravery you may be rewarded with some suggestions that could help you nail your next interview.

Alternatively, you may be heartened to learn that the hiring decision turned on factors, such as veterans' preference, that were unrelated to your credentials. And it is even possible that your hiring manager may still help you land employment paydirt; I have heard of a number of instances where an interviewer was so impressed by a runner-up that s/he immediately helped that applicant land another current opening.

Establish a Rolodex Contact

If you've established a positive rapport with the selecting official (particularly if you sent him/her a post-interview thank-you letter) even if you weren't selected, occasionally touch base with the selecting official; s/he may provide you with future leads.

PART III

THE TALKING STAGE

Welcome to the home stretch of your job campaign: the talking stage—which includes interviewing, negotiating your salary, and responding to agency decisions. To get here, you skillfully created a written application that proved that you are a top-tier professional . . . the cream of the crop . . . a potential keeper. Now, at last, your paper chase is, for the most part, over.

Instead of hinging entirely on what you write, your ability to beat out your final few competitors and then convince hiring managers to give you a top salary will largely hinge on what you say and how you say it during, at most, a few short meetings. Do you feel the pressure build?

But no worries, as the Aussies say. This chapter and the cheat sheets on this book's CD will tell you everything you need to know to confidently, coolly, and compellingly talk yourself into your target job and target salary.

Like the preceding parts of this book, Part III features pivotal advice, available nowhere else, straight from federal hiring managers—the gatekeepers to federal jobs. I know that this advice can vault you ahead of the competition and raise your salary offer, because it has done so for hundreds of my clients.

CHAPTER **13**

Interviews That Nail the Job

"Forget gimmicks like echoing the body language of your interviewer. Any intelligent interviewer sees right through that. What I look for is evidence that the applicant understands my agency and its goals, and is going to work like the dickens."

—HOWARD HYMAN, FEDERAL HIRING MANAGER

Congratulations! The powers that be were so impressed by your written sales pitch that they have summoned you for an interview. This means that you probably beat out dozens, or even hundreds, of competitors to rank among the best and the brightest.

So go ahead, savor your victory, crank up the sound track of *Rocky*, and do some victory laps around your cube. But once the music stops, it's time to start preparing for your interview.

What Interviewers Want

What does your interviewer expect from you during your interview? Your interviewer wants to check that you look as good/qualified in person as you did on paper and to confirm that you're the zero-risk employee who:

➤ Will solve the organization's problem, not create more problems.

➤ Can do the target job well.

➤ Really wants to work there, cares about the organization, and is positive and upbeat. (Look ma, no cattle prodder!)

➤ Is mentally stable, reliable, team-friendly, and will fit with the organization's culture.

Remember that during the interview phase of the selection, you're competing against the cream of the crop; you and your competitors probably comprise the top 5 percent of the applicant pool. And because each of you is highly qualified and could probably do the target job well if given the chance, petty differences between you that would not matter one bit in other contexts may assume heightened importance during interviews.

"O.K., which cup is your job under now?"

Unfortunately, you only have one or maybe two relatively brief interviews to pull ahead of your highly qualified competitors and prove that you're the one percenter, the zero-risk applicant who deserves to be hired. To do so, aim to:

➤ Do everything better than your competitors during your interview(s).

➤ Milk every interview minute for all it's worth; devote all your interview time to proving that you're the one percenter, the zero-risk applicant; don't waste any time on irrelevant aspects of your background, such as what city you were born in or your latest basket-weaving coup or topics, like religion, that could alienate interviewers.

The best way to achieve these goals and beat your competition is to prepare more for your interview than your competition does. I promise you that most of your competition won't prepare for their interview at all; they will wing it and therefore risk crashing and burning. By contrast, if you prepare for your interview by using the techniques explained in this chapter, you will significantly improve your interview performance, and thereby significantly increase your chances of beating out your competition.

Interview

Research the Hiring Agency

I'll bet that you would rather form a personal relationship with someone who recognizes and appreciates your uniqueness than with someone who is obviously desperate to start a relationship with someone . . . anyone. Likewise, employers would rather form a professional relationship with an applicant who recognizes and appreciates their organization's uniqueness than one who is obviously desperate to land a job . . . any job.

In other words, if you saunter into your interview with the attitude of, "If it's Tuesday, it must be the Transportation Department," you will turn off interviewers. Instead, seize interview questions, such as "Why do you want to work here?" as invitations to describe your long-term passion for the issues addressed by your target organization and your understanding of how the organization works. Prepare to do so by following tips on researching federal agencies covered in Chapters 2 and 11, and by "Googling" your interviewer(s).

However, if your research reveals that the hiring agency is mired in scandal, or that your interviewer has been tainted by "youthful indiscretions," well . . . um . . . er . . . the less said about such unpleasantries, the better.

During a *Good Morning America* segment about job hunting, Diane Sawyer said: "I'm so surprised by the way a lot of kids come in to see me to talk about getting jobs . . . And I'm amazed how few of them have watched the shows they want to work on."

If you neglect to research your target organization before your interviews, you will come across as apathetic and unprepared as those hapless applicants to *Good Morning America*. But if, by contrast, you show your interviewers that you're knowledgeable about your target agency, you will prove that you care about it (whether or not you really do), and you will thereby win over your interviewers in a BIG way.

Craft Answers to Common Questions

"It usually takes more than three weeks to prepare a good impromptu speech."
—MARK TWAIN

Ironically, the more you prepare for interviews, the more spontaneous and articulate you will sound during interviews. You can craft winning answers to interview questions by:

➤ Rereading the description of your target job and your application. (You may be asked your KSA or ECQ questions again during the interview.)

➤ Researching your target agency.

➤ Listing your relevant credentials and success stories so that you can incorporate them into your answers. Review Chapter 7 for tips on how to convey your successes in impressive terms.

➤ Reviewing the rest of this chapter as well as the interview and application prep cheat sheets included on this book's CD.

➤ Preparing concise answers to the list of common interview questions provided on this book's CD. Federal hiring managers rely heavily on these common questions. Therefore, if you prepare for them, you will be prepared for most of your interview questions.

   A case in point: I recently rehearsed common interview questions with a college senior before she interviewed for a job as a policy analyst at EPA. After the interview, she said we had nailed over 80 percent of the interview questions. The result: she got the job.

➤ Remembering that you will only have a few brief minutes, at most, to answer each question during interviews and time zooms by when you are under pressure. So time your answers during practice sessions and limit each answer to a max of about 1½ minutes. If, while answering questions during interviews, you're not sure whether or not to keep talking, ask your interviewer, "Would you like more information on this?"

➤ Anticipating other likely questions by asking your colleagues what questions they think you will be asked. Also inventory the types of challenges that your target job will probably present and practice discussing specific examples of how you've successfully tackled such challenges. For example, will your target job require you to meet tight deadlines or mediate conflicts or develop new training programs?

➤ Conducting mock interviews with your trusted advisors. The more people you role play with the better. Why? Because each person you practice with will give you different and complementary advice—most of which will help you on your day of reckoning.

Two Main Types of Questions

The real question behind most interview questions is, "Why should we hire you?" Common "Why should we hire you?" questions include:

➤ Tell me about yourself.

➤ What do you do on your current job?

➤ Why do you want to work here?

When I ask hiring managers why they selected a particular applicant, they invariably answer that their pick had the most experience in the areas required by the opening. They consider past experience important because they operate on the "past is prologue" ethic. They assume that if an applicant did the target job well before, she/he will do so again in the future.

So use "Why should we hire you?" questions as invitations to show hiring managers that you could do the job because you have already done it in the past, and have done it well. Prove it by citing your successes that parallel the demands of the opening and the positive feedback they drew.

The real question behind many other common interview questions is, "Why shouldn't we hire you?" Common "Why shouldn't we hire you?" questions include:

➤ What are your weaknesses?

➤ What don't you like about your job?

➤ What is your 5-year-plan?

By hiding the "Why shouldn't we hire you?" question behind other questions, your interviewer hopes to trick you into revealing why you would be a problem, not a problem-solver.

If you fall for this trick, you will probably be rejected. Don't do your interviewer's work for him. It's his job to identify your foibles and your job to conceal them. Does this sound to you like a game of hide and seek? In a way, it is. Although you shouldn't lie in interviews, you also shouldn't volunteer self-incriminating information; unfortunately, if you do, you will lose points for your deficiencies—not gain points for your candor.

Possible answers for many common interview questions appear in Table 13-1. More tips:

➤ Whenever discussing mistakes, focus on something that happened a long time ago, was relatively trivial, and is irrelevant to the opening's demands. Emphasize how you learned from your mistakes and how you would act differently now.

➤ Never criticize a previous boss, colleagues, or job. Why? Because whenever you trash anything or anyone, you invariably raise doubts about whether the problem was caused by you or the trashee, no matter how blameless you actually were, and you thereby stop being a zero-risk applicant. By the same token, don't criticize yourself or even imply that you have personality defects, judgment problems, family challenges that could interfere with your job, or any other characteristics not possessed by the zero-risk employee.

(*text continues on page 198*)

TABLE 13-1	Answers to Common Interview Questions	
Question	**Avoid Unimpressive Answer**	**Give Impressive Answer**
Tell me about yourself.	Save your biographical filibuster for your retirement party. Don't give a long review of your entire career, and don't provide personal background info that is irrelevant to your target job and may alienate hiring managers.	Provide a quick, concise, logically organized summary of your most relevant academic and professional credentials—even if they're included on your résumé. Emphasize your recent achievements over ancient ones. Only cite personal background info that is relevant to your target job. See template for answering this question on this book's CD.
What is your weakness?	Consider yourself Miranda-ized from the minute you arrive at your interview: everything you say can and will be held against you. So don't say anything that will confirm your unworthiness for the job. Also avoid clichés like: "I don't have any weaknesses," "I'm a perfectionist," or "I work too hard."	Craft your answer to demonstrate your self-awareness, humility, or commitment to self-improvement. Here are some techniques that have helped professionals land jobs in various government organizations, including The White House: 1. Describe how you stay current in your field, and identify training that you would like to take. 2. Describe a non-deal-breaking gap that you've fixed. For example: "I previously underestimated the importance of X. So now I emphasize that more." Or "I used to shy from public speaking. So I joined Toastmasters, and I now enjoy it." 3. Acknowledge that, as a new employee, you would have a lot to learn about your target organization; explain how you would quickly get up to speed and have previously done so. 4. Say: "I inventory lessons learned after each project, and so I try never to repeat mistakes. I also incorporate lessons learned into instruction to others."

Question	Avoid Unimpressive Answer	Give Impressive Answer
What are you most proud of?	Before consulting me, one of my clients answered this question by referring to his role as husband and father. In response, "My interviewer's face fell," he recalls. P.S. He didn't get the job.	Describe a high-impact project that parallels the demands of your target job, how your results improved your organization's operations, and positive feedback you received. That's what my client—the proud parent and husband—did when asked that question again in his next interview. P.S. He got the job.
Why should we hire you rather than another applicant?	If you say, "I don't know the other applicants so I can't compare myself to them," your interviewers will hit the eject button. Don't be meek, overly humble, or apologetic.	Identify your unique, desirable skills, strong work ethic, and team-friendly approaches. Also cite your reputation, as reflected in your record of excellent performance reviews and awards. Express confidence without cockiness.
Can we call your current boss?	Don't say, "We don't get along. Please don't call him."	If you don't want your interviewer to call you current boss, say, "I would prefer if my current boss didn't know about my job search. Here's a list of my references, including several previous bosses."
What would your boss and colleagues say about you?	Don't spread negative gossip about yourself.	Cite positive feedback you have received and your team-friendly approaches. For example, "If the comments I have received on my performance evaluations are any indication, my boss would praise my contributions. Moreover, my ability to work well with others is reflected in my record of earning team awards and the fact that a share a spirit of camaraderie with my colleagues."
How do you deal with conflict?	Don't say, "I won't compromise when I know I am right."	Say something like, "I look for common ground and ways to compromise. For example . . . Also, I believe that disagreements don't have to become conflicts. Colleagues should be able to discuss disagreements amicably. When I get overruled or overrule someone else, I just do it graciously, and move on."

(continues)

TABLE 13-1	Answers to Common Interview Questions *(continued)*	
Question	**Avoid Unimpressive Answer**	**Give Impressive Answer**
What is your management style?	Don't just pound your chest and say you're the boss.	Say something like, "I am a decisive, effective, and fair manager who creates a collegial office. I believe that a manager's job is to get the work done. To do that, s/he must understand the work and relevant obstacles, understand the people who do the work, and make sure they have the guidance and resources they need to do it."
What would you do during your first week on a management job?	Don't pledge to buffalo through the office and immediately overhaul it.	Say something like, "During my early days, I would hold off on making any big decisions, even though I know a lot of people would probably immediately suggest changes to me. Instead, I would initially talk to as many people as possible and read whatever I could to really understand the organization and its constraints."

HOT TIP

If you must travel a long distance to get to an interview or to start your job, ask your hiring manager if the agency would be willing to cover your travel expenses. Federal agencies do have discretion to cover such costs. Alternatively, a federal agency can opt to interview you by phone.

➤ Reassure the employer that you're a goal-oriented professional, not a job-hopping flake. You may also mention additional education that you might want to eventually pursue.

➤ You may also be asked some "What would you do in this situation?" type of questions. You may answer some of these types of questions by explaining how you would research your options and weigh alternatives. But if you're asked a hypothetical question that tests your willingness to break laws, pass the test by stating that you would refuse to break them.

Prepare Questions to Ask Your Interviewer(s)

Your opportunity to ask questions is another opportunity to impress your interviewer; don't waste it with silence. So even if you already know more than you ever wanted to know about your target job, prepare insightful questions to ask your interviewer(s). See the list of possible questions on this book's CD.

Save your questions about salaries and benefits until after you receive an offer. Why? Because the goal of your interview is to reel in an offer. Your questions about salary and benefits probably won't help you achieve that goal because they are about what you want rather than about what your hiring managers care about: what they want. Therefore, questions about salary and benefits are unlikely to help you win over hiring managers. What's more, such questions may even provide grist for rejections. So wait until you have reeled in an offer to ask them.

HOT TIP
Interviews: What Works, What Doesn't Work

According to a survey of 300 recruiters by Korn/Ferry International: "The strongest candidates effectively correlate their experience in a concise and compelling manner."

Survey results also indicate that about 33 percent of interviewees are unprepared; 24 percent show overinflated egos; and large percentages strike out because they talk too much, show bad hygiene, or are poorly dressed.

Prepare to Give the Portfolio Treatment

One important way to stand out of the pack is to use my patented "portfolio treatment" on your interviewers. That is, bring to your interview a sample of your work products and positive feedback generated by them. I know this technique can help you wow hiring mangers because it has helped scores of my clients do so.

The portfolio treatment works so well because:

➤ Actions speak louder than words. So sales pitches that incorporate tangible work products are more impressive and convincing than uncorroborated promises of future productivity.

➤ By giving a copy of your portfolio to your interviewer(s) to keep, you will leave them with an indelible impression that will linger long after you have left the interview.

➤ Tangible, eye-catching work products appeal to multiple senses and so are more vivid and memorable than oral pitches alone.

Your competition probably won't give the portfolio treatment to interviewers. Therefore, by giving the portfolio treatment, you will help prove that you are the most organized and forward-thinking applicant in the competition. A case in point: I recently coached a federal IT specialist at the U.S. Mint who was applying for a job in another agency. During his interview, he submitted to his interviewers a neatly packaged portfolio of print-outs of eye-catching Web pages he had produced. The result? The IT specialist was told by his interviewers he was the only applicant who had shown them work products, which BOWLED them over. The result: the IT specialist got the job.

To prepare to use the portfolio treatment, bring to your interview a portfolio with pockets that holds several copies of your well-formatted hard-copy résumé, business cards, reference list (see "Template for Reference List" on this book's CD), and a sample of documents that validate your relevant successes. These documents may include:

> ➤ Writing samples such as reports, articles, newsletters, press releases, press clips, or printouts of PowerPoint presentations that you wrote or that cover your projects.

> ➤ Programs from events you organized or conferences that featured your presentations.

> ➤ Explanatory maps, charts, and photographs.

> ➤ Samples of artwork, manufactured products, catalogues, or packaging that you designed.

> ➤ Praising e-mails from managers, colleagues, or clients; positive performance evaluations; evaluations from conferences or trainings you organized; justifications for major awards; or written recommendations from your references—even if you are not asked for them. (Remember: you can stand out from the pack by doing more than the pack.)

> ➤ Students and recent grads: copies of your relevant papers (preferably with praising comments from professors) or a list of relevant papers and their high grades.

Label your portfolio to be self-explanatory to hiring managers who may review it when you are not with them and to identify your contributions to group projects. Make sure your labels and your portfolio's contents are typo free!

Before your interview, practice quickly walking your interviewers through your portfolio's contents. As you do so, point to relevant sections and look up! During your interview, give a copy of your success portfolio to each interviewer for keeps, if possible.

The Morning of Your Interview

> ➤ Get pumped by listening to energizing music, reciting motivating slogans, and getting pep talks from friends.

> ➤ Wear to your interview a new, crisp outfit that is in a contemporary, professional style. A pants suit or the equivalent is fine for women. Make sure that your personal hygiene, including your hair and nails, are in tip-top shape.

> ➤ Arrive at the interview office about 10 minutes early. But build plenty of extra travel time into your schedule for traffic, getting security cleared into the building, finding your interview office in a large labyrinth, primping, and de-jittering.

> ➤ Treat phone interviews just as seriously as you would other interviews. Suspend call waiting and lock yourself inside your phone room: keep out all pets and people. Strategically position yourself in front of your résumé, cheat sheets, and the names of your interviewers.

During Your Interview

➢ Even if you're regularly tossing back fistfuls of horse tranquilizers, be cheerful, re-laxed, and friendly—no one wants to hire a sourpuss. Exude confidence without acting cocky or superior. This is important because an applicant who has gusto can beat out more qualified but uninspired applicants.

➢ Congratulate your interviewer for any major awards or recent major accomplishments earned by your target organization, the effectiveness of its website, or any other worthy achievements you discovered during your research. When delivered in a sincere manner, your flattery will reinforce your enthusiasm and knowledge for your target job and help ingratiate you to your interviewers.

➢ Assume no prior knowledge about your credentials from your interviewers. Feel free to incorporate into your interview answers/descriptions of your credentials that are included on your application. Why? Because your interviewer will proba-bly either neglect to read your résumé or forget what it says by the time your inter-view rolls around. And, even if your interviewer does remember your application, she/he wants to hear you describe your selling points.

➢ Describe your successes to interviewers just as you would describe them to strangers, even if you're interviewing for another job within your current organiza-tion and already know your interviewers. Why? Because it's dangerous to rely on the selective, defective memories of decision-makers who hold your fate in their hands. Moreover, if you don't tell you interviewer what you offer and why s/he should hire you, you will likely be overshadowed by applicants who do tell them so.

➢ Beware: many federal hiring managers have told me that they have rejected inside applicants because they treated the interview too casually, acted entitled to their target job, or neglected to sell themselves during the interview; instead, these hir-ing managers offered the job to the outsider who treated the interview with seri-ousness and deference, and persuasively sold themselves.

➢ Incorporate plenty of specific examples of your successes into your interview answers. (This will be easy if you memorize some of your biggest successes before the interview.) In addition to citing your on-the-job and academic successes in your answers, you may also cite successes from volunteer work or your contribu-tions to professional organizations, jury duty, the PTA, or any other important organizations.

➢ Exploit any common ground that you share with your interviewer. Why? It may sound hokey, but it's true: people tend to like people with whom they share some-thing in common, whether it's a hometown, a mutual friend, or unbridled passion for Tibetan dance.

➢ Take notes during the interview or check your list of questions.

➢ Artfully weave into the conversation your success portfolio and explain that you brought it to show the range of experience you offer your target organization.

➢ Pause briefly before answering a question if you need to think it over.

➤ If you're asked about a skill you lack, admit it—don't lie. But after you acknowledge your lack of a credential, quickly mention a similar credential that you do offer and emphasize that you are a fast learner and give an example of how you have previously demonstrated this skill. As one hiring manager advises: "Don't just say that you haven't done X and leave it at that. Give me something to work with . . . some reason to think that you will be able and willing to rise to the occasion."

➤ During phone interviews, if you pause to answer a question, gently state "I'm thinking . . . " so that your interviewer doesn't wrongly assume that your phone connection was lost. Also, occasionally address your interviewer by name, as do guests on radio interviews. For example, "Well, Mr. Smith, I think that . . ."

➤ If you face a firing squad . . . I mean a panel interview . . . focus on each interviewer as s/he asks a question, then move down the line to other panelists.

➤ Recent grads: emphasize your knowledge of the latest developments in your field.

Your Close

➤ Collect the business card of everyone who interviews you.

➤ Ask your interviewer when s/he expects to make a decision. That way, you will know when you should call to follow-up in case you don't hear from him/her.

➤ Ask your interviewer whether the agency's snail mail is slowed by security screens. (This information will help you decide whether to send your thank-you note by snail mail or e-mail.)

➤ Offer a parting salvo that summarizes your key credentials. Then say, point blank, "I'd like to work here." Otherwise, your interviewers won't necessarily know that you want the job.

BLOW AWAY YOUR COMPETITION!

I know a federal Human Resources (HR) Specialist who was invited to an interview for a very appealing but highly competitive job. During the interview, her interviewer mentioned that the hiring agency was having trouble motivating employees who lacked promotion potential.

Even though the interviewer did not solicit a solution to the problem, the HR Specialist developed a creative problem-solving plan after the interview and then presented it during a follow-up interview. By contrast, all of her competitors had either ignored the problem altogether or had proposed pat, obvious solutions. The result: the HR Specialist was offered the job immediately after her interview. She was later told by her interviews that her success was largely due to her problem-solving initiative.

To similarly stand out of the pack, ask your interviewer to identify some of the big challenges currently facing the hiring office. If you can provide a thoughtful solution right away, do so. Otherwise, concisely sketch out your approach in your post-interview thank-you letter or your next round of interviews.

Don'ts

Some rules should go without saying, but I'll say them anyway, because many applicants ignore them.

➤ Don't be late to your interview.

➤ Don't leave your cell phone or BlackBerry on during your interview.

➤ Don't forget to listen to your interviewer(s) and don't talk too much. As one hiring manager put it, "When I interview people, I ask myself whether I would want to spend lots of time with this person." No one wants to be hermetically sealed in meetings with an unstoppable yacker.

➤ Don't be negative about anyone or anything.

➤ Don't mention your personal problems. (Basket cases need not apply.)

➤ Don't slam the selection process, no matter how many Byzantine hoops you were forced to conquer to land the interview. Don't express doubt over whether you would take the job, if given the choice.

➤ Don't curse and don't use sexist language. One federal applicant recently nixed his chances by referring to his female interviewers as "you gals."

➤ Don't act annoyed if the interviewer is delayed or interrupted, no matter how disgusted you are.

➤ Don't lie or try to fake skills that you don't have. For example, an applicant whose résumé boasted of fluent French recently lost out on an overseas job because she responded with a deer-in-headlights stare to a basic interview question that was asked of her in French.

➤ Don't reveal that you are a loose canon by admitting to breaking rules in previous jobs.

➤ Don't act desperate, no matter how desperate you feel.

➤ Don't challenge the judgment of the interviewer or be argumentative about anything.

➤ Don't answer questions with empty responses, such as "that is a tough one" or with mere "yes" or "no" answers. If an answer doesn't occur to you right away, pause for a moment and think about your response. If you need clarification of the question, ask for it.

➤ Don't bring anyone with you to the interview. The blooper-of-the-century award goes to an applicant who brought her mother with her to the interview. When the interviewer asked the applicant to identify her goals, she responded, "To move out of my mother's house." (I suspect that the applicant's mother shared that same goal for the applicant!)

➤ No matter how chummy your interviewer may act or how comfortable s/he may make you feel, don't get lulled into a false sense of friendship with your interviewer. Don't spill any information about yourself that you wouldn't print on your résumé.

Guerilla Interviewing Tactics

Most interviewers are not full-time interviewers; they are full-time managers and technical experts. And sadly, in many cases, their lack of interviewing expertise shows.

Many interviewers, for example, will fail to prepare questions or neglect to read your résumé before your interview. Some interviewers will prattle about their own rise to the top without asking you about your credentials. Others may ask irrelevant questions that recall the Barbara Walters' "What type of tree would you like to be?" school of interviewing.

If you don't seize control of such lousy interviews, your interviewers will—through no fault of your own—be left without a clear, let alone a favorable, impression of you. Here are several ways to rescue such wayward interviewers and score your break-out performance:

> ➤ If your interviewer is endlessly prattling about the job without asking you any questions, say something like, "If I understand the position correctly, you are looking for X, Y, and Z skills. May I illustrate how my background reflects these requirements?"

> ➤ When the interviewer asks you whether you have any questions, say: "Yes, I do have several questions. But first, if you don't mind, I would like to tell you a little about some of my important qualifications that we haven't yet had a chance to cover."

At the end of the interview, say, "I just want to mention before I leave that there are three main reasons why my background has prepared me to contribute to this organization . . . "

A JOB INTERVIEW THAT CHANGED HISTORY

Know what sunk Senator Edward Kennedy's presidential aspirations? Not Kennedy's fatal car accident in Chappaquiddick, MA, in 1969. Rather, what doomed Kennedy's presidential bid was an interview that he gave during his campaign for the 1980 democratic nomination during which he was asked why he wanted to be president—the political equivalent of the "Why should we hire you?" job interview question. In response, Kennedy fumbled, stammered, and then petered out altogether. Kennedy's unpersuasive answer is widely cited as the last nail in his presidential possibilities.

If you are ever similarly stricken by hoof-in-mouth disease during a job interview, you can at least be grateful that your performance will not be replayed over and over and over again on national television.

The Fear Factor: Sidestepping Employers' Secret Fears

So you think that looking for a job is scary? Well, here's a shocker: many hiring managers are just as afraid of the hiring process as you are.

So what are hiring managers so terrified of? The possibility of making bad hiring decisions—bad hiring decisions that they will have to live with for a loooooooooong time.

The fear of selecting the wrong job applicant is especially strong in government, where it is particularly hard to fire employees; federal hiring managers may literally have to live with their bad hires until death do they part. This principle was recently underscored by a federal executive after I asked him whether he had ever made any bad hiring decisions during his 25 years in government. In response, he offered to introduce me to his staffing mistakes, "They all work right over there," he said, pointing to a cubicle farm that encircles his office.

But as pivotal as a hiring manager's fears may be, they are almost never openly acknowledged during the selection process. Indeed, the hiring manager's secret insecurities are like the proverbial elephant in the closet—the huge, dominating presence that is carefully avoided without being discussed.

But even though you probably won't be directly asked to address hiring managers' secret fears, you can head them off. Table 13-2 provides profiles of the five most common types of problem employees and strategies for reassuring interviewers that you will not present such problems.

(text continues on page 208)

TABLE 13-2	Proving That You are a Problem-Solver, Not a Problem
Profile of Problem Employee	**How to Prove That You Are a Problem-Solver**
The Wolf in Sheep's Clothing: This type of employee looks great on paper, interviews well, and appears well-adjusted. But lurking beneath a presentable veneer is a sociopath who lies, cheats, or steals, or behaves otherwise unstably or unreliably. Because of hiring managers' fears of saddling themselves with a wolf in sheep's clothing, objective validation of an applicant's mental stability may even trump professional qualifications. Many hiring managers have told me, "I would rather hire someone who is technically mediocre but who I know is sane and reliable than an off-the-street applicant who is a first-rate technician but whose personality is an unknown quantity."	1. If you have inside contacts, name them in your cover letter, application, and interviews. 2. Arrange for your inside contact to vouch for you as early in the selection process as possible. (I have heard many hiring managers profess regret that an inside contact endorsed a candidate too late—after the candidate's application had already been rejected.) 3. Even if you do not have inside contacts, during your interviews, mention the names and titles of people who will provide you with exemplary references. 4. See "Prepping Your References."
The Team Wrecker: A government employee who doesn't work well with others is usually an employee who doesn't work out at all. In the words of one hiring manager, "When I hire someone, I want to know that they are not going to run out of the office crying because someone looked at them the wrong way and leave me in the lurch right before a critical deadline."	Cite examples of your team and leadership successes, including team awards, contributions to important work-groups, and elected positions in professional organizations. Show your interviewer thank-you letters or e-mails from managers, staffers, customers, or stakeholders. Also mention that you take suggestions/criticism well. Students: Cite your contributions to group projects, team sports, musical groups, theater projects, school papers, volunteer work, or your participation in Outward Bound-type programs. You may also mention how your experience in a large family taught you how to work with varied personalities or how your travels increased your cultural sensitivity.
The Outshiner: Virtually every hiring supervisor wants to hire staffers who will help improve their stature without outshining them. But The Outshiner diminishes the stature of supervisors by hogging the limelight and/or going over their heads.	Mention that you understand that your first loyalty is to your supervisor and that you would keep him/her informed of important developments that warrant his/her attention. Cite examples of how you have flagged hot-button issues in a timely manner for your previous supervisors, if possible.
The Lazy Bones: This type of employee needs constant nagging, hand-holding, and prodding to get anything done.	Convince hiring managers of your dogged work ethic by: 1. Citing your work ethic if you are asked about your strengths or what you are proud of. Say something like, "I consider myself reasonably smart, though I am not the smartest person in the world. But I won't let anyone outwork me. I am the employee who will be here until 10:00 PM, if necessary. And I have a record for reliability. I am my office's Cal Ripkin."

Profile of Problem Employee	How to Prove That You Are a Problem-Solver
	2. Citing projects that you completed with little supervision and instances when you took the initiative, put in long hours, and did what was needed to get the job done . . . no matter what. 3. Citing your record of meeting deadlines and multi-tasking many projects. 4. If you're student or a recent grad, citing your independent projects, your demanding electives, and your record of simultaneously working toward a degree and managing a grueling work schedule, if appropriate. 5. Asking your hiring manager to consider hiring you as a temporary employee for an initial 90-day trial period and then, at the end of this trial period, converting you into a permanent employee if you measure up. (Agencies can accomplish such conversions relatively easily.) This suggestion will provide employers with a no-risk option for evaluating you. Moreover, because you will probably be the sole candidate to propose a trial period, you will stand out from the pack.
The Pointy Headed Pontificator: This type of employee might as well wear a sign across their forehead that reads, "I don't do projects." The Pointy Headed Pontificator has no specialized knowledge, contributes little to tangible work products, and fancies him/herself as decision-making management material: a thinker, not a doer. Though most managers do value the critical thinking skills, their main, burning desire is to hire go-getters who get things done.	Don't describe yourself as a "big-picture generalist" who is above getting your hands dirty. Instead, bill yourself as the "go-to person," the super-charged, indispensable, unflappable professional who managers consult when they need a question answered, a problem solved, a customer satisfied—immediately.

Prepping Your References

Offer your interviewer a list of at least three references. (See the Template for References List on this book's CD.) Select references that are:

➤ **Respected:** your references should be people of professional stature, not your bowling buddies. If you have contacts at your target agency, or if you know anyone in common with your interviewer(s) who would vouch for you, cite them. You will thereby go a long way toward proving that you're the zero-risk applicant. Why? Because interviewers generally trust references from people who they know more than references from strangers.

BLOW AWAY THE COMPETITION

One of my clients learned through the grapevine that his interviewer suspected he would not be assertive enough to carry out some of the management tasks required for his target job. In response, my client strategically defused his hiring manager's hesitation by asking his references to artfully weave into their reference his ability to get tough when necessary. The result: he got the job.

If you can cite your current supervisor as a reference, do so. But if not, tell your interviewer that you don't want your current supervisor to know about your job search. Your references may also include previous bosses and supervisors, colleagues, clients, contractors, or anyone else who is familiar with your work and thinks highly of it.

➤ **Enthusiastic:** before you ask a contact to serve a reference, ask whether she/he can give you an enthusiastic endorsement. If your contact expresses any reluctance or hedging, don't use him/her as a reference. After all, if you detect his/her ambivalence, so will hiring managers. As one hiring manager recalls, "When I call the former employer of a job applicant, I always ask them if they would hire the applicant again. If the reference pauses at all before responding, I know what their true answer is, and I won't hire the applicant."

➤ **Prepared:** don't assume that your references will be able to spontaneously describe why they think highly of you. Prepare them to do so by giving them your résumé and reviewing your salient qualifications with them. You may also remind your references of projects you completed for them and positive feedback they provided you on those projects. To this end, give your references copies of the write-ups for awards or positive performance evaluations that they gave you. Also describe to references your target jobs and which aspects of your background you would like them to emphasize. In particular, if you suspect that your hiring manager has any hesitations about your credentials, ask your references—if appropriate—to provide hiring managers with reassurance that will defuse those hesitations.

ON THE CD...

This book's CD features copies of my *Washington Post* articles on how to answer the "What are your weaknesses?" interview question and how to prepare your success portfolio for interviews. It also features lists of frequently asked interview questions, potential questions for you to ask interviewers, a template for providing references to interviewers, an interview preparation checklist, and other cheat sheets to help you ace your interviews.

➤ **Accessible:** don't use references who are on vacation, irresponsible about returning calls, or otherwise potentially unreachable when you need them. If, for example, your reference is losing his inner bureaucrat by yak-riding through Nepal, don't use him. Also, confirm your references' contact info before you give it to hiring managers. (I have heard of finalists getting rejected simply because their interviewers reached the references of other worthy applicants before reaching theirs.)

INTERVIEW SUCCESS STORY

By Heidi McAllister, Environmental Educator

While living in Mexico, Heidi McAllister, a U.S. citizen, nailed a federal job in Washington, DC, solely through her application and a phone interview; she never even had a face-to-face interview with a hiring manager. Heidi explains here how she learned how to give a killer phone interview.

I had been living in Mexico and working as a consultant in environmental education mostly to the Mexican government for about 13 years when I started applying for jobs back in the United States.

Soon after beginning my job search, I had about six phone interviews. All of them seemed to go smoothly, but none led to a job offer. As the rejection letters rolled in, it became obvious that something was wrong with my interviewing skills.

So I researched interviewing strategies and soon realized that I hadn't been selling myself enough. I know why I had been holding back: I am self-deprecating; I like to poke fun at myself. So tooting my own horn doesn't come naturally to me.

But my research showed me how I could sell myself without coming off as egocentric. All I had to do was cite concrete examples of my achievements that matched the requirements of my target job. No need to sound pompous, haughty or conceited; I just had to be factual and specific.

I used this technique for the first time during my phone interview for a federal job as an Environment Program and Training Specialist. For example, in response to the question, "What are the necessary components of an environmental education program?" I ticked off the countries where I had helped design environmental programs and described the sponsoring organizations, target audiences and components of my programs, and the positive feedback they earned.

I previously would have answered this question by naming the essential components of environmental education programs. But I think the adage "actions speak louder than words" applies here. By showing that I had taken action—that is, set up successful environmental education programs—I impressed my interviewers more than if I had merely talked about what an environmental education should be.

Likewise, I incorporated into many of my other interview answers specific examples of my achievements as well as objective evidence of my success. I was able to quickly identify these examples because I had studied my résumé just before the phone interview began and because I could quickly glance at my résumé, which was strategically positioned in front of me throughout the session. I know that my interviewing strategy worked because, within several weeks, I was offered the job, which I enthusiastically accepted.

HOT TIP
Deflecting Your Liabilities

What are your unspoken liabilities—aspects of your application that you suspect may, rightly or wrongly, turn off interviewers? Perhaps, for example, you sense that you're perceived as too young, too old, an outsider, too entrenched, or a job-hopper.

Instead of letting your interviewer's unspoken fears silently sabotage your application, you could gingerly address them in an oblique way. For example, suppose you find yourself sitting across from an interviewer who is significantly younger than you. You could say something like: "You may think that, because I have a significant amount of experience . . . that I might be rigid and might not take direction well. But I want to assure you that I understand that you would be my supervisor and that it would be my obligation to support you. I am certainly prepared to accommodate and profit by any approaches that you may suggest. I also want to emphasize that I am energetic and flexible."

Explain how the combination of your knowledge of the latest techniques in your field together with your extensive experience make you a uniquely well-rounded applicant.

Also, make sure that your grooming and dress don't reinforce negative stereotypes and prejudices; dress in neat, up-to-date styles.

Post-Interview Thank-You Efforts

Question: What is the first thing you should do when you get home from an interview (after you rip off your uncomfortable interview outfit but before you pour yourself a stiff, cold drink)?

Answer: Write a thank-you letter to everyone who interviewed you.

It may seem unfair that you are obliged to thank an interviewer(s) who hasn't really helped you yet. Indeed, if you are like most job applicants, you think that your interviewer(s) should thank you for trucking down to their office, submitting to the Spanish Inquisition, and perhaps even graciously agreeing to itemize some of your weaknesses during your interview. But, like it or not, your fate hinges on the decision of your interviewer(s). And by thanking them, you may win them over because:

> ➤ Very few applicants bother to write thank-you letters. Therefore, your thank-you letter will help you stand out from the pack.

> ➤ A thank-you letter will remind the interviewer of your strengths. As one hiring manager put it, "If a letter is right in front of me, it is a tangible nudge that forces me to think about the candidate again." This is important because an interviewer who screens many candidates can, soon after the interview, easily forget the credentials of even outstanding candidates.

> ➤ By thanking your interviewers, you'll prove that you really want the job, and that you're polite, conscientious, and demonstrate follow-through—all prized traits.

Content and Format

A thank-you letter should be brief and zippy, no more than several paragraphs. It should:

➤ Thank the interviewer for their time and trouble.

➤ Summarize what you discussed in the interview.

➤ Reaffirm your interest in the position.

➤ Concisely summarize relevant qualifications.

➤ Add any important information that you neglected to mention during the interview.

➤ Be error-free. Spell check and proof your letter, and then get a second opinion on it.

A thank-you letter sent by overnight delivery generally makes a stronger and better impression than e-mails that are almost instantly read, deleted, and forgotten. But speed does count—your thank you should arrive before your interviewers make a decision. So if your target agency's snail mail is delayed by security screens, consider personally dropping off your thank-you letter the day after your interview.

Alternatively, if you have no other options, e-mail your thank you letter immediately after your interview. (But as one hiring manager observed, "E-mails are just one step above doing nothing.")

Note that your thank-you may be formatted as a printed business letter or a hand-written card written in neurotically neat penmanship. See Figures 13-1 and 13-2 for samples of thank-you letters.

Checklist for Interview Success

❑ Ask for the name and title of each interviewer when you're invited to the interview.

❑ "Google" your interviewers.

❑ Research your target organization: review its website, particularly its annual report, strategic plan, and recent press releases. Also, search major publications for recent coverage of your target organization's hot-button issues, as discussed in Chapter 11.

❑ Craft answers to common interview questions. (See list on CD.)

❑ Prepare a few questions to ask your interviewer(s). (See list on CD.)

❑ Role-play interviews with as many friends and colleagues as possible.

❑ Pack your briefcase with a pad, pen, and success portfolio containing your résumé, business cards, list of references, and documents that validate your ability to succeed on your target job.

❑ Prepare your references to be contacted by your interviewer.

❑ Prepare your interview outfit.

➤ Plan to arrive at your interview location early, to leave time for traffic jams, getting cleared into the building, and finding your interview office in a large building.

➤ After interview: send thank-you letter or e-mail.

➤ If you're rejected from your target job, ask your interviewer for feedback on how you may improve your interview skills. Also, occasionally contact any interviewers who are encouraging to you, and inquire about any additional upcoming openings they may have.

May 1, 2008

Mr. John Doe
Office of Legislative Affairs
National Science Foundation
4201 Wilson Blvd., Suite 1245
Arlington, VA 22230

Dear John:

Thanks so much for explaining to me the ins-and-outs of working at NSF. I would like to reaffirm my enthusiasm for the Legislative Affairs Specialist opening.

I would be very excited to contribute to the fascinating and important scientific issues addressed by NSF and to work in the agency's uniquely academic environment. Moreover, the creative possibilities and *esprit-de-corps* offered by joining a new "class" of Legislative Affairs Specialists would be extremely appealing.

I greatly appreciate the time you took to explain the challenges of the job. I believe that I am prepared for the task; I am experienced in handling ever-changing priorities and deadlines.

I trust that all my references will confirm that I have the skills you seek. In particular, Jane Smith, the Legislative Director of the Mine Safety and Health Administration, can offer insights into my adaptability, which I understand is an important job requirement. (Jane's work number is 111-012-2345)

Again, I would welcome the opportunity to join your staff, and I very much appreciate your time and consideration.

Sincerely,

Jane Q. Public

Figure 13-1. Sample thank-you letter: business format.

Dear Mr. Harris:

It was a pleasure discussing the opening for a Public Affairs Officer and meeting Jack Gold and Cindy Smith. Your energetic presentation, your office's congenial atmosphere and your office's many new dynamic programs added to my enthusiasm for the opening.

As I mentioned when we met, I have four years of experience producing the same type of employee newsletter that Public Affairs will soon launch. In addition, my editorial experience at ABC News and my writing experience at MSNBC.com would allow me to make immediate contributions to your multimedia outreach campaign.

My cell phone number is (123) 123-4567, and my e-mail is JHarris@e-mail.com. I hope I will have the opportunity to contribute to the Office of Public Affairs. And thanks again for your personal attention.

Sincerely,

Sam Murphy

Figure 13-2. Text of sample hand-written thank-you card.

CHAPTER **14**

Commanding a Top-Dollar Salary

"By negotiating the salary of my first federal job, and successfully campaigning for promotions I received since then, I increased my total take-home pay for the last 16 years by more than $200,000."

—LILY WHITEMAN, AUTHOR OF THIS BOOK

So you've received an offer for a federal job. As Sally Field might say, "They like you! They really like you!"

The mere utterance of an offer from a hiring manager may flush your nervous system with happy hormones and send you into raptures of relief. But don't let the thrill of your victory compel you to accept an unacceptable salary. Remember: many employers in all sectors—including the federal sector—offer new hires the lowest salaries they can get away with. That's simply how the game is played.

But the federal government has even more leverage over most new recruits than do other types of employers. Why? Because the typical federal job seeker wrongly believes that federal salaries are nonnegotiable. Such unfortunates usually cave to lowball salaries without so much as asking, "Is this salary negotiable?" They may thereby unwittingly sacrifice hundreds of thousands of dollars in salary over the course of their career.

"We reward top executives at the agency with a unique incentive program. Money."

Don't Buy Into the Myth of the Non-Negotiable Federal Salary

The real deal is that salaries for many federal jobs—like those of private sector jobs—are flexible. But the raw reality is that you are unlikely to ever receive your full worth without asking for it. Even if the meek shall inherit the earth, they shan't earn a decent salary without negotiating for it.

In order to help backfill for the ongoing federal retirement wave, many federal organizations have adopted new flexibilities on pay and benefits. This means that the bargaining power of federal selectees is currently at an all-time high.

This chapter introduces the various pay scales used by federal agencies and then reviews tried-and-true methods for negotiating for top-dollar salaries. I know that these negotiating methods work because I have personally used them many times, as have my clients—much to the benefit of their bank accounts.

Show Me the Money: Federal Pay Scales

Salaries in Federal Agencies

A variety of pay scales operate in federal agencies. Most of these pay scales incorporate annual cost-of-living increases from 2 to 5 percent. In addition, many feds receive annual bonuses. (But, before you start drooling, be aware that the average federal bonus equals 1.6 percent of annual salary.) Also, some pay scales provide locality pay for feds working in cities where the cost of living is high. And commuting feds may receive free metro tickets or free or discounted parking. Additional possible perks include on-site daycare and work-out facilities.

Listed here are the most common federal pay scales. To access current salary tables for these and other pay scales, enter *salary tables* into the search window at http://www.opm.gov/.

1. **General Schedule System:** General Schedule (GS) jobs are graded from GS-1 to GS-15. Each GS grade has 10 steps. Salaries rise with each increase in grade and step. Entry-level jobs are usually graded through GS-9; mid-career jobs are graded GS-11 to 13; senior level jobs are graded GS-14 and 15, and also include all jobs in the senior executive service (SES).

   Feds working in cities where the cost of living is particularly high receive locality pay, which can boost pay by as much as 12 percent over base pay rates.

   Most feds in the GS system receive a grade increase after satisfactorily completing their probationary period on their 1-year federal anniversary. Thereafter, they automatically receive a step increase every 1, 2, or 3 years, depending on their position on their career ladder. (For more info, type *within-grade increases* into the search window at http://www.opm.gov/.)

   Feds are also eligible for merit-based promotions consisting of a grade or step increase. The following rules govern such merit-based promotions:

   ➤ Above the GS-5 grade, feds must remain in each grade and step for at least 1 year before being promoted to the next grade or step. (But at press time, the federal government was considering eliminating this 1-year time-in-grade requirement.)

   ➤ Feds generally cannot skip grades as they advance up the career ladder. (An exception: GS-14s can move directly into SES jobs without first landing GS-15 jobs.)

   ➤ To rise above the ceiling grade of his/her current job, a fed must convince supervisors to raise his/her ceiling or move into another job with a higher ceiling.

These regulations frequently work like speed bumps on federal careers. Moreover, employees do not necessarily receive merit-based promotions after fulfilling their time-in-grade or step requirements; they frequently wait longer than minimum waiting periods for such promotions.

Although the GS pay system is the most common pay system for federal white-collar employees, more and more federal agencies are currently abandoning it.

2. **Pay Banding Systems**: Most agencies and jobs in the excepted service are on "pay banding" systems that consolidate many pay grades into fewer, more flexible pay bands. (Agencies and jobs in the excepted service are listed at http://www.makingthedifference.org/federaljobs/exceptedservice.shtml.)

    Pay banding systems generally pay better than the GS system. But many pay banding systems have replaced automatic raises with raises that reward employees for good performance. In addition, it's generally easier (though still relatively hard) to fire pay banded employees than to fire GSers.

3. **High-Demand Professionals**: Special salary rates apply to some high-demand professionals, including some IT specialists, medical specialists, scientists, and engineers.

4. **Senior Executive Service (SES)**: If you're new to the SES, your hiring agency should top your previous salary. Some agencies always offer new SESers a set percentage increase (usually 10 to 15 percent) over his/her previous salary; other agencies are free of such restrictions.

    But SES salaries vary from agency to agency. Agencies that have been certified by the Office of Personnel Management for adopting performance-based appraisal systems for SESers can pay higher SES salaries than can uncertified agencies. The performance-based systems of certified agencies reward high performers with raises but eliminate automatic annual raises. SESers receive annual bonuses between 5 and 20 percent of basic pay. Also, SESers accrue 8 hours of vacation time every 2 weeks.

5. **Law Enforcers:** A patchwork of laws has created differences in salaries and benefits for law enforcers across the government. What's more, the types of jobs that are classified as law enforcers vary inconsistently. Therefore, some security professionals who do law enforcement work are not officially classified as such.

6. **Blue-Collar Workers:** They are covered by the Federal Wage System.

LOOK UP THE SALARIES OF CURRENT FEDS

Several tantalizingly voyeuristic sites that have been widely compared to "salary porn" reveal the salaries of current feds. Look up the salaries of employees of federal agencies on the "Gannett searchable database" of federal employee salaries at http://php.app.com/fed_employees/search.php. Or look up the salaries of Congressional staffers at http://www.legistorm.com/.

Variation of Salaries Among Agencies

It is important to understand that federal salaries for the same job can vary considerably from agency to agency. And as more and more agencies abandon the GS system for their own pay systems, such variation is increasing. A few tips: agencies in the excepted service generally pay better than agencies in the civil service—many of my clients have received large pay increases just by moving from the competitive service to the excepted service. In addition, particularly high salaries tend to be paid by agencies addressing corporate finance because they compete with Wall Street to recruit staffers. These agencies include the Securities and Exchange Commission, the Federal Reserve, the FDIC, the Commodities Futures Trading Commission, and some Treasury Department agencies.

Salaries of Congressional Staffers

Each Congressional office and committee establishes its own policies on pay, student loan repayments, and leave. Therefore, salaries and benefits for the same job may vary considerably from office to office.

Most offices only allow staff to take vacations when Congress is not in session. And staffers are frequently expected to remain on the job through late-night sessions. Some positions are eligible for comp time and overtime pay; some are not.

Generally, Congressional staff jobs pay much less and offer much less job security than do comparable jobs in federal agencies. A few rules of thumb within those constraints:

1. Jobs on Congressional committees usually pay better than jobs on the staffs of Congressional members.

2. Jobs on Senate staffs tend to pay better than jobs on House staffs.

3. Most jobs in Congress offer less negotiating leeway than those in federal agencies. But any job may offer wiggle room. So it never hurts to diplomatically ask hiring managers if they are willing to negotiate salary or offer tuition reimbursement, parking or metro tickets, or other benefits.

Negotiating Basics

The Basis of Any Agency Offer

Each vacancy announcement for an agency job on USAJOBS identifies a salary range for the opening. How does a hiring agency determine what salary to offer you? Usually based on your salary history.

> ➤ If you're currently employed, the hiring agency will usually match or best your current salary or a current, reasonable competing offer. Professionals who transfer from nonprofit jobs, Congressional staff jobs, or other sectors that pay much less than federal agencies may get considerable salary bumps when moving to federal agencies. But conversely, professionals who transfer from corporations paying extravagant salaries may not fare quite as well.

> ➤ If you're currently unemployed, the hiring agency will, in many cases, match or best your most recent salary or a current and reasonable competing offer.

> ➤ If you're a new college grad, the hiring agency will probably offer you its standard offer for recent grads, or match or best a current and reasonable competing offer. Here are the guidelines for standard offers for new graduates under the GS pay system:

>> ➤ An applicant with a college degree but without any specialized experience in their field qualifies for a GS-5 position. But an applicant who has at least a B average or other desirable college credentials can expect to start at a GS-7 position.

>> ➤ An applicant with a master's degree qualifies for at least a GS-9 position.

>> ➤ An applicant with a Ph.D. qualifies for a GS-12 position.

> ➤ If you're a recent high school grad with no work experience, you will qualify for GS-2 jobs. But if you have some work experience, you may start at the GS-3, 4, or 5 levels.

A few more rules of thumb: the more work experience you have in addition to degrees, the higher grade you will probably land. But keep in mind that the hiring agency will probably offer you the lowest step in your grade level, unless you negotiate for a higher step.

Wiggle Room

Although you probably can't raise the ceiling of your opening's salary range, you probably can negotiate for a higher offer within your opening's salary range. Nevertheless, many job seekers accept a federal salary offer without negotiating—only to regret upon discovering that:

> ➤ Colleagues with comparable credentials are earning more than them.

> ➤ Grade increases are not necessarily granted frequently, and their pace generally declines as employees move up the federal career ladder.

The brutal truth is that you may be locked into your starting grade, or close to it, for a significant chunk of time. This possibility increases the importance of negotiating the highest starting salary that you can up front.

The Power Play

The time between your receipt of an offer and your response to it is the only time during the selection process, and perhaps the only time during your career, when the tables are turned in your direction and you get to call the shots. Yes, until the salary negotiations began, the hiring agency ran the show, and the selection process revolved entirely around its demands.

Finally, during salary negotiations, you can assert your salary and benefits needs, and the agency—temporarily rendered powerless—twists in the wind awaiting your next move. But don't get too excited. Once you accept or reject the offer, the tables will turn again . . . the natural order will return . . . and the hiring agency will once again wield the upper hand.

Salary-Boosting Research

Before you negotiate, improve your bargaining position by taking these actions:

1. Study the vacancy announcement for the opening and identify how your credentials exceed its requirements. Also, visit the career section of the hiring agency's website and the salary table on http://www.opm.gov/ that covers your job.

2. Get a competing salary offer from another employer in writing, if you can swing it. As previously mentioned, a hiring agency will usually match a current and reasonable competing offer from another employer. This is one of the best kept secrets in government!

    To get a competing offer, you might have to apply for jobs that you don't even want. Granted: this requires work. But, this strategy may boost your federal salary by thousands of dollars per year—not a bad potential payback for your efforts.

3. Get a copy of the classification standards used by the hiring agency to determine the grade level of the position. Access these documents by typing *classification standards* into the search window at http://www.opm.gov/. Alternatively, you can probably obtain a copy of the classification standards that apply to your opening from the agency contact person identified on its vacancy announcement.

4. Discuss your offer with any feds that you know. Your federal contacts should be able to help you gauge the reasonableness of your offer. (Probably because federal salaries are part of the public record, they are generally not protected by the kind of "cone of silence" that protects private sector salaries. So feds are relatively open about their salaries.)

Your Move: The Negotiation
You Get That Call: You're Offered the Job

When you're selected for a federal job, the human resources (HR) officer will probably call you with a job offer. In response, express enthusiasm for the offer, but don't commit to it. Ask the HR officer to specify your salary offer, if s/he hasn't done so. In response, say that you would like to clarify the offer because you would appreciate being considered for a higher salary. Ask, "Is this salary negotiable?" You may also ask about other benefits, such as student loan repayments and coverage of your moving expenses. (See negotiating checklist.)

Keep in mind that your selecting official probably has much more power to raise your offer than does the HR officer; in most cases, the HR officer's hands are tied. So if the HR officer doesn't respond to your negotiating invitation by referring you to the selecting official, ask the HR officer if you can discuss your offer with the selecting official.

It is always more effective to negotiate in person than over the telephone, where facial cues are obscured. So if possible, make an appointment to discuss the position in person with the selecting official.

HOT TIP
Body Language
Speaks Volumes

When you negotiate, convey confidence with your body language and speaking style. Sit in a slouch-free posture, maintain eye contact, keep your hands folded on your lap or the table, smile, suppress nervous/jittery mannerisms, and don't speak too fast no matter how eager you are to conclude your negotiations.

Revving Up for the Negotiations

Few people enjoy negotiating their salary. It feels uncomfortable, undignified, and even somewhat unseemly—disturbingly similar to haggling over the price of a used car. But, distasteful though the process is, you owe it to yourself to advocate for what you deserve. Remember: if you don't ask for what you deserve, you probably won't get it.

And for a few minutes of uncomfortable assertiveness, you may earn thousands of additional dollars or more per year. Isn't that worth a few minutes of discomfort? In other words, the fact that negotiating is uncomfortable is not a good enough reason to avoid negotiating (Table 14-1).

The Face to Face

Open your meeting with your hiring manager by briefly mentioning some of the reasons why you were so pleased to receive an offer and how you would add value to the organization.

Then go into negotiating mode. If you really do want this job, don't issue any ultimatums or deal-breaking demands. Instead, open the negotiation with a question and then proceed gingerly and gently.

No Flexibility

If, by chance, your hiring manager responds by stating that there is no flexibility in the offer, you may still negotiate. How? First, emphasize concessions you are making. For example, mention that the job change would be just a lateral for you; or requires you to sacrifice vacation, sick leave, or other benefits; or requires you to pay moving expenses or significantly raise your living costs.

TABLE 14-1	Negotiate Rather Than Demand
Ultimatum or Demand	**Negotiating Questions**
Thanks for your offer. But I need a much higher salary and reimbursement for my moving expenses to take the job.	I am so excited about the possibility of contributing my skills to this organization. But is there any flexibility or wiggle room in your salary offer and could your office help cover my moving expenses?
I appreciate your offer. But I'm afraid that compensation might be a deal-breaker.	I'm excited about this job. I'd like to work out an agreement that would make both of us feel great. Would it be possible for you to raise your salary offer? I think I deserve consideration on this because . . .

Then, ask your hiring manager to consider evaluating you in 6 months if you take the job, and agreeing to give you a merit-based step increase or cash award if s/he is happy with your productivity, as you are certain will be the case. (Agencies can grant an employee a cash award based upon a favorable rating totaling up to 10 percent of salary.)

In the unlikely event that your hiring manager does not offer you any concessions, you've lost nothing just by attempting to negotiate. And if nothing else, you have established yourself as an assertive, goal-oriented professional and have set the stage for future promotions.

Yes, We Do Have Flexibility!

Alternatively the hiring manager may respond to your invitation to negotiate by saying something like, "What did you have in mind?" Provided below are some possible responses:

1. **Suppose you've received a competing offer**: Present documentation of your competing offer, and say, "I understand that the government usually matches reasonable competing offers. I wonder whether you could match or come closer to my other offer." Alternatively, if your research has revealed that another agency is paying people at your level better than your agency's offer, ask whether your agency could pay comparably.

2. **Suppose you're a current fed**: If you're currently eligible for a grade or step increase, tell your hiring manager about your eligibility for a promotion and why you deserve it. Note that when a GS employee is promoted to a higher grade, he/she may receive a pay increase equal to two steps above their current grade and step.

   If you're a current fed who is ineligible for a promotion because you have not yet fulfilled your time-in-grade or step requirements, ask your hiring manager if s/he can commit to giving you a grade increase or a merit-based step when you do fulfill whatever time requirements apply to your situation and/or a bonus after 6 months if s/he is happy with your contributions.

3. **Suppose you're a new grad with outstanding student loans**: Ask your hiring manager for coverage in the Student Loan Repayment Program. (See Hot Tip.)

HOT TIP
Pick an Employer That Can Help You Lose Your Loans

Federal agencies can repay up to $10,000 of an employee's academic debt per year, up to a total of $60,000. In return, the employee must agree to stay with the agency for at least 3 years.

Some agencies use the student loan repayment program more than others. To find out which agencies use this program, type *Student Loan Repayment Program* into the search window at http://opm.gov/.

BENEFITS THAT MAY BE NEGOTIABLE

- Salary
- Student loan repayments, if you have outstanding loans
- Relocation bonus, travel, and/or moving expenses, if you're moving to take the job
- Recruitment bonus
- Accelerated vacation accrual rate
- Start date
- Alternative work schedule or telecommuting options
- Tuition reimbursement, if you want to take job-related courses or earn another degree
- Parking, if you will drive to work
- Access to childcare facilities
- Date of your first review
- Salary advance

4. **Suppose you're an experienced nonfed or a returning fed:** Request authorization to accrue vacation time at the same rate as feds whose experience levels are similar to yours instead of at the standard accrual rate for new feds—4 hours per 2-week pay period. Your hiring manager can credit your previous work experience so that you will meet seniority requirements for accelerated leave rates. (Feds with 3 years of seniority earn 6 hours of vacation every 2 weeks, and those with at least 15 years of seniority earn 8 hours.) Strengthen your request by telling your hiring manager how much vacation time you will sacrifice by leaving your current job.

5. **Suppose you've received bonuses on previous jobs:** Cite these awards as evidence of your superior performance and evidence that your previous salary was underestimated by your previous base pay, which provided the basis for the hiring agency's salary offer.

6. **Suppose your qualifications match the ceiling of your opening's grade range:** Show your hiring manager the position classification criteria for the higher grade and explain how your credentials match the criteria for the higher grade.

7. **Suppose you have truly superior qualifications:** Your hiring agency can set your pay at a middle step—instead of at the lowest step—of your grade level. Explain why your educational and/or work experience exceeds your opening's basic requirements and ask whether you qualify for Superior Qualifications and Special Need Pay-Setting Authority. If you have a security clearance, mention it. If you're a recent grad, underscore your exceptional academic record and the relevance of your major or degree to your target job. For more info, type *superior qualifications and special need pay-setting authority* into the search window at http://www.opm.gov/.

"I can only discuss salary and benefits. You'll have to analyze the babe situation yourself."

8. **Suppose you want to continue your education**: Request reimbursement for your tuition. Agencies can pay for job-related degrees and non-degrees. For more info, type *training and development policy* into the search window at http://www.opm.gov/.

9. **Suppose you're a nonfed who has been offered a job in a high-demand field:** Ask your hiring manager if s/he will authorize a recruitment bonus for you. A recruitment bonus may range up to 100 percent of your annual salary. For more info, type *recruitment and relocation incentives* into the search window at http://www.opm.gov/. (Chapter 2 identifies many agencies that offer recruitment bonuses.)

10. **Suppose that taking the job would require you to move to a new location:** If you're a current fed, ask your hiring manager for a relocation bonus. (The cap for a relocation bonus is 100 percent of your annual salary.) Alternatively, if you're currently a nonfed, ask whether your hiring agency would cover your transportation and moving expenses. For more info, type *recruitment and relocation incentives* into the search window at http://www.opm.gov.

11. **Suppose you want scheduling flexibilities**: Request telecommuting or an alternative work schedule involving working 9 hours per day in exchange for a long weekend every other week or working four 10-hour days per week.

12. **Suppose you plan to drive to work:** Request free parking. In some cities, this benefit is worth several thousand dollars per year. In a lesson in creative negotiating, one new recruit convinced her new boss to give her the parking privileges of her predecessor and thereby enabled her to avoid joining the agency's waiting list for free parking.

13. **Suppose you're short on cash:** Your hiring agency can advance up to two paychecks to a new fed.

Sealing the Deal

Your hiring agency may pressure you to make a quick decision on an offer. Nevertheless, you are completely within your rights to ask for a day or two to consider any offer. Also, request an offer letter.

CHAPTER **15**

Responding to an Agency's Decision

"The world is all gates, all opportunities, strings of tension waiting to be struck."
—RALPH WALDO EMERSON

You Got the Job!

So you've received an offer! You won the jackpot . . . the grand slam . . . the ultimate prize. Give yourself a big fat slap on the back and collect some kudos from friends and relatives.

You Want the Job

Sometimes, the decision on an offer is a no-brainer. The job would be perfect for you, and you're chomping at the bit for it. But no matter how heavenly an offer may be, consider negotiating your salary, as well as other benefits covered in Chapter 14.

Here are some additional tips for what to say when you accept a job offer:

> ➤ Thank the hiring manager for the offer.

> ➤ Express excitement about the job and say something like, "I will make sure that you will be pleased that you selected me."

> ➤ Politely request an offer letter that summaries the terms of your agreement, including your start date, salary, and title.

Uncertainty

Although it is always flattering to be selected for a job, do not reflexively accept a questionable job just because it was offered to you or because it represents a new opportunity. Change merely for the sake of change will not necessarily make you happier or advance your career. You should only accept a job because you *really* want it, or *really* need income . . . now!

Yes, bills or the need "to get your foot in the door" might justifiably compel you to accept a questionable job—despite its imperfections. But in such cases, be honest with yourself (but not with your hiring manager) about your needs and continue your job search accordingly.

But don't accept an unappealing job just to escape a current unappealing job. By doing so, you will only jump from the fire to the frying pan. After all, if a potential boss or a job description rubs you the wrong way, your affection for them is unlikely to grow once you dive into the job's day-to-day drudgery. Moreover, remember that the demands of a new job would probably complicate your continued job search.

If you feel undecided about an opening, more information about it might help you clinch your decision. So if this is the case, when you talk to the hiring manager, thank him/her for the offer, express enthusiasm about the job, and then ask for a meeting to clarify a few points. If salary is the sticking issue, see Chapter 14 for negotiating tips. Once you gather more information, ask the hiring manager for a day or two to finalize your decision, if you need it.

Rejecting an Offer

If the offer isn't right for you, let the hiring manager down courteously, quickly, and graciously. Don't burn any bridges unnecessarily; you never know if you might cross paths again with the hiring manager. Here are some tips for turning down an offer:

> ➤ Thank the hiring manager for taking the time to interview you and for selecting you.

> ➤ Cite something impressive about the organization.

> ➤ Say that you gave the offer much thought and that turning it down was a tough decision.

> ➤ Give a specific reason for turning down the offer, such as the salary, or leave your reasons vague by saying something like, "It wasn't the right fit for me right now."

If at First You Don't Succeed

> *"Success is the ability to go from failure to failure without losing your enthusiasm."*
> —WINSTON CHURCHILL

Although it is understandable to be disappointed by a rejection, never regard your standing in a job competition as a referendum on your credentials, smarts, or personality. As one recent rejectee sensibly explained, "I don't take it personally. It's not like the hiring managers *really* knows me or what I can do."

Also, take solace in the fact that almost everyone—even the most fabulously successful people—have, at one time or another, been rejected for a job that they *knew* they were perfect for. Indeed, many roads to success are rutted with potholes, riddled with speed bumps, blocked by barricades, and traversed by blind alleys.

And even if you're rejected for a job that seemed like it was the BEST JOB IN THE WORLD, another exciting opportunity will almost certainly eventually develop.

Keep On Keeping On

Many job searchers let their fear of failure derail their job search. Instead of rolling with the punches, they let rejections confirm their conviction that that they are destined to fail, and so they suspend their job search—sometimes indefinitely. They thereby succumb to a self-fulfilling prophecy: by stopping their job search, they guarantee that they will not find a job and thereby further reinforce their poor self image.

THE POWER OF PERSISTENCE

If you recently experienced a professional disappointment, you're in good company. In fact, many of the most fabulously successful people have overcome setbacks that would have thwarted less determined people. For example:

- The Beatles were turned down by Capitol Records *four* times before Capitol signed them.

- *Chicken Soup for the Soul* is one of the best-selling nonfiction books in United States history. But the proposal for the book was rejected by more than 24 publishers before it found a publisher.

- Screenwriter Marc Cherry spent three staffing seasons without so much as an interview, let alone a job. He told *The Washington Post* that his spec script for the blockbuster *Desperate Housewives* was itself "born of desperation" and was initially turned down by all four networks.

- High jumper Dick Fosbury failed at conventional straddle jumping. So he pioneered the goofy backward "Fosbury Flop," and won the Gold in the 1968 Olympics.

Remember: the quality that distinguishes many successful people from others is neither intelligence, nor talent, nor luck, but sheer persistence. Successful, persistent professionals take setbacks in stride; instead of turning away from obstacles, they step around or over them. They incorporate any lessons that might be gleaned from setbacks into their strategies without losing their resolve, their determination, their self-confidence.

Indeed, many high-profile people only achieved their goals after tenaciously toiling through humiliating defeats. Consider, for example, politicians—many of whom apparently regard a lost election as encouragement to run for an even higher office. And why not? After all, many Presidents—including Lincoln, Nixon, Reagan, Clinton, and both Bushes—lost major elections before ultimately winning the White House.

Maximizing Your Odds

I have frequently been amazed to hear unemployed job seekers say things like, "I once got rejected from a federal job, so it would be useless for me to apply for another federal job." By contrast, no reasonable person would ever say, "I once got rejected from a private sector job, so it would be useless to apply for another." Nevertheless, it is just as unreasonable to paint all federal jobs with a broad brush as it is to paint all private sector jobs with a broad brush.

Why? Because federal agencies are as different from one another as private sector organizations.

Every federal office is run by different people with different priorities, and every opening is screened by different mangers. So any rejection you receive in a federal job competition would not impact your standing in any others.

But the raw reality is that no matter how impressive your application is, there will always be uncontrollable factors that can nix your application. For example:

➤ Another applicant may have pivotal connections or more experience than you.

➤ You may be beaten out for a job by a veteran who has veterans' preference.

➤ A hiring manager may have a wacky bias against some innocent and even admirable aspect of your background. For example, I know of a professor at a top university who automatically rejects any applicant for a professorship who does not cite her articles in their own scholarly publications. (The nerve!)

➤ A hiring manager may have poor judgment.

➤ The selection may hinge on unstated criteria. For example, a hiring manager recently told me that he based a selection on his "sense that my pick would thrive in this office's chaos." But an "ability to thrive in chaos" was never identified as a selection criterion.

➤ Your target job may be cancelled because of hiring freezes or changing priorities.

➤ You may be overqualified—a particular liability before insecure hiring managers who fear being outshined by subordinates. (Remember why the first President Bush selected the inexperienced lightweight Dan Quayle as his running mate?)

To a large extent, hiring decisions are based on chance; they hinge on the vagaries of your hiring manager's judgment, your competition, and other fluky and sometimes kooky factors. You can always increase your odds by acing your application and interview. But no matter how impressive you are, success is never guaranteed.

The best way to improve your odds in the job searching numbers game is to apply to as many jobs that suit you. Moreover, the more logs you keep in the fire, the less disappointed you will be if any one of them is snuffed out.

TORN BETWEEN TWO AGENCIES?

If you receive an offer from your "second choice" opening before receiving a decision from your "first choice" opening, here is what to do: Ask your contact at your second choice opening for time to think over their offer. Then, call your contact at your first choice opening, explain the situation to him/her, and ask whether a decision about you has already been made.

If your first choice opening won't give you a decision before you must repond to your second choice, accept your second choice. But back out of it if you are later offered your first choice. Remember: you should accept the best offer you receive at any time, even if doing so would—through no fault of your own—unfortunately inconvenience an employer.

HAS YOUR JOB HUNT SENT YOU OUT ONTO THE LEDGE?

"And this, too, shall pass."
—Unknown

One of my clients observed, "When you're looking for a job, you feel particularly fragile, insecure, and nervous." Another says that "a job search is about has much fun as unrequited love." As you thanklessly pound the cyber-pavement day after day searching for a break, it can be tough to maintain your morale and fighting spirit. Some tips for staying off the ledge:

- Continually give yourself things to look forward to and celebrate every little victory, like finishing a long application. After receiving good or bad news, splurge on special treats for yourself—even modest ones, such as time off with a great book, a movie, a walk through the park, or a special meal.

- This one is *not* negotiable: Keep up your exercise program. If you don't have one, start one. (I would have attached a free pair of sneakers to each copy of this book if I could have.)

- Don't bottle up your frustration: Discuss it with friends and relatives and seek pep talks from them. And if you live in an isolated area, occasionally open the window, stick your head out the window and yell: "I'm mad as hell and not going to take it anymore." (Then close the window and get back to work on your job search.)

- Harden yourself to rejections. Because of the unpredictability and capriciousness of selection processes, there is an excellent chance that you won't hit employment paydirt on your first try. Many extremely qualified job seekers receive a number of rejections before they ultimately get hired. As one successful EPA attorney recalls, "Before I landed my EPA job, I received enough rejections from EPA to wallpaper my apartment."

- If you are currently unemployed, consider working a temp or contract job during your job search. By doing so, your will add credentials to your résumé, increase your cash flow, and generate contacts that could lead to permanent jobs. (See Chapter 2 for leads.)

- Throughout your job search, keep participating in activities, including professional activities and hobbies, that you enjoy and are good at—whether they be playing musical instruments, painting, gardening, cooking, coaching sports teams, volunteering for an advocacy group, organizing community events, or anything else. The emotional lift and positive feedback you receive through such activities will help you maintain your equilibrium throughout the vicissitudes of your job search.

- Remember that your fortunes can, and probably will, change on a dime. A case in point: a federal IT expert who had submitted fantastic applications consulted me in tears because her job search had generated a 4-inch folder of applications without a single job offer. But 1 week after her tearful meltdown, my client was invited on three interviews. And 2 weeks after that, she received an offer for a choice job.

- **Never let anyone, particularly strangers, make you feel bad about yourself. As Eleanor Roosevelt said, "No one can make you feel inferior without your consent."**

Reevaluate Your Approach

If employment paydirt is eluding you, you would be wise to calmly and objectively evaluate your strategy, and to—if possible—seek a fresh, objective perspective from a trusted source. Some ways to do so:

➤ Check that you are qualified for your target jobs and are not overreaching.

➤ Call a previous interviewer and ask for candid suggestions on how you could improve your performance in future interviews.

➤ Ask friends, relatives, and colleagues to give you honest feedback on your résumés and essays, and to practice interviewing with you. Incorporate any reasonable advice that you receive into your job searching strategy.

➤ Review this book's application and interviewing advice again.

"I'm not against public service. I just think I can do more damage in the private sector."

➤ Seek advice from a career coach. Yes, such advice may cost you. But if your career is stalled, the real question is, can you afford *not* to seek it?

Remember: perseverance is a critical component of success. If you keep improving your application, keep plugging, and keep applying, you will eventually land a career-boosting job.

PART IV

ACCELERATING YOUR ASCENT

Two new feds who start out on the same rung on the career ladder can soon find themselves on different rungs, with the distance between them only growing with time. Why? Because the speed of a fed's climb up the career ladder—just like in the private sector—usually depends not only on each professional's smarts and dedication, but also on each professional's savvy use (or lack of use) of go-getter strategies for speeding their career ascent.

Part IV provides a bevy of career-accelerating strategies—available nowhere else—for earning an enviable reputation, generating high-level connections, getting the credit you deserve, amassing key credentials, boosting your salary, and making the right moves at the right time.

This is the kind of practical, potentially pivotal advice that they never taught you in school, your friends don't know, and your boss won't tell you.

CHAPTER **16**

The Fed "Get Ahead" Guide

"Luck is what happens when preparation meets opportunity."
—Seneca (5 BC–65 AD)

237

What Is Success?

"Did you think the ladder of success would be straight up?"

You're successful at work when you're doing the most interesting and important work possible, getting the recognition you deserve, and making as much money as possible.

This chapter is loaded with tips for achieving work success and accelerating your ascent. Some of them may be more appropriate for you at certain times than others. So as you review these tips and strategies, don't pressure yourself to do them all at once, or even to ever do them all.

Instead, cherry pick the strategies that suit you now, and then periodically review this chapter to remind yourself of strategies that will help you keep improving and advancing.

Why Initiative Beats Inertia

HOW FAST WILL YOU MOVE UP?

There are no formulas for how fast feds rise.

The speed of your climb will depend on many factors—some that you can control and some that you can't. For example, your agency's budget will probably influence how generously it rewards producers. Nevertheless, by continuously gathering résumé-stuffing experiences and seizing opportunities to grow and excel, you will surely accelerate your ascent.

Even if you have the best boss in the world, you are, at most, only your boss's second most important priority. Indeed, no matter how kind and caring your boss is, how much camaraderie you share with your colleagues and how loving your family is, you're the only person in the world who has true pride of ownership over your career; it is *your* career.

Sure: managers, colleagues, and your inner circle may provide guidance and support. But whether you're in government or the private sector, you can't expect anyone else to vigilantly look out for your career, make sure you get the recognition you deserve, and devote themselves to your advancement.

Also, remember that opportunities to shine and advance probably won't just drop into your lap. To find and pursue them, you must be enterprising, show initiative, and apply savvy strategies.

First Impressions

When you start your job, your main goal should be making a good first impression with your boss. Why? Because the single most important factor determining your quality of life on any job is your boss. In fact, your boss is as critical to your happiness at work as your parents were to your happiness at home while you were growing up.

HOT TIP
Getting to Know You

Position a candy jar near the entrance to your cube or office. Your candy jar will entice your new colleagues to stop by and introduce themselves.

Moreover, first impressions make lasting impressions. That's why it's much easier to make a good first impression than to correct a bad first impression. So if you get off to a good start with your new boss, you will help pave the way for a smooth long-term relationship with him/her.

Start working on your relationship with your boss even before your first day on the job. How? By asking your future boss what you should read to be able to hit the ground running, and then read what s/he suggests. Also, if possible, take off a few days before you start your new job so that you will arrive rested and energetic, and not frazzled from finishing up old commitments. Then, once you start your new job:

➤ **Give your all to your job for at least the first few months.** Go above and beyond the call of duty whenever possible, even if you slack off later; be punctual; work extra hours if necessary; double-check and proofread your work; and meet your deadlines.

➤ **Ask for "getting started" suggestions.** On your first day, ask your boss which people you will be working with most closely and frequently so that you can introduce yourself to them. Follow-through on any other "getting started" suggestions your boss offers.

➤ **Be enthusiastic and positive.** Act like you feel privileged to work there, even if you had to miss a free Hawaiian vacation to take the job. Be friendly and courteous to everyone.

➤ **Charge out of the gate.** During your first couple of week(s) on the job, bite off a contained, easy-to-accomplish project and finish it quickly and effectively, if possible.

Second Impressions

An axiom of life is that if you make life easier for people, they will probably like you and seek out your company. If you make life harder for people, they probably won't. Apply this principle to your relationship with your boss: in other words, win your boss over by solving problems—not creating them. Some ways to do so:

➤ **Priorities, priorities.** Identify your boss's priorities and, as much as possible, make them your own. Why? Because by helping to push his/her agenda, you will make his/her life easier and thereby make your life easier as well. After all, your efforts will take you further if you swim with the tide rather than against it.

➤ **No cattle prodders.** Finish assignments quickly, enthusiastically, and without prodding, even taxing, nonscintillating projects. If you need clarification of assignments, request it. If you have ideas on how to improve projects, suggest them tactfully.

➤ **Volunteer to do more.** If you're underbooked or you would like to do higher-level projects, ask your boss point blank, "How can I make a bigger contribution here? Is there something else I could take off your plate? Don't worry about giving me tough assignments. I will do what it takes to get them done."

➤ **Do crisis management.** Be the unflappable, indefatigable trouble-shooter during crises.

➤ **Don't be a clock watcher.** Work extra hours, if necessary and if you can.

➤ **No disappearing acts.** Your boss shouldn't have to put your photo on milk cartons in order to find you. A case in point: I once had a colleague who arrived on time every morning only to strategically place his jacket over his seatback in order to create the impression that he was in the building. Then, he would run out to who-knows-where for most of the rest of the day. My colleague's gimmick fooled his boss… but only for a while.

➤ **Be a problem solver.** If you can independently troubleshoot through obstacles and problems without supervision, do so, and then tell your boss about such successes. Generally speaking, your boss will be happier to hear about problems you solved than problems you created or can't solve.

➤ **No surprises.** If you anticipate missing a deadline, don't blindside your boss. Instead, warn him/her of the problem while there is still time to develop work-around strategies. And even though you should attempt to work as self-reliantly as possible, by the same token, if you need help tackling important technical or administrative obstacles, ask for it. Remember: part of your boss's job is to make sure that you have everything you need to do your job.

HOT TIP
Free Advice on Career Advancement Strategies

My recent "Career Matters" columns in *Federal Times* cover everything from avenues into the senior executive service to landing overseas jobs to effective communication skills. To access an archive of my columns, visit the *Career Information* section of http://www.FederalTimes.com. Additional free advice is posted on my website at http://www.IGotTheJob.net.

In addition, if you're involved in snags that your boss will inevitably learn about from others, break the news to him/her first yourself. Why? For the same reasons that a defense attorney presents the weaknesses of their own case to the jury before the prosecution does: to establish credibility, put bad news in the best possible light, explain mitigating circumstances, and steal the thunder of those who would joyfully harp on their misfortune.

> ➤ **Schmooze.** Managers are more likely to trust members of their inner circle with important, career-boosting assignments and promote them than hostile outsiders. So try to become one of the gang. When appropriate, engage your boss, other managers, and colleagues in conversation and attend office parties and outings.

> ➤ **Never say this line: "That's not my job" (even if you're thinking it).**

Start Spreading the News

As your projects progress, ask yourself whether you think your boss knows what you do. I mean *really* knows what you do, as in all the trouble shooting, barrier busting, and going the extra mile-ing that you do.

The Danger of Communication Gaps

Unfortunately, many bosses—overtaxed and untrained in supervising—rarely take the time and trouble to say to their staffers those five little words, "What are you working on?" This principle was underscored to me by the manager of a large federal accounting office who confessed as we strolled through his staff's cubicle farm, "I probably know about 10 percent of what each of these people does daily." The problem with such communication gaps for employees is that they generally don't get credit on their annual evaluations for achievements that their bosses don't know about. In other words, what your boss doesn't know about you can hurt you.

But beware, your annual evaluations are important to you for several reasons. For one thing, pay for performance evaluation systems, which base annual raises on employees' evaluations instead of on automatic increases, are proliferating throughout the government.

In addition, your evaluations will probably impact your prospects for promotions. This is because many federal job applications require submission of recent annual evaluations. And even if your future applications don't require you to submit your evaluations, you may want to cite your record of earning positive evaluations and quote praising comments from your evaluations in your résumé and application essays in the future.

> **"***If you done it, it ain't bragging.***"**
> —WALT WHITMAN, WRITER

If you feel self-conscious about encouraging positive feedback, remember:

➤ You're as entitled to your hard-won positive feedback, such as positive annual reviews, as to your paycheck—you worked hard for it and you deserve it. So if it doesn't come to you spontaneously, go get it, just like you would if you were denied your paychecks.

➤ Bad news and criticism travels on its own wings, but good news needs a nudge. Yes, when things go wrong for you, news of the problem will fly up and down the gossip wires. But when things go right for you, you may have to telegraph the news yourself.

➤ Your work won't speak for itself because inanimate objects can't talk.

➤ No one is going to advocate for you. So if you don't advocate for yourself, you will be advocate-less. It is up to you to sing your own praises... toot your own horn... and trumpet your achievements. And if you do so by sticking to the facts without exaggerating, and by using tact, common sense, and moderation, you won't sound egocentric and brassy.

Nine Ways to Close Communication Gaps

1. **Introduce yourself.** If your boss is replaced, your new boss probably won't know anything about what you have already done or can do. And so you'll probably have to re-reestablish your reputation from scratch with him/her.

   Don't just settle for a hallway handshake introduction with your new boss. Instead, make an appointment to introduce yourself to him/her. During your meeting with your new boss, tell him/her about your biggest projects; show him/her some of your relevant work products; identify your upcoming projects and the approvals you will need on them; and suggest some future projects. One more thing: no griping or complaining in this first meeting!

2. **Cultivate a friendly rapport.** Without being obsequious, complement your boss on his/her successes and chat with you boss when you both have the chance. By doing so, you will make it easier to deliver your good news as it develops.

3. **Be direct.** Many professionals only hint about their extra efforts. For example, they assume that if they send their boss an e-mail late at night, their boss will notice the time stamp on the e-mail, make a mental note of their long hours and remember those efforts at review time. But will s/he? And isn't it risky to rely on the selective and perhaps defective memory of a pressured, distracted boss?

   Alternatively, when you're working like a harnessed beast, take the bull by the horns and tell your boss about your extra effort. Say something like, "I just wanted to let you know we are making good progress on Project X... Sharon and I are working hard on it; we put in 12-hour days on it every day this week."

   In addition, if you put in extra hours, claim it on your time card. You shouldn't anonymously donate your time to your office any more than you would make anonymous financial donations to your office.

4. **Provide updates.** Establish a regular method for updating your boss on your projects. This mechanism may involve some sort of cyber or paper trail—such as regularly e-mailed status reports. Be sure to describe in your updates special obstacles you conquered, such as repeated system crashes or staff shortages. Also mention in your updates how you are going the extra mile.

5. **Participate in meetings.** If you've completed an important phase of a project, tell your colleagues about it in staff meetings. Also, mention any major positive feedback you've received. For example, if your office's top banana just approved your organization's annual report that you wrote, say so.

6. **Show-and-tell.** Show to your boss or leave in your boss's in-box documents that validate your success. These may include, for example, evaluations from trainings or events you organized; complimentary e-mails from top managers; agendas from conferences at which you gave presentations; articles you published; or printouts from web pages you created. Also, invite your boss to presentations, trainings, or other events that you organize.

7. **Convey compliments.** If another manager besides your boss or a client, stakeholder, colleague, or any other noteworthy figure compliments your work orally, say to him/her: "I'm sure my boss would like to know that my contributions were helpful to you. Would you mind e-mailing her/him a short note telling her/him what you just said to me, and c.c.-ing me on that as well?"

In government, your reputation serves as your calling card.

I taught this technique to one of my clients—a Treasury Department Webmaster—who used it to convey to his boss his client's satisfaction with a website he created. His payback? The praising e-mail he requested inspired his boss to give him a $500 cash award that he otherwise would not have received.

8. **Write about it.** Offer to write articles about your projects for your office's newsletter or Intranet site or for professional publications.

9. **Express gratitude.** When projects that you lead conclude, e-mail each member of your team a thank-you note that cites some of the team successes and c.c. your boss on it.

Get Juicy Projects

Some ways to get assigned to interesting, important projects:

➤ **Be proactive.** Read everything you can about your office's activities, ask your colleagues about their work, and stay alert at staff meetings. By doing so, you will find ongoing projects that interest you. Volunteer to contribute to them instead of passively waiting to be assigned your next projects.

➤ **Create new projects.** Identify new projects that would fill unrecognized needs, explain to your boss how your office would benefit from these projects, and then offer to do them yourself. I can personally testify to this approach because I have used it to my own advantage many times. For example, some years ago, I worked for the Plain Language Initiative (PLI)—a government-wide campaign to improve federal communications. Because I am interested in science communication, I suggested to my boss that I develop communications trainings for various science-based agencies, and so began my training career. What's more, the experience I gained on that job training scientists in communication skills helped me land my current job as a science writer at the National Science Foundation.

➤ **Be a pinch hitter.** When your colleagues permanently leave their jobs or go on extended leave, offer to cover projects for them. Opportunities for doing so will probably increase as the retirement tsunami washes over the federal workforce. I know, for example, a federal accountant who was itching for a career switch. So she volunteered to help the director of her agency's Alternative Dispute Resolution (ADR) program manage some of her cases. Some months after the accountant started her ADR work, the director went on maternity leave, and so the accountant slid into her job as a temporary substitute. Then, when the director finished her maternity leave, she decided not to return to work, and so the accountant was selected to replace her.

➤ **Track changes.** When you attend staff meetings and read publications targeting feds, stay alert to mentions of reorganizations, the creation of new offices, and government-wide commissions and task forces. Why? Because such organizations may need your temporary or permanent help. This principle was exploited by a U.S. Postal Service (USPS) professional that I know; immediately after hearing about the creation of new USPS division, he e-mailed the chief of the new division a summary of his credentials and a description of some ways that he could contribute to the new division. Two weeks later, he was on staff in the new division, and 6 months after that, he was promoted.

➤ **Get supervisory experience:** Experience supervising others in any capacity—even without serving as a direct-line supervisor—is an excellent credential for landing senior-level jobs. So if your office has interns, entry-level employees, or experienced employees whom you are qualified to supervise, guide, or mentor in any way, volunteer to do so, if appropriate. Also, make yourself available to serve in "acting" positions, when possible. Brandish any resulting supervisory experience in your job applications.

Grow Your Reputation

Do you have fantasies of being plucked from the obscurity of your cube and being instantly elevated into the lofty position you deserve, like Lana Turner was "discovered" at the soda fountain in that old "we're going to make you a star!" Hollywood legend? Sorry to be the bearer of bad news, but your agency's star-making machinery is about as likely to unexpectedly visit your cube as Ed McMahon of the Publishers Clearing House is to ring your doorbell.

But take heart, here are simple things you can do to progressively spread your reputation so that:

> ➤ Your boss won't be the only manager who knows what a great job you're doing. This is important because, after all, your boss could leave her/his job at any time. And if s/he does leave before you, you don't want your reputation to walk out the door with her/him.

> ➤ You will get the credit you deserve.

> ➤ Managers will invite you to work on hot-button projects, provide you with good references, and maybe even recruit you onto their staffs.

Some ways to shine:

> ➤ **Follow the power.** Pounce on any and all opportunities to interact with the front offices of your agency and department. Even better, arrange a detail or transfer into a front office, if possible. Why? Because the front offices of your agency and department are loaded with highly-graded positions, big budgets, and senior managers who have the power to promote. So it's usually easier to move up in front offices than in backwater offices. Moreover, if you hitch your wagon to one of the front office's rising stars, you may rise with him/her. Remember: when it comes to success, in many cases, it's not about who you know but who knows what you can do.

> ➤ **Follow the controversy.** If possible, volunteer to work on your organization's high-profile, high-priority projects. Your contributions to such projects will be more appreciated and will provide more exposure to high-level officials than will your contributions to back-burner projects.

> ➤ **Talk to the crowds.** Offer to help work on high-profile events that will draw staffers from various offices. Also, don't wait to be invited to give presentations before large groups, volunteer to do so. If, for example, you know of an upcoming conference in your field, offer to give a presentation at it. To select good topics to cover, consider what specialized knowledge you have that others would find useful. For example, describe a successful case study, provide how-to instruction, or discuss lessons learned from a policy or system implementation. Alternatively, summarize the state of knowledge on a topic, or discuss ways to adapt to changes in your field.

> ➤ **Bust out of your office.** Join interoffice and interagency workgroups that will help you generate outside contacts. Tell your boss about your desire to join such groups.

➤ **Advertise your availability.** When your office is short staffed, tell your office director that you're available to help. For example, a Policy Analyst at the Department of Housing and Urban Development did just that on July 3, after most of her colleagues had already left for the holiday. The result: by the end of that July, the Policy Analyst had been hand-picked by the Assistant Secretary to become her Special Assistant.

➤ **Develop a useful high-demand specialty.** This technique helped a young financial planner catapult into the senior executive service. He explains: "I volunteered to distill complex data and trends into bite-sized descriptions and easy-to-understand graphs for managers. I thereby helped them find good answers to hard problems. Soon I was getting invited to high-level meetings where these conceptual skills were useful. And those meetings provided a good vantage point for me to spot opportunities for advancement."

➤ **Be a "friend in need."** Extend yourself to managers and colleagues in need, even if doing so requires you to do menial tasks. That way, they will see for themselves what a trooper you are, and reciprocate when you're in a crunch. (And believe me, you *will* have at least a few crunches of your own.)

➤ **Solicit advice.** Many people who would be happy to help you won't volunteer their help; they'll only give their help if asked for it. So seek career advice from people you admire inside and outside your office.

➤ **Stay in touch.** Keep in contact with as many of your current colleagues as possible. And whenever you change jobs, send out a global e-mail with your new contact info to your contacts. Why? Because as you move up the career, so will your current colleagues and supervisors. So even if they can't hire you now, they may be able to do so in the future. In addition, some of your current contacts will inevitably move into different organizations. Therefore, if you stay in touch with them, they will serve as your tentacles throughout the government.

Join Professional Organizations

You're probably already taxed to the max with work and nonwork commitments. So why should you try to squeeze time into your jam-packed schedule for professional organizations? Because these organizations provide excellent opportunities to:

➤ **Meet kindred spirits.** Each professional group brings together professionals who belong to the same demographic group, minority group or profession, or have another interest in common. By interacting with one another and sharing ideas, these like-minded professionals find camaraderie and achieve strength in numbers.

➤ **Stuff your résumé.** Because professional groups are smaller and more nimble than federal organizations and because they are run by volunteers, they offer great opportunities to gain top management experience. This type of experience usually impresses hiring managers as much as paid experience. For example, one of the founders of Young Government Leaders (YGL)—a turbo-charged professional organization of 22- to 40-year-old feds from over 30 agencies—says, "at YGL, I am doing things I want to do on a grand scale." His achievements include building YGL's IT infrastructure, appearing on national radio shows, delivering presentations to executives about federal recruitment at Brookings Institution conferences, and receiving Federal Computer Week's Rising Star Award.

➤ **Find new jobs.** Professional organizations provide informal and formal mechanisms to inform members of job openings that they would not otherwise learn about. They also provide platforms for members to exhibit their skills to hiring managers.

➤ **Advocate for important causes.** Professional organizations create opportunities for their members to get published, make media appearances, give presentations, and organize events that are of common concern to their members.

➤ **Get mentored.** Professional organizations provide training to feds of all levels and offer advice on varied issues, such as strategizing career moves, dealing with difficult bosses, fighting discrimination, and motivating staffs.

➤ **Meet colleagues from other agencies.** Professional organizations provide all-too-rare opportunities for employees of different agencies to interact with one another. They thereby enable members to broaden their perspectives and make more informed professional and life choices.

➤ **Socialize.** Professional organizations sponsor happy hours, networking events, lectures, cultural outings, vacation packages, and other recreational activities.

ON THE CD...

This book's CD includes: (1) a list of professional organizations for feds of various career levels and in various fields; (2) my *Washington Post* article on the career-boosting advantages of participating in professional organizations; and (3) a cheat sheet to help you ace annual reviews.

Details, Details

What a Detail Is

A "detail assignment" is a temporary assignment for a specified period of time in another office or agency. While detailed, an employee remains an employee of his/her home office and continues to be paid by it, but works for another organization.

You may want to do a detail to get experience working on new and different issues from your current ones, completing different types of assignments, networking, working for a more prestigious organization, or scoping out another organization. Moreover, detail assignments, like rental-with-option-to-buy agreements, frequently lead to permanent jobs.

Where to Find Details

Details are occasionally posted on USAJOBS; you may find them by doing keyword searches on the word *detail*. However, many details are never advertised. You may find them by asking around among your current and previous colleagues.

Also, when you read the newspaper and publications that target feds, look out for discussions on temporary government-wide organizations, like task forces and commissions, that may need temporary staff; call the staff directors of those that interest you and volunteer your services. Alternatively, contact the managers of agencies where you would like to work, describe your credentials and your interest in joining his/her staff, and then ask if she/he would be interested in helping you arrange a detail.

Your boss is most likely to approve your request for a detail if s/he tends to encourage professional advancement; believes that you will return from your detail with new skills that will be helpful to your home office; or is sympathetic with your desire to jump ship. One way to encourage your boss to approve your detail is to arrange for a senior executive from the detail agency to contact your office director and request you for the detail. The more senior your requesting official is, the better.

Training and Education

Continuing to Learn

By pursuing training and education opportunities on your government job, you will:

➤ **Stay current.** Every field, no matter what it is, is continually advancing. So if you just tread water without advancing with your field, and without learning the latest methods and software tools, you will fall behind. Alternatively, if you stay on top of your field, your commitment to staying current will serve as a great selling point to hiring managers.

➤ **Keep evolving.** As you evolve, your interests may change. By getting training in your new areas of interest, you will improve your ability to pursue them further.

➤ **Become management material.** No matter how good your leadership, communication, team-building, and project management skills already are, you can improve them more. And the more you do, the more you will increase your credentials for moving into management.

➤ **Network.** Classes provide great opportunities to interact with feds from other agencies.

"It's the old story. I was in the middle of a successful acting career when I was bitten by the accounting bug."

Where to Get Training

These sources provide training to feds:

> ➤ More and more agencies are sponsoring formal mentoring programs for their employees. Ask your boss and your agency's training department if your agency has one. If it doesn't, seek out mentors on your own.

> ➤ The U.S. Office of Personnel Management's Federal Executive Institute and Management Training Centers in Virginia, West Virginia, and Colorado. See http://www.leadership.opm.gov/.

> ➤ Fed LDP: the Catalogue of Federal Leadership Development Programs at http://www.opm.gov/fedldp/index.aspx.

> ➤ The USDA Graduate School offers day and evening classes and certificate programs especially for feds. See http://www.grad.usda.gov/.

> ➤ Various degree programs and classes for feds listed on the training tab at http://www.govleaders.org.

> ➤ Fellowships for current feds covered in Chapter 3 and this book's CD.

> ➤ Professional organizations.

> ➤ Federal Executive Boards, which are located throughout the U.S., provide leadership training programs and classes. See http://www.feb.gov.

In addition, various federal organizations provide training in specific disciplines. For example, The Federal Acquisition Institute (http://www.fai.gov/) and the Defense Acquisition Institute (http://www.dau.mil/) provide training to federal contract managers. In addition, since 9/11, many defense and intelligence agencies have created new training programs for their employees.

Getting Trained on the Government's Time and Dime

Many agencies allocate a certain amount of money to each employee's training and/or attendance at conferences per year and associated travel expenses. They also allow employees to use work time to attend such events. If your boss hasn't already explained your agency's training policy, ask him/her or your agency's training department to do so.

Note that if you pursue a college or advanced degree related to your job, you may be able to cover some or all of your tuition through your annual training allocation or through your agency's student loan repayment program. I know, for example, a GS-14 Public Affairs Specialist at EPA whose department covered her entire tuition for a Masters in Public Administration that she earned at night; this degree helped her qualify for a GS-15 position.

In addition, find out if your agency has an employee scholarship program. Also, the University of Maryland's Robert H. Smith School of Business in College Park, Maryland, offers partial-tuition scholarships to federal managers.

Your Success Portfolio

No matter how preoccupied with your current projects and proud of your achievements you are now, I guarantee you that your memory of them will soon fade as you move onto new projects. Moreover, the evidence of your success will vanish as websites are revised, key documents get lost, and supervisors who witnessed your achievements leave your organization.

Nevertheless, you will need a complete inventory of your achievements and resulting positive feedback to ask for promotions and land your future jobs. So continually track your achievements and preserve the evidence of your success. For guidance on how to do so, see the discussion of the "Validating Your Success" in Chapter 7, "The Portfolio Treatment" in Chapter 13, and my *Washington Post* article, "Make Every Interview a Show and Tell," which is included on this book's CD.

Getting Great Evaluations

Make it easy for your boss to give you a great review by:

➤ **Answering the question: what have you done for me lately?** If your boss was replaced midyear s/he probably doesn't know much about what you did before she/he arrived. And even if you have had the same boss all year, she/he probably doesn't remember all of your important accomplishments for the year.

So instead of relying on your boss's selective or defective memory, submit to your boss a concise, bulleted list of this year's achievements before review time. That way, s/he will have sufficient time to incorporate it into your review.

Your achievements list should succinctly review your success portfolio's recent additions, describe how your achievements added value, and review the positive feedback you received. Also describe how you went above and beyond the call of duty, exceeded your grade level, and stayed current in your field. Attach any relevant documents to your list. (See Chapter 7 and the "Cheat Sheet for Annual Review Prep," which is included on this book's CD.)

If your boss ignores your list, during your review meeting request that s/he attach it to your review. That way, it will become a formal part of your record. So even if you receive a comment-less review, you will still get credit for your achievements and the positive feedback they drew.

➤ **Making detail assignments count.** If you're detailed to another office for any extended time period, ask your detail boss for a written evaluation when your assignment ends, and then give it to your permanent boss.

➤ **Requesting what you need.** Your review is a great time to request training, discuss the types of projects you would like to take on, and ask for an additional administrative or equipment supports you need.

➤ **Proactively defusing criticism.** If you had any significant setbacks this year, acknowledge them and affirm your commitment to doing better in the future. Even if you had a great year, solicit suggestions from your boss on potential improvements.

➤ **Doing better next time.** If you get a poor review, develop with your boss an action plan for improvement and follow through on it. Ask for another review in 6 months.

➤ **Asking for what you deserve.** If you had a good year but your boss doesn't schedule a review meeting, schedule a meeting for a review with your boss. Then, during the meeting, explain to your boss what you accomplished during the year and show him/her evidence of your success.

Alternatively, if your permanent or temporary boss is too busy to write your evaluation, politely volunteer to write it yourself for his/her signature. By using this technique myself when I completed a detail at the White House Conference on Aging, I earned a positive evaluation that I deserved but otherwise wouldn't have received. Then, I submitted my detail evaluation to my permanent boss in the Treasury Department, and thereby bolstered my reputation on my permanent job. Finally, by incorporating comments from my detail evaluation into job applications (as explained in Chapter 7), I helped generate many interviews when I was job-hunting.

Asking for a Promotion

Do you think that your boss will automatically give you a promotion when you deserve it, or that promotions only come to those who don't ask for them?

Well, think again. Remember that your boss's primary concern is probably not your wellbeing, but his or her own wellbeing. And to be brutally honest, she/he probably remembers her/his fifth grade report card better than what you did 5 months ago. So if you have done a stellar job on a demanding project, put in a banner year, or are handling increased responsibility, your boss may need a tactful reminder that you are due for some financial positive feedback.

Under the General Schedule (GS) pay plan, a supervisor usually can:

➤ Give you a cash award worth up to 20 percent of annual salary.

➤ Give you a Quality Step Increase (QSI), which will move you up one step within your grade before the required waiting period has passed. (In some agencies, employees who receive the highest rating in tiered annual evaluations must receive either a QSI or a cash award.) If you have a choice between a cash award and a QSI, you should usually opt for the QSI because its long-term value will probably exceed that of a cash bonus; unlike a one-time bonus, a QSI is a gift that keeps on giving.

➤ Give you a grade increase, if your job has promotion potential. In most cases, you would become eligible for a grade increase after spending one year at your current grade. This means that you would probably become eligible for a grade increase on the first anniversary of your first day in the government.

But if your position doesn't currently have promotion potential, your boss might be able to give you a grade increase by upgrading your job because of additional duties and responsibilities under an "accretion of duties." To do so, your boss would have to submit a justification to your agency's Human Resources Office that explains how your duties increased and so now warrant classification at a higher grade level. Alternatively, your boss may be able to give you a grade increase by advertising a job with a higher grade level than you now have, and putting it out to competition. Under this alternative, you would have to apply for the job and win the competition to land the higher graded job.

Whenever you request a promotion, QSI, or cash award, give your request extra oomph by submitting a clear justification of why you deserve it—including a concise explanation of how your responsibilities have increased, a bulleted list of your achievements, and how they benefited your organization and a description of the positive feedback they generated.

A particularly strategic time to remind your supervisor of your recent glories is before your annual review, and in time for your supervisor to incorporate your list of successes into your review. If you're confident that your boss values you but is resistant to rewarding you, you may want to put the squeeze on him/her. How? By getting a better, competing offer from another organization, and then asking your boss to match it.

One more thing: if your boss announces his/her impending departure from your agency, be sure to ask him/her to finalize any promotions s/he has promised you before departing. This is important because your boss's replacement will be about as likely to honor your current boss's promises as the next U.S. President will be to honor the current President's promises.

Moving On to Move Up

Here are some ways to boost your salary besides, as discussed above, earning a promotion:

1. **Get a retention bonus.** You may be eligible for a retention bonus if you're a prized employee and are considered likely to leave the federal government for any reason, including retirement. (You can help prove that you may be likely to leave the government by providing letters for other job offers.) For more info, type retention bonus into the search window at http://www.opm.gov/.

2. **Get a better job.** To keep moving up in government, you may have to keep moving on to different jobs, different offices, and different agencies—just as many private sector employees must do.

   Why? Because even if your job was perfect for you when you were hired, perfection is usually a temporary state with only a limited lifespan. Any number of circumstances can damage the magic of a great job. For example, opportunities on your job might not evolve as quickly as you do. Your relationship with your boss may deteriorate. Your agency may have thorny organizational problems. Or you may deserve a promotion that you're not getting.

Deciding to Make a Move

How do you know when it's time to go? Someone once suggested to me that as soon as you land a new job, you should start looking for your next job. While instant job searching may be a bit premature, it's a good idea to:

1. Continually scope-out opportunities in your field even if you like your current job. Why? Because by doing so, you may get ideas on how to slant your career or unexpectedly stumble across a job that you like even better than your current job

2. Cultivate and maintain a broad array of professional relationships throughout your career, not just when you're in crisis-management mode or when you're job hopping. Once you're in a crisis or ready to bolt, it's too late to stock your Rolodex with contacts who can provide advice, feedback, and job leads.

As a general rule of thumb, it's time to start looking to jump ship when you realize that your current job doesn't offer advancement, interesting projects, and/or a respectful, dignified work environment—and probably won't do so in the future.

However, I have known many intelligent, energetic, and accomplished feds who—almost resembling the victims of Stockholm Syndrome—stayed in jobs long after they had, for one reason or another, become hopelessly unrewarding and unpleasant. Why? Usually because these stagnating feds were afraid of change.

But to be successful, and keep advancing, your fear of not achieving your potential must exceed your fear of change. If your fear of change or anything else is blocking your ascent, it's a good idea to address your fears by discussing them with friends, reading self-help books, joining self-help groups, or getting professional help. After all, if you don't wrestle your fears to the ground, they will wrestle you to the ground.

And if you expect things to get better by themselves even when management is not even addressing the situation, ask yourself whether your expectations are reasonable. In my experience, problems rarely fix themselves.

Here's another way to look at it: Conventional wisdom says that about 50 percent of all marriages end in divorce, even though most marriages were formed out of love. Most employee/employer relationships were formed out of a lot less than love, and so are destined to ultimately end in divorce.

Landing Your Next Job

As a current fed, you may find openings in your current agency and other agencies by:

1. Regularly checking USAJOBS and the other sources of openings listed in Chapter 2. If you apply to openings that are advertised through multiple announcements, be sure to apply to the announcement that is only open to current and former feds. For more info of this, see "Steps for Reading a Vacancy Announcement" in Chapter 5.

2. Finding hiring managers who will either create a position for you or hire you into an existing opening. You may find such networking contacts among your existing contacts or through networking activities discussed in Chapter 2 or in this chapter.

A few tips on moving around in the government:

1. If you're willing to accept a position at your current step and grade without a promotion, in many cases, you can be lateraled into any equivalent position within your current agency or another agency without competition. That is, a hiring manager can select you without considering any other applicants. Unfortunately, this option is not well publicized. So if you suspect a federal manager might be interested in hiring you, consider tactfully reminding him/her of it.

"*Actually, it was more of a lateral move than a promotion.*"

2. If a federal position is created for you, ask your hiring manager to build promotion potential into it; otherwise, you will probably eventually have to land another job or have the position redesigned in order to move up.

3. Because excepted service agencies generally pay better and have more flexibility in setting pay than competitive service agencies, if you switch from the competitive service to the excepted service, you will have an excellent chance of getting a big salary boost.

4. No matter where you land your next job, see Chapter 14 to prepare for salary negotiations.

Becoming Executive Material

Thinking about aiming for a job in the senior executive service (SES)? If so, the first thing you should do is confirm that you do, in fact, want to be an SESer.

Indeed, there are many good reasons to set your sights on the SES. After all, the SES is an elite, prestigious organization composed of the federal government's leaders. Each SESer has big opportunities to make big changes in the federal government. And the salaries and bonuses of SESers are significantly higher than those of nonSESers.

But the SES is not for everyone. Why not? For one thing, SESers devote the majority of time to leadership activities, such as setting goals for their organizations, marching their organizations toward those goals, and making decisions about organizational management and the allocation of resources. (READ: death by meeting!) So if you would prefer to devote your time and energy to advancing in your technical field rather than in management, the SES is not for you.

Moreover, the SES is high-profile and high-pressure. If you don't like the limelight or being accountable for organizational results, the SES is probably not for you.

To decide whether you want to aim for the SES, read the discussion of the SES in Chapter 5, review the SES website at http://www.opm.gov/ses/; interview current SESers about what they do; and discuss your goals with your boss, your agency's SES training coordinator, and your colleagues.

If you decide to pursue the SES, be aware that you can apply directly from a GS-14 job (or the equivalent) for SES jobs without first landing a GS-15 job. More tips that may help you get into the SES:

> **Chart your course.** Identify which route you want to take to get into the SES. To do so, take an SES prep class at the Federal Executive Institute and discuss your goals with your boss and managers at your agency's SES Candidate Development Program.

> **Fill your gaps.** Compare your experience to the Executive Core Qualifications for the SES and fill your gaps by asking your boss for relevant projects, identifying and volunteering for new projects, and getting training. If your current job will not provide the experience you need, transfer to another job that provides better opportunities, even if doing so requires you to lateral into another position.

> Also, consider participating in fellowships sponsored by the Council for Excellence in Government designed to prepare feds for the SES, and other fellowships for current feds that provide leadership experience. These fellowships are discussed on the list of fellowships provided on this book's CD.

> **Be a leader.** Lead projects, task forces, committees, and change management programs whenever possible. Also volunteer for leadership positions outside your job. Yes, your nonwork leadership experience will help you get into the SES. For example, you could gain budget experience by becoming treasurer of your condo board or by running charity fundraisers.

DISCOUNTS AND FREEBIES FOR FEDS

- **Computers:** Feds get hardware discounts ranging from 6 to 10 percent, and software discounts up to 18 percent at most Apple Stores (bring your federal ID) and online at http://www.apple.com/r/store/government/. Many PC vendors also give discounts to feds. Apple and PC vendors that give discounts to feds are listed at The Army Small Computer Program's website online at https://ascp.monmouth.army.mil/scp/content/gepp.jsp.

- **Hotels:** Many hotel chains give their government rate to feds even when they're on personal time. (But don't pretend you're on government travel when you're not in order to get the federal rate.) See the Federal Discount Lodging Directory at http://www.hotels.idt.net/.

- **Insurance and Other Services:** Geico offers discounts to feds. See http://www.geico.com/information/geicoprograms/federal/discounts/. Also, the National Active and Retired Federal Employees Association offers various types of insurance and discounts on moving expenses to its members. See http://www.narfe.org/departments/hq/guest/home.cfm/.

- **Scholarships and Loans:** The Federal Employee Education & Assistance Fund provides scholarships and emergency financial assistance to feds and their families (see http://www.feea.org). Some professional organizations for feds also offer scholarships.

- **Agency-Sponsored Services:** Many federal agencies sponsor employee assistance programs that offer free confidential support, including emotional counseling, legal services, and financial advice. So check whether your agency has such a program.

- **Cell Phones:** Some major cell phone companies give discounts to feds on their monthly bills. Ask for the discount when you buy your plan.

- **Rental Cars:** Many major rental car agencies give discounts or offer their government rates to off-duty feds.

CAUTION

Feds may only accept discounts that are offered to feds from all or multiple agencies, not just to those of particular offices or to particular employee(s). (This is an anti-bribery restriction). If you're unsure whether to accept a particular discount or gift, ask your agency's ethics attorney.

"I say, if at first you don't succeed, redefine success."

➤ **Schmooze with SESers.** Contribute to associations for federal executives (which are listed in the directory of professional organizations on this book's CD), because they provide ideal opportunities for impressing potential hiring managers, receiving mentoring and participating in formal leadership training programs. Many of these groups invite feds at the GS-13 through GS-15 levels to join.

➤ **Soak-up knowledge.** Throughout your career, seize formal and informal opportunities to learn the nuts and bolts of running federal offices by learning about budget management, human resources, information security, communications, and procurement. As one SESer observes, "If you're going to run a large department, you need to know it all."

APPENDIX **1**

Tip Sheet for Veterans and Their Families

The federal government is a very veteran-friendly employer.

➤ More than 425,000 veterans currently work for the federal government.

➤ Veterans currently account for about 25 percent of the federal workforce, which is more than double the percentage in the private sector. What's more, more then 40 percent of upper-level hires are currently veterans.

➤ The representation of veterans at all levels of the federal workforce is steadily rising.

Described below are various widely used programs that give veterans important advantages over non-veterans in landing federal jobs.

Get Hired Through a Competition

Several programs give veterans an edge in landing federal jobs that are filled through open competitions involving the rating and ranking of applicants and interviews.

Veterans' Preference

Veterans' preference gives points to qualified veterans in competitions for federal jobs, and requires federal agencies to hire a qualified veteran over an applicant who scores similarly in a job competition. Veterans' preference has make-or-break power; it often serves as the deciding factor in selections.

There are two types of veterans' preference:

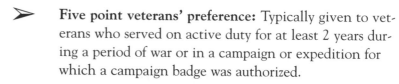

> **Five point veterans' preference:** Typically given to veterans who served on active duty for at least 2 years during a period of war or in a campaign or expedition for which a campaign badge was authorized.

BOOKMARK THESE SITES

For more info on federal programs for job seeking veterans, visit http://www.jobsearch.usajobs.gov/veteranscenter/ and http://www.vetsuccess.gov/.

> **Ten point veterans' preference:** Typically given to a disabled veteran, a Purple Heart recipient, the mother of a veteran who is disabled or who died in active duty, and the spouse of certain disabled or deceased veterans.

To determine whether you have veterans' preference and to count your points, go to http://www.jobsearch.usajobs.gov/veteranscenter/. Additional information about veterans' preference, including a videotaped webcast, is posted at http://www.opm.gov/veterans/. To learn about your rights if you believe your veterans' preference has not been honored, go to the Labor Department's Veterans' Preference advisor at http://www.dol.gov/.

Note that veterans' preference counts in competitions for most jobs that are: (1) in the competitive service or excepted service; *and* (2) open to the public. But because veterans' preference does not count in competitions for jobs that are only open to current feds (feds with status), veterans usually can't use it to land promotions. Another restriction: applicants for senior executive service jobs cannot count veterans' preference.

Other Competitive Programs

These programs allow nonfeds who are vets to compete for federal jobs that are otherwise open only to all current feds (feds with status):

HOT TIP

In some cases, late applications from veterans are accepted by federal agencies. For more information, type *filing late applications* together with *veterans* into the search window at http://www.opm.gov/.

> **The Veterans Employment Opportunities Act of 1998 (VEOA).** Note that veterans using VEOA cannot count veterans' preference and so VEOA does not give veterans an advantage in job competitions; it only allows them to compete in competitions that would otherwise be off limits to them.

> **Reinstatement eligibility:** The right of former feds with veterans' preference and former career feds to apply for jobs that are only open to current feds (feds with status). For veterans with veterans' preference and former career feds, reinstatement eligibility never expires; for many other types of former feds, it lasts for 3 years after their federal job ended.

Get Hired Without a Competition

The following programs enable veterans to be selected for jobs without competing against other applications:

➤ **Veterans' Employment Recruitment Act (VRA):** Enables veterans to be non-competitively hired into 2-year temporary jobs at or below the GS-11 level or equivalent. (A GS-11 job is a mid-level position.)

➤ **Thirty Percent or More Disabled Program:** Enables veterans who have a service-connected disability of 30 percent or more to be noncompetitively hired into temporary jobs that may be converted at any time into permanent positions. There is no grade level limitation to this program. Note that more positions are available under this program than under VRA.

➤ **Reinstatement Eligibility:** In addition to the rights described above, reinstatement eligibility allows former feds with veterans' preference to be noncompetitively hired into positions at grades that are equal or lower than those previously held.

Some openings that can be noncompetitively filled by veterans through the above programs are not advertised. You may find them by contacting your target agencies' Selective Placement Coordinators; these Coordinators stay current on noncompetitive hiring and match applicants with openings. To obtain a list of Coordinators, type *Selective Placement Coordinators* into the search window at http://www.opm.gov/. You can also find these Coordinators by "Googling" that phrase with the names of your target agencies.

Military Spouse Preference

The spouses of active duty military members who move with their spouse to new active duty stations receive priority consideration for many types of federal jobs in the Defense Department. For more info about military spouse preference, see http://dod.mil/mapsite/spousepref.html. At press time, the federal government was considering expanding military spouse preference to all federal agencies.

THE OPERATION WARFIGHTER PLACEMENT PROGRAM

DOD's Operation Warfighter Program matches veterans who are receiving treatment at DC-area facilities with temporary federal jobs that match their skills and interests. Many of these temporary jobs lead to permanent jobs. To access this program's website, "Google" the program name.

Find Opportunities

➤ You can find openings that accept VEOA, VRA, or the 30 Percent or More Disabled Program by doing keyword searches of vacancy announcements using the names of these programs at http://www.usajobs.gov/.

➤ Some federal agencies recruit veterans from lists of job seekers provided by the VA. For more info, contact your state VA office, which you can find on http://www.va.gov/.

➤ Federal organizations with particularly good track records in hiring veterans include the intelligence community, and the Departments of Homeland Security (DHS), Defense (DOD), Labor, Transportation, Energy, Agriculture, and Labor, and the VA.

➤ Key federal websites for job-hunting veterans: The career website of the intelligence community is http://www.intelligence.gov/index.shtml. The CIA's career website (https://www.cia.gov) and DHS's career website (http://www.dhs.gov) each have special pages for military transitioners. DOD's website for military transitioners is http://www.dodtransportal.dod.mil/dav/lsnmedia/LSN/dodtransportal/, and its website on civilian DOD careers is http://www.go-defense.com/. The Defense Logistic Agency's website for military transitioners is http://www.hr.dla.mil/prospective/military.

Note that agencies in the intelligence community, DHS, DOD, the FBI, and State frequently hold job fairs throughout the nation that are announced on their respective websites. In addition, DOD's Hiring Heroes program sponsors job fairs (frequently located near military hospitals) that match veterans with government organizations. (See Chapter 2 for tips on faring well at career fairs.)

The Labor Department's site for job-hunting veterans is http://www.dol.gov/vets/ and its program for military transitioners is described at http://www.dol.gov/vets/programs/tap/transition_assistance_program.pdf.

➤ Key federal websites for job-hunting disabled vets: See DOD's jobs website for disabled vets at http://www.dodvets.com/vetinfo.asp; the website of the Army Materiel Command, which helps disabled veterans find jobs, at http://www.amc.army.mil/AlwaysASoldier/; and the website of the VA's Vocational Rehabilitation & Employment Program at http://www.vba.va.gov/bln/vre/.

➤ See internship and recruitment programs that are covered in Chapter 3 and on this book's CD, and discussions of BRAC, contract, and temp jobs requiring security clearances that are covered in Chapter 2.

➤ The Office of Personnel Management runs Veterans Outreach Offices at the Brooke Army Medical Center in San Antonio, Texas; Walter Reed Army Medical Center in Washington, DC; and Brooke Army Medical Center in San Antonio, Texas. These offices provide wounded veterans with info about federal jobs and other transition issues.

> ➤ Also do "Google" searches on terms like *military transition*. In recent years, many new websites connecting veterans with employers have appeared. Moreover, since 9/11, defense contractors—particularly DC-based ones—have grown like gangbusters.

> ➤ The Small Business Administration's nationwide offices help veterans start and run their own businesses by providing them with grants as well as free training, help winning federal contracts, mentoring, and other resources. For more info, type *veterans* into the search window at http://www.sba.gov/.

On Your Application

The federal government's special programs for veterans never guarantee jobs to applicants. To be offered a job, you must, at the very least, prove that you meet the job's minimum requirement. Also, be sure to clearly and prominently identify on your applications all of the relevant veterans' hiring programs that you're using.

To translate your military experience into civilian terms:

> ➤ Identify your final rank, promotions, medals, honors, the number of people under your command, and the training you received.

HOT TIP
If You Have Security Clearance...

Identify your current or previous security clearances prominently on your cover letter, résumé, KSAs, and mention them in your interviews. Such clearances may increase the number of jobs that you qualify for and significantly boost your salary offers for federal and contracting jobs.

> ➤ Clearly identify the challenges you faced in the military and the generic skills they taught you. For example, describe how your experience as a combat infantry leader sharpened your leadership skills, ability to quickly make high-stakes decisions, allocate assignments to team members based on their skills, develop quick responses to threats, adapt to changing circumstances, quickly communicate with people of diverse backgrounds, and conduct post-action reviews. Other important selling points frequently offered by military experience include high technological proficiency, loyalty, self-diligence, experience managing confidential information, troubleshooting skills, attention to detail, international experience and knowledge or particular regions, language skills, team-friendly approaches, strategic planning skills, grace under pressure, and ability to excel in high-pressure environments.

> ➤ Remember that a hiring manager won't be impressed by your application if s/he doesn't understand it. So avoid or define technical terms and acronyms that are commonly used in the military but will stump civilians, and explain the importance of your contributions. Here's an excerpt of a federal job application from a veteran who unfortunately violated these principles:

> *I wrote Mission Need Statements (MNS) and Capstone Requirements Documents (CRDs) that were mandated when Joint Strike Fighters or IMDs are introduced. The audience of these documents was the Flag-level officers in the J1, J2, and J3 Directorates.*

One more thing: are you a current or former fed with veterans' preference applying for a federal job that is open to the public? If so, you can apply under Competitive Procedures or Merit Promotion Procedures. Look up these terms in the Glossary in Appendix 4 to evaluate the relative pros and cons of applying under each of these Procedures.

CAUTION
Submit All Required Documents

Many veterans inadvertently sabotage their applications by neglecting to submit or failing to label documents proving their military service and/or disability or by neglecting to bring such documents to career fairs.

Tip Sheet for Applicants with Disabilities

The federal government is the largest employer of people with disabilities; it employs about 125,000 people with disabilities and almost 20,000 people with severe disabilities. About 7 percent of feds have a disability.

Job applicants with disabilities may be hired for federal jobs through the same competitive procedures as non-disabled applicants. But disabled applicants may also be hired through special procedures that allow them to bypass job competitions. These procedures are called noncompetitive Schedule A Appointments.

Under a noncompetitive Schedule A Appointment, a federal agency can simply hire an applicant with a disability into an opening without considering other qualified applicants—as long as the disabled applicant meets at least the opening's basic requirements. This means that an applicant with a disability does not necessarily have to be the best qualified applicant to get the job; she/he only has to be qualified.

Using Schedule A Appointments minimizes red tape for federal agencies and applicants, and helps agencies fulfill their obligation to increase their hiring of people with disabilities.

Get Certified

To be considered for a noncompetitive Schedule A Appointment, you must have a severe physical disability, psychiatric disability, and/or be mentally retarded. You must also have proof of your disability and a certification of your job readiness that describes your ability to perform the essential duties of your target positions. You can obtain these documents from any of these sources:

> ➤ A licensed medical professional (e.g., a physician or other medical professional certified by a state, the District of Columbia, or a U.S. territory to practice medicine);

> ➤ A licensed state or private vocational rehabilitation specialist;

> ➤ Any federal agency, such as the Department of Veterans Affairs, state agency, or agency of the District of Columbia or a U.S. territory that issues or provides disability benefits.

If you have proof of disability but don't have a job readiness certification, you may be hired into a temporary federal job. Once you obtain the job readiness certification or your on-the-job productivity convinces your agency that you are able to fulfill the duties of the job, you may be hired into a permanent job or into another temporary job.

Find Openings

> ➤ Some federal agencies do not advertise some openings that they want to fill with disabled applicants. Instead, they may recruit for these openings via methods that target disabled applicants. Once you get certified, find these openings by contacting the Selective Placement Coordinators at your target agencies. These Coordinators stay current on job openings for disabled job seekers, including unadvertised openings, and match applicants to them. To find these coordinators, type *Selective Placement Coordinators* into the search window at http://www.opm.gov/. Also "Google" *Selective Placement Coordinators* along with the names of your target agencies.

> ➤ If you're a veteran, see Appendix 1.

> ➤ If you're a student or recent grad, review the internships and recruitment programs discussed in Chapter 3 and listed on this book's CD, particularly the Workforce Recruitment Program and other programs that are flagged for favoring people with disabilities.

> ➤ Some federal agencies recruit applicants with disabilities from state vocational rehabilitation agencies. Therefore, you may find some unadvertised federal openings by contacting your state agency. To access a list of vocational rehabilitation agencies, "Google" *state vocational rehabilitation agencies*.

> ➤ Some agencies recruit people with disabilities through organizations such as the American Association for People with Disabilities, Easter Seals, and The Arc and by advertising in *CAREERS & the disAbled Magazine*.

➤ The Computer/Electronic Accommodations Program (CAP) provides assistive technology and services (at no charge) to employees of dozens of federal agencies. See http://www.tricare.mil/cap/. The CAP website also posts updates on federal disability hiring and links to other sites addressing federal opportunities for people with disabilities.

➤ Bender Consulting Services, Inc., places professionals in varied fields in federal jobs throughout the United States. See http://benderconsult.com/index2.html.

➤ USAJOBS works with screen reading software like JAWS (Job Access with Speech). You can increase the font size of USAJOBS screens on Internet Explorer. Access USAJOBS by phone at 703-724-1850 or TDD at 978-461-8404.

Reasonable Accommodation

The federal government is required by law to make reasonable accommodations for a worker's disabilities. Examples of reasonable accommodation include providing interpreters, readers or other personal assistance, modifying job duties, restructuring work sites, and providing alternative work schedules and/or work-at-home options.

Hiring agencies also provide special accommodations to help disabled applicants take tests or be interviewed for openings if they are asked to do so. For more information on reasonable accommodation, go to http://www.eeoc.gov/; then type *reasonable accommodation* into the search window.

On Your Application

➤ If you want to be considered for a job opening under a noncompetitive Schedule A appointment, say so in your cover letters of paper applications, in the short-answer questions addressing Schedule A appointments in online applications, and in any other opportunities you identify. Although you are not required to do so, you may provide assurance in your application that you could get the job done with reasonable accommodation.

➤ You will probably want to begin your cover letter just like any other applicant for a competitive appointment would begin their cover letter. (See Chapter 11 for more instruction on writing cover letters.) But after you identify your target job, and review your credentials, you could say something like this:

> *Please consider me for the [name of the position goes here] opening under a noncompetitive Schedule A appointment because I am deaf. I assure you that I am a top-notch producer, and I could perform the job effectively; my certification letter is attached.*
>
> *I can communicate articulately as long as I have an interpreter for meetings and telephone calls. I offer a solid record as a team player. My contributions to group projects are reflected in my successful completion of [cite specific types of projects you completed and objective validation of your success, as discussed in Chapter 7].*
>
> *I would be happy to show you my portfolio of work and discuss my communication abilities in person. My references can verify my skills, positive attitude, and reputation as a team player, as well.*

➤ In job interviews, employers are technically restricted by law to asking if the applicant could do the job and, in some cases, to asking the applicant for an illustration of how he/she would do so. This means that interviewers are prohibited from asking you questions about your disability that are irrelevant to your functioning on the job and you are not required to discuss your disability during interviews. Nevertheless, you are certainly permitted to answer the unspoken questions that may loom large in the interviewer's mind. For an excellent article on how to address disabilities in interviews, see http://www.quintcareers.com/disabled_job_strategies.html.

➤ You may ask your references to specifically discuss your disability with potential employers and provide additional validation of your effectiveness.

HOT TIP
Agencies with Good Track Records

• The U.S. Postal Service and the Defense Department (DOD) have won awards from *CAREERS & the disAbled* magazine for their records in disability hiring. To access DOD's website on civilian jobs for people with disabilities, go to http://www.go-defense.com and click on the *People with Disabilities* tab.

• In 2004, The Department of Homeland Security launched an initiative to hire more people with disabilities. For a list of Homeland Security's Selective Placement Coordinators, type that phrase into the search window at http://www.dhs.gov.

• In addition to the above-mentioned agencies, agencies with particularly good track records in disability hiring include the VA and The Departments of Treasury, Energy, Housing and Urban Development, Agriculture, Commerce, and Labor.

More Resources

> ➤ For the federal government's fact sheets on federal disability hiring, type *Federal Employment of People with Disabilities* into the search window at http://www.opm.gov/.

> ➤ Professional organizations for disabled feds include Deaf and Hard of Hearing in Government at http://www.dhhig.org/ and the Association of Persons with Disabilities in Agriculture at http://www.apda.usda.gov/.

> ➤ For the U.S. Labor Department's one-stop website for government disability info, go to http://www.dol.gov, and then select *disability resources* in the A-to-Z site index.

> ➤ See *Job Hunting for the So-Called Handicapped or People Who Have Disabilities* by Richard Nelson Bolles and Dale Susan Brown. This book explains rights guaranteed by the Americans with Disabilities Act and provides insightful job-hunting tips. (Bolles also wrote the job-hunting blockbuster *What Color Is Your Parachute?*)

> ➤ *CAREERS & the disAbled* magazine provides insightful job-searching articles. See http://www.eop.com/cd.html.

APPENDIX 3

Formatting Tips

The most important formatting principle is: *WHAT STANDS OUT ON THE PAGE IS WHAT WILL STAND OUT IN THE READER'S MIND.*

In order to format your most important credentials to leap off the page and into the reader's mind, you must use effective formatting techniques. This appendix provides tips for attractively formatting your documents in Microsoft Word XP. (Instructions for formatting online documents are provided in Chapter 8.) Note that this Appendix explains all of the formatting features used in the hard-copy résumés on the CD that accompany this book.

To Add Special Characters

The diamonds in the résumé header below are an example of a special character.

JOE SIXPACK
Certified IT Specialist

1234 Yellow Brick Road ◆ City, State, Zip Code
Work: (123) 123-4567 ◆ Home: (123) 123-4567 ◆ E-Mail: JSixpack@E-mail.com

---

Steps to Add Special Characters

1. Position your cursor where you would like to position a special character.

2. Click on the "Insert" pull-down menu.

3. Select "Symbol."

4. Click on the symbol you would like to select.

5. Click "Insert."

6. Click "Close."

To Create Bulleted or Numbered Lists

Capitalize each item in a bulleted list. If each item in a list consists of a word or just a few words, don't punctuate listed items with periods. If each listed item is a sentence, end each item with a period. Use numbers when rank or sequence is important. Use bullets when rank or sequence is not important.

Steps to Format and Position Bullets

1. Select text to be bulleted.

2. In your toolbar, access the "Format" pull-down menu.

3. In the pull-down menu, select "Bullets and Numbering."

4. At the top of the menu box, select "Bulleted."

5. Select the desired symbol for bullets from menu box options.

6. At the bottom right of the menu box, select "Customize."

7. At the left side of the customized bulleted list menu box, fill in numbers for "Bullet Position" and "Text Position." To position bullets flush with the left margin, select "0" for "Bullet Position," and a higher number, such as .3, for "Text Position." The higher the numbers selected for "Bullet Position" and "Text Position," the further bullets and accompanying text will be indented from the left margin.

8. Select "Font" in the middle of the Customized Bulleted List menu box if you want to adjust the font or size of bullets or bold bullets. Bullets should usually be about the same size font as the text they accompany.

9. Select "OK."

10. Type text to accompany the bullet and then hit "enter." After you do so, your next bullet will appear.

Alternatively, create a bulleted list by typing each item of the list on a separate line, selecting the entire list, and then hitting the icon representing bullets located in the toolbar at the top of the page.

Steps to Create a Bulleted List Inside of Another Bulleted List

1. Complete steps 1 to 5 from above.

2. Select a different symbol for subbullets than bullets in Step 5.

3. Specify higher numbers for "Bullet Position" and "Text Position" for subbullets than selected for bullets, such as .3 and .6 respectively.

4. Select "OK."

Steps to Format Numbered Lists

Follow steps provided above in "Steps to Format and Position Bullets" as those for formatting and positioning bullets—except at step 4, select "Numbered" in the "Bullets and Numbering" pull-down menu, instead of "Bulleted."

To Create and Manipulate Tables

You may want to include a *Your Needs/My Skills* table in your cover letter, as discussed in Chapter 11.

Steps to Create a Table

1. On the toolbar, access the "Table" menu.
2. In the pull-down menu, click "Insert Table."
3. Enter the number of columns and rows that you want your table to have.
4. Adjust the sizes of the table's columns and rows by clicking on gridlines and moving them.
5. Bullet items in the table's cells, if you so desire.
6. Bold the table's headings.

Steps to Delete a Table and Its Contents

1. Click inside the table.
2. On the toolbar, click on the "Table" menu.
3. Point to "Delete."
4. Click "Table."

Steps to Delete a Row or Column of a Table

1. Click inside the table.
2. On the toolbar, click on the "Table" menu.
3. Point to "Delete."
4. Click "Row" or "Column," as appropriate.

To Adjust a Document's Margins

Steps to Adjust a Document's Margins

1. From your toolbar, select the "File" pull-down menu.

2. In the pull-down menu, select "Page Setup."

3. Make sure that the "Margins" tab on the upper left side of the menu box is selected.

4. To create ample white-space with your margins, set the top, bottom, right, and left margins to one inch each.

5. At the bottom of your menu box, click "OK."

To Create Horizontal Lines Across the Page

You can sandwich text, such as a heading in a résumé or KSA, between various types of lines—some of which are showcased below.

A HEADING SANDWICHED BETWEEN HORIZONTAL LINES

- -

A HEADING SANDWICHED BETWEEN DASHED HORIZONTAL LINES

- -

A HEADING SANDWICHED BETWEEN THICK HORIZONTAL LINES

Steps to Sandwich Text Between Lines

1. Select the text that you want lined. If you want the sandwich lines to extend across the entire page, extend the selected area beyond the last letter in the text to be lined. Alternatively, if you want the lines to end where the text ends, end the selected area where the text ends.

2. In your toolbar, access the "Format" pull-down menu.

3. In the pull-down menu, select "Borders and Shading."

4. On the top of your menu box, select "Borders."

5. Under "Setting" in your menu box, select "Custom."

6. Under "Style" in your menu box, specify a style.

7. On the right side of your menu box under "Preview," select the icon representing a line positioned above your selected text, and the icon representing a line positioned below your selected text.

8. At the bottom of your menu box, click "OK."

9. Justify or center the text between the lines by selecting the text and then clicking the appropriate justification icon on the toolbar at the top of the page.

Steps to Create a Single Horizontal Line Under Text

1. Complete steps 1 to 6 as explained above.

2. On the right side of your menu box under "Preview," select the icon representing a line positioned below your selected text.

3. At the bottom of your menu box, click "OK."

4. Justify or center the text.

Steps to Create a Single Horizontal Line Without Text

1. Hit the "Shift" key.

2. While keeping down the "Shift" key, hit the dash key (the key next to the zero key) at least three times.

3. Release the "Shift" key.

4. Hit the "Enter" key.

To Shade a Heading

You can emphasize text, such as a heading in a résumé or KSA, by shading it.

Steps to Shade a Heading

1. Select the text to be shaded. If you want the shading to extend across the entire line, extend the selected area beyond the last letter of the text. Alternatively, if you want the shading to end where the text ends, end the selected area where the text ends.

2. In your toolbar, access the "Format" pull-down menu.

3. In the pull-down, select "Borders and Shading."

5. At the top part of your menu box, select "Shading."

6. On the left side of your menu box under "Fill," select the "fill" box representing the desired darkness of your shading.

7. At the bottom of your menu box, click "OK."

8. Justify or center shaded text by selecting the text and then clicking the appropriate justification icon on the toolbar at the top of the page.

To Shade and Sandwich a Heading Between Lines

To shade and sandwich a heading between horizontal lines, combine the instructions provided above for shading a heading and sandwiching a heading between horizontal lines.

SHADED AND SANDWICHED TEXT BETWEEN THICK HORIZONTAL LINES

SHADED AND SANDWICHED TEXT BETWEEN DASHED HORIZONTAL LINES

SHADED AND SANDWICHED TEXT BETWEEN HORIZONTAL LINES

To Erase Lines and Shading

Use the steps below to erase lines and/or shading that you have just created:

1. Select the box, shading or line to be erased.

2. In your toolbar, access the "Edit" pull-down menu.

3. In the pull-down menu, select "Undo Borders and Shading."

Alternatively, you can erase lines and/or shading around text by selecting the shaded or lined text; then accessing the "Borders and Shading" menu and selecting the "No Fill" option for shading and the "None" option for borders.

To Expand the Spacing Between Letters in a Heading

You can emphasize a heading by expanding the spaces between its letters. Here are the steps for doing so:

1. Select the text that you would like to expand.

2. From your toolbar, select the "Format" pull-down menu.

3. In the pull-down menu, select the "Character Spacing" tab.

4. In the pull-down menu next to "Spacing," select "Expanded."

5. In the adjacent box next to the word "by," insert a number.

6. Click "OK."

To Create Borders Around Each Page

Steps to Create Borders Around Each Page

1.   From your toolbar, select the "Format" pull-down menu.

2.   In the pull-down menu, select "Borders and Shading."

3.   On the top of the menu box, click on the "Page Border" tab.

4.   In the "Style" box, select the desired style of your borders.

5.   If you do not want your pages bordered on all four sides of the page, click on the lines in the picture in the preview box that represent the sided of the page that you would like to be free of borders.

6.   Click "OK."

Steps to Erase Borders Around Each Page

1.   From your toolbar, select the "Format" pull-down menu.

2.   In the pull-down menu, select "Borders and Shading."

3.   On the top of the menu box, click on the "Page Border" tab.

4.   In the "Setting" box, select "None."

5.   At the bottom of your menu box, click "OK."

Space-Saving Tips

You can save space by shrinking the size of the empty line between items in bulleted or numbered lists (without shrinking the font of listed items) and/or by shrinking the size of empty lines before or after headings (without shrinking the font of the heading) to an 8-point font.

Steps to Shrink the Size of a Line

1.   Select the empty line that you would like to shrink.

2.   Access the "Format" pull-down menu from the toolbar.

3.   Click on "Font."

4.   Change the font size to "8."

5.   Click "OK."

To Make Long Lists Readable

By using headings to break up lists of achievements, training courses, or other credentials, you will make them easier to skim and remember. This principle is demonstrated by the two lists of training courses provided below, which contain the same course titles. Isn't List #2, which has headings, easier to skim and remember than List #1, which is long and unbroken?

List #1: Long, Unbroken List—Training Courses

- ➤ PowerPoint—January 2007
- ➤ Using Spreadsheets—November 2006
- ➤ Direct Marketing Math & Finance Seminar—November 2005
- ➤ High Impact Business Writing—October 2004
- ➤ Public Speaking—September 2007
- ➤ Mediation and Conflict Management Skills—January 2001
- ➤ Project Management Principles—March 2005
- ➤ Crash Course in Direct Marketing—September 2000
- ➤ Diversity Training—August 2007
- ➤ Dispute Resolution—October 2007
- ➤ Fundamentals of Writing—February 2006

List #2: List Broken Up With Subheadings—Training Courses

Management

- ➤ Diversity Training—August 2007
- ➤ Project Management Principles—March 2005

Marketing

- ➤ Direct Marketing Math & Finance Seminar—November 2005
- ➤ Crash Course in Direct Marketing—September 2004

Conflict Resolution

- ➤ Dispute Resolution—October 2007
- ➤ Mediation and Conflict Management Skills—January 2001

Communication

➤ Public Speaking—September 2007

➤ Fundamentals of Writing—February 2006

➤ High Impact Business Writing—October 2004

Software

➤ PowerPoint—January 2007

➤ Using Spreadsheets—November 2006

Essential Features for Hard-Copy Applications

1. Print your name and the title of your target job at the top of each page.

2. Number your pages.

3. Answer your essays in the same order in which they appear on the application.

4. Include each essay question with its answer.

5. Use margins that are between 1 and 1.5 inches wide. Instructions for manipulating margins are provided in this Appendix.

6. Limit each essay to 1 or less than 1 page. If your essay runs over 1 page, fit it onto a single page by eliminating irrelevant information and unnecessary words and manipulating font sizes and margins. (But do not resort to minuscule margins.)

7. Use a font size of at least 9 or 10 points.

8. Use plain fonts such as Arial, Helvetica, or Trebuchet.

9. Print your applications on a single side of the page so that hiring managers can copy it without losing content.

10. Do not print your application on odd-sized paper.

11. Print your application on white or off-white paper. Do not print your application on colored paper or include any other formatting gimmicks.

Glossary

30 Percent or More Disabled Program: Program that makes some disabled veterans eligible to be directly hired into some federal jobs without competing against other applicants.

Appointment: A federal job. Each federal job is filled either through a competitive appointment or noncompetitive appointment.

Basic Qualifications or Minimum Qualifications: The criteria that applicants must meet to be seriously considered for the job. Applications that don't meet these qualifications are rejected.

Best-Qualified Applicant: An applicant who was among one of the top scorers in a job competition. (In government lingo, the applicant has "made the cert.") The applications of best-qualified applicants are forwarded to the selecting official for further consideration; other applications are rejected.

BRAC: The Defense Department's (DOD) Base Realignment and Closure program. This program is shutting down some DOD facilities and expanding others.

> **FOR MORE INFO...**
>
> For more definitions, see the Glossary in "The Info Center" at http://www.usajobs.gov/.

Career Appointment: Type of position held by feds after completing career-conditional appointment in the competitive service. It usually takes 3 years to progress from career-conditional appointments to career appointments with career status (or tenure). If you have career status, you have two main advantages: (1) it would be harder to lay you off than career-conditional feds; and (2) if your resign you federal job, you can be rehired by the federal government at any time in the future without competing with the general public. Also see "Status."

Career-Conditional Appointment: Type of position held by most new feds in the competitive service. The first year of service in a career conditional appointment is usually a probationary period. Usually after serving 3 continuous years in a career conditional appointment, an employee automatically receives a career appointment. If you have conditional status *and*: (1) if your agency is involved in a layoff (RIF in government lingo), then you are more vulnerable to being RIFed than feds who have career status; (2) if you resign from federal service, then your ability to be later re-employed without having to compete for a job with the general public is limited to the 3-year period after resignation. Also see "Status."

Career Transition Assistance and Special Selection Priority (CTAP): Program that gives selection priority to displaced federal employees for some job openings in their own agencies before their federal employment ends.

Certification List: The list of most qualified or best-qualified applicants developed either by a peer-review panel or an online hiring system during a competitive examination for a federal job. The certification is given to the selecting official who makes a final selection. In government lingo, applicants listed on the certification "made the cert."

Civil Service: Includes the competitive service, excepted service, and senior executive service.

Civil Service Laws: Laws designed to ensure that hiring is strictly merit-based. Civil service laws apply to all jobs in the competitive service. The Office of Personnel Management establishes regulations for implementing civil service laws. Jobs in the excepted service are specifically exempted from civil service laws.

Closing Date: The deadline for applications for federal openings. Late applications are almost always rejected. On rare occasions, a closing date is extended to encourage more applications or because of other reasons.

Competitive Appointment: A federal job that is filled through a merit-based competition.

Competitive Examination: A merit-based competition that is used to screen applications for federal jobs that are open for competition. In a competitive examination, applications are rated and ranked with a numerical score based upon merit and veterans' preference; an applicant who ranks as most qualified for the position is selected. (Only relatively few competitive examinations involve tests or exams.) Most jobs posted on http://www.usajobs.gov/ are screened through competitive examinations.

Competitive Procedures: Procedures used to rate outside applicants to vacancy announcements that are open to the public. Under competitive procedures, applicants may use their veterans' preference. But applicants hired under competitive procedures must undergo a 1-year probationary period that is not required under Merit Promotion procedures. (See "Merit Promotion Procedures.")

Competitive Service: Includes all jobs covered by federal civil service law. (Civil service laws are designed to keep hiring procedures strictly merit-based.) Competitive service jobs are filled through open job competitions (competitive examining procedures). Most federal jobs are in the competitive service. All federal jobs that are not in the competitive service are exempt from civil service laws and are in the excepted service. Personnel regulations for competitive service jobs are set by the Office of Personnel Management.

Competitive Status: See "Status."

Contact Person: Agency employee identified on a vacancy announcement who answers questions about the job opening.

Detail Assignment: A temporary assignment of a federal employee to a different position for a specified period, with the employee returning to his or her regular duties at the end of the detail.

Direct Hire Authority: Special streamlined procedures used to quickly fill openings when there is a severe shortage of candidates or when there is a critical mission need.

Excepted Service: Includes all jobs exempted from civil service laws. Excepted service jobs can be filled via more flexible procedures than competitive service jobs. That is, an agency can decide to select an applicant for an excepted service job without a competition designed to identify the best-qualified applicant. Agencies set their own qualification requirements and salary rules for excepted service jobs, but some excepted service agencies do follow some Office of Personnel Management regulations. Excepted service jobs are civil service jobs that do not confer competitive status. Excepted service jobs include:

> All political positions in the federal government.

> All federal jobs filled through special appointments instead of through competitive procedures.

> Some categories of jobs in all federal agencies such as attorneys, chaplains, doctors, dentists, and nurses. All jobs in some federal agencies—including the Central Intelligence Agency, Foreign Service, Federal Bureau of Investigation, State Department, and Postal Service. To access a list of excepted service agencies, look up *excepted service* on Wikipedia.

> Some jobs in the Department of Veterans Affairs and Department of Defense.

> Most jobs on Congressional staffs and in the Judiciary.

The classification of some federal jobs can change. For example, when a competitive service job is filled through a noncompetitive appointment under a special hiring authority, it becomes an excepted service job. If this excepted service job is then filled again through a competitive appointment, it converts back into the competitive service.

Executive Core Qualifications (ECQs): Qualifications required for obtaining a senior executive service (SES) job. Essays addressing ECQs are required in applications for SES jobs. Note that ECQs are very similar to KSAs.

Federal Wage System: The personnel and salary scale for blue-collar federal employees.

Federal Résumé: Type of résumé required for applying for jobs in federal agencies. Federal résumés are required to contain more information than standard résumés.

Foreign Service: The federal government's diplomatic corp that helps design and support U.S. foreign policy from Washington, DC, at over 250 international posts and runs all U.S. embassies, consulates, and other diplomatic missions. The foreign service is comprised of branches from the Departments of State, Agriculture, and Commerce and The U.S. Agency for International Development. The foreign service is part of the excepted service.

General Schedule (GS) Pay: The pay scale for most federal white-collar positions. GS positions range from GS-1 to GS-15.

Interagency Career Transition Assistance Plan (ICTAP): Program that gives selection priority for some federal openings to displaced federal employees after their jobs have ended.

Knowledge, Skills, and Abilities (KSAs): Main criteria used to judge federal applications. Applications for many federal jobs are required to include essays addressing KSAs.

Locality Pay: Special pay increases that apply to federal workers in cities with high costs of living such as New York City, San Francisco, and Washington, DC.

Merit Promotion Procedures: Procedures used to rate and rank applications for vacancy announcements that are only open to current and former feds. (Specifically, merit promotion procedures may apply to applicants who have status or reinstatement eligibility.) Applicants hired under Merit Promotion Procedures cannot count their veterans' preference; but, if hired, they do not have to fulfill a probationary period. By contrast, applications for vacancy announcements that are open to the public are rated and ranked according to competitive procedures. Table Appendix 4-1 explains the differences between merit promotion and competitive procedures.

Noncompetitive Appointment: A federal job that is not filled by the hiring agency through a merit-based competition involving the rating and ranking of applicants; noncompetitive appointments are filled by agencies by using special hiring programs for veterans, returned Peace Corps volunteers, students, former feds, or others who can bypass competitions under some circumstances or by transferring, reassigning, or promoting current feds. Each vacancy announcement for a noncompetitive appointment specifies what types of noncompetitive appointments can be used to fill the position.

APPENDIX 4-1 TABLE	Merit Promotion vs. Competitive Procedures	
	Merit Promotion Procedures	**Competitive Procedures**
Coverage	• Applicants with status. • Applicants with reinstatement eligibility.	• All applicants without federal experience. • All applicants who have status or reinstatement eligibility and opt to be covered under competitive procedures.
Veterans' Preference	Veterans' preference does not count. Applicants who are rated and ranked under merit promotion procedures do not gain points for veterans' preference.	Veterans' preference counts. Applicants who are rated and ranked under competitive promotion procedures may gain points for veterans' preference.
Probation Period, if Hired	No probation if applicant is hired.	One-year probation period if applicant is hired.

Noncompetitive Schedule A Appointment: A federal job that can be made available to disabled applicants without competition. See Appendix 2.

Office of Personnel Management (OPM): Sets hiring procedures for all federal agencies in the competitive service. Some excepted service agencies also follow some OPM procedures, but the degree to which they do so varies from agency to agency.

Optional Application for Federal Employment (OF-612): Form that can be submitted with federal job application instead of a résumé. However, hiring managers generally prefer résumés over this form, which have a bureaucratic, hard-to-read format.

Personal Service Contract: A contract between a federal organization and a professional for providing specific services during a specified period of time.

Probation: The first year of service of employee who has a career or career-conditional appointment in the competitive service. After an employee completes probation, it becomes much harder to fire him/her. In practical terms, the overwhelming majority of employees complete the probationary period without any problems. See also "Trial Period."

Promotion Potential: The promotion potential assigned to each job defines the highest level that can be reached by a person holding that job without competing against other applicants. To climb higher than his/her current job's promotion potential, a fed must either land another job or convince their boss to extend their current job's promotion potential.

Reinstatement Eligibility: Right of former feds who held career appointments and former feds with veterans' preference to: (1) be noncompetitively rehired into federal jobs at grades equal or lower than those previously held; and/or (2) apply for jobs that are open only to applicants with status. For former career feds and former feds with veterans' preference, reinstatement eligibility never expires. For other former feds, it usually expires 3 years after end of federal employment.

Reduction-in-Force (RIF): The federal government's version of a lay-off. RIFed feds receive priority for other federal openings.

Security Clearance: Authorization awarded by the federal government to a fed or contractor to access classified materials needed to do a job. You can only get a security clearance if you: (1) work for a federal agency or a federal contactor who requests a security clearance for you because you must access classified materials to do your job—you cannot get a security clearance by applying for it yourself—and (2) pass a security investigation. Your security investigation, which may last months, may involve reviews of where you've lived, worked, and gone to school; checks of credit and police records; interviews; and a polygraph. The main types of clearances from lowest to highest level of security are: (1) confidential, (2) secret, (3) top secret, and (4) sensitive compartmented information. Some job offers are contingent upon receipt of a security clearance. In recent years, the processing of security clearances has been significantly speeded.

Selecting Official: Person who makes a hiring selection from best-qualified candidates in a job competition (competitive examination). The selecting official usually interviews at least some of the best qualified candidates to help them make the decision, but does not always do so. The selecting official is usually the supervisor of the new employee.

Senior Executive Service: The federal government's corps of executive managers.

Special Hiring Authorities: Authorities that enable federal agencies to hire applicants who meet specified criteria without an open competition. Special hiring authorities are commonly used to noncompetitively hire veterans, people with disabilities, RIFed feds, returned Peace Corps volunteers, applicants for internships and student jobs, and former feds. Note that applicants in these categories are not guaranteed jobs. To be hired for a job, an applicant must meet or beat its minimum qualifications.

Status: Possessed by career employees and career-conditional employees who have served at least 90 days. (Includes employees hired under noncompetitive appointments working in the competitive service; excludes employees of agencies in the excepted service.) It is advantageous to have status (also known as "competitive status") because some federal jobs are only open to those who have it. In addition, a status employee may be promoted, transferred or reinstated without an open competition. Take care not to confuse "competitive status" with "career status" possessed by feds with career appointments.

Temporary Appointment: Temporary job that lasts 1 year or less; usually benefits are not provided.

Term Appointment: Temporary job that usually lasts 1 to 4 years. Benefits are usually provided.

Trial period: The excepted service's version of the probationary period. This period may last up to two years.

USAJOBS: The federal government's official jobs website. See http://www.usajobs.gov/.

Vacancy Announcement: The announcement of a job description(s) and application requirements for one or more federal job openings.

Veterans Employment Opportunities Act of 1990 (VEOA): Program that allows veterans to apply for some federal jobs that would otherwise be off-limits to them.

Veterans' Preference: Preferential treatment given to the applications of some veterans, and some spouses and mothers of veterans for federal jobs. See Appendix 1.

Veterans Recruitment Appointment (VRA): Program that enables veterans to be hired into temporary positions that may lead to permanent positions.

Index

About the Author

A Leading Authority on Federal Careers

Lily Whiteman is a:

> **Federal Career Coach:** Lily has helped hundreds of professionals of all levels—from recent grads to executives—land jobs and earn promotions.

> *Washington Post Contributor* and *Federal Times* **Columnist:** Lily has written for the "Jobs" section of *The Washington Post* and *WashingtonPost.com,* and her "Career Matters" column appears twice a month in *Federal Times.* Her career advice has also been featured by *Newsday,* XM Satellite Radio, WTOP Radio Network, and other outlets.

Lily doesn't work *all* the time. Here she is on vacation.

> **Savvy, Seasoned Fed Who Knows the Federal System Inside Out:** Currently a senior science writer at the U.S. National Science Foundation, Lily has climbed the career ladder at six agencies, including the White House Conference on Aging and the Vice President's National Partnership for Reinventing Government. As an experienced job seeker herself, Lily relates to other job seekers with empathy and humor.

> **Hiring Manager:** Lily knows how to instantly impress federal hiring managers because she has served as a hiring manager herself and has interviewed hundreds of others about their hiring decisions.

> **Award-Winning Communicator:** Lily received two "Awards of Excellence" from the National Association of Government Communicators in 2008.

Communications Consultant

Known for her informative, entertaining approaches, Lily has led seminars for many organizations including the American Association for the Advancement of Science, the Council of Science Editors, and the Performance Institute. Dozens of her articles have appeared in national publications including *Audubon*, *National Parks*, and in-flight magazines.

Education

Lily has a Master's degree in Public Health and a Master's degree in Environmental Management from Yale University. She received her BA in Earth Science from Wesleyan University in Connecticut.

Websites

http://www.IGotTheJob.net

http://www.CrystalClearCommunication.com